THE KID

THE KID

A Season with Sidney Crosby and the New NHL

SHAWNA RICHER

McCLELLAND & STEWART

Library and Archives Canada Cataloguing in Publication

Richer, Shawna
    The Kid : a season with Sidney Crosby and the new NHL /
Shawna Richer ; foreword by Roy Macgregor.

Originally published under title: The rookie.
ISBN 978-0-7710-7521-6

    1. Crosby, Sidney, 1987-. 2. Hockey players–Canada–Biography.
I. Richer, Shawna. Rookie II. Title.

GV848.5.C76R52 2007   796.962092   C2007-901074-1

We acknowledge the financial support of the Government of
Canada through the Book Publishing Industry Development
Program and that of the Government of Ontario through the
Ontario Media Development Corporation's Ontario Book
Initiative. We further acknowledge the support of the Canada
Council for the Arts and the Ontario Arts Council for our
publishing program.

Typeset in Sabon by M&S, Toronto
Printed and bound in Canada

This book is printed on acid-free paper that is 100% recycled,
ancient-forest friendly (100% post-consumer recycled).

McClelland & Stewart Ltd.
75 Sherbourne Street
Toronto, Ontario
M5A 2P9
www.mcclelland.com

    2 3 4 5   11 10 09 08

For my parents

CONTENTS

Foreword by Roy MacGregor   ix

Acknowledgements   xvi

1. The Arrival   1
2. The Crosby Show   19
3. Born to Play Hockey   44
4. Under a Penguin's Wing   57
5. Rough Start   75
6. A Dream Come True   88
7. The Flyers   103
8. The Other Rookie   121
9. Grey December   130
10. Heart Break   137
11. A Fresh Start   149
12. The Olympics   163
13. Backlash   175
14. Oh Canada   190
15. Groaning Pains   203
16. New Year's Leave   219
17. Au Revoir, Le Magnifique   228
18. Lessons in Losing   237
19. The Kids Are All Right   252
20. Chasing 100   264
21. Following Sidney Crosby   277

Epilogue   292

What a Difference a Year Makes   300

Appendix I: The Pittsburgh Penguins 2005-2006   328

Appendix II: Sidney Crosby's Season Game-by-Game Results   336

FOREWORD

By Roy MacGregor

In the summer of 2005, I had a singularly brilliant idea. I immediately dispatched it, by e-mail, to Ed Greenspon, the editor of the *Globe and Mail* and my boss. How could he resist? I would, I selflessly offered, be willing to bail from my regular column – writing about such profound, and perhaps even related, topics as puppy training and parliamentary behaviour – and return, briefly, to my first love: covering hockey.

Why not? The 2005-2006 National Hockey League season was certain to be the most interesting in decades, perhaps the most significant since the league's beginning back in 1917. The bitter labour dispute that had turned professional hockey into the first major sport to lose an entire season was finally over. The long lockout had, to many of us, been the best possible solution to a game that had, in recent years, become almost unbearable to watch. It had forced the owners – seeking economic certainty through a salary cap – to think, finally, about the *product* they would offer to entice increasingly disenchanted fans back to the game. It was far more than just getting the books in order; it was about, finally, getting the game in order.

That summer, the storylines were already bursting like a lawn sprinkler. The small-market teams – declared doomed only a few seasons earlier – were now likely to survive, perhaps even thrive. The new rules proposed looked like they had the potential to open the game up again and to reward speed and skill over obstruction and interference.

And there were now *two* years of fresh faces and new talents to meet – those young players who had been denied the 2004-2005 season and the new top draft picks of this year, chief among them a then seventeen-year-old from Cole Harbour, Nova Scotia, by the name of Sidney Crosby.

I fired my e-mail off and soon realized I was probably but one of dozens of political and city and arts and business writers offering to *sacrifice* a year of routine boredom for a year of the exciting unknown.

Ed took little time in responding. Stay where you are, he said. Keep doing what you're doing. We have something else in mind.

That "something else" turned out to be a far more original idea than even I had imagined. It was, in many ways, the precise reverse of what I had suggested.

The *Globe*'s Atlantic bureau chief, Shawna Richer, had proposed that she view the coming NHL season through the eyes and experience of that teenager who had been virtually an afterthought in my pitch. She would write about this pivotal year in hockey by using Sidney Crosby as the starting point rather than the finishing. He would be the way in which to look at the new rules and how they affected a playmaking genius with considerable speed and not a great deal of size. He would be the manner in which she could study the new collective bargaining agreement's effect on small-market teams, particularly one that was flirting with bankruptcy, which was precisely the case of the new team Crosby was off to join. He would be Canada's next great hope in the national game, the heir to Rocket Richard and Jean Beliveau and Bobby Orr and Guy Lafleur and Wayne Gretzky and Mario Lemieux. To make the storyline even more perfect, Crosby would not only be playing with Lemieux in the aging star's final seasons, but he would be living with him. It was the *arrival* of the prodigal son.

"I like it," the editor said.

"I'm terrified," the writer said when she called.

Shawna Richer was as worried they might accept her idea as she was concerned they might not go for it. It was, after all, an audacious notion: to spend an entire season following around a kid who would be all of eighteen when you were completing what would stand, in essence, as his life story . . . so far.

She called and we talked about it, and I said I thought it was an idea filled with possibilities – though, frankly, neither of us could even remotely imagine what would happen. A few weeks later, the *Globe* decided it was a go and told her to relocate to Pittsburgh for the year and prepare to spend the entire season with Sidney Crosby.

There was no doubt Shawna could do the job. She had, even before this assignment, a reputation as a stellar reporter. I had covered provincial elections and federal elections with her, and even the World Junior Hockey Championships in

Halifax. She had started out as a sports reporter, was excellent at it, and knew the game she would be covering. But there was more to it than that. Shawna Richer burns with a passion for reporting that is, perhaps, fitting for one with the best head of red hair in the business. She is dogged, determined, fair, and thorough. She also writes wonderfully well. It may be sexist to suggest this – yet even more foolish not to – but the fact that she is a woman writing in what has unfortunately usually been a male domain is also significant. In thirty years of writing about sports off and on, I have long been aware that a woman writing about sports comes at it from a welcome and different perspective. Less complicated statistics, more simple equations. Less what is going on in the game than what might be going on in the head or in the life away from the playing field. The ability of Shawna Richer, and so many other women sports reporters, to draw male athletes out and reveal their inner thoughts is something most male sports reporters can only envy.

Sidney Crosby might have been an obvious choice at first, but he grew into an inspired choice – even if no one, himself included, quite saw what was coming. He was immediately seen in Canada as the answer to tomorrow; the gifted player who could accept that clichéd "torch" and carry Canada on to presumed glory in the game we so desperately wished the world to take up, but equally desired the world not to take up quite as well as it had in recent years. Gretzky and Lemieux had restored Olympic glory to Canada; if anyone could sustain it, it would be this kid from Cole Harbour with the low centre of gravity and the slightly goofy smile.

The weight of this role is difficult to comprehend for those who have never felt it on their shoulders. Hockey is not just the national game of Canada, but, as poet Richard Harrison once put it, "the national id." It is how Canadians define themselves, see themselves, imagine themselves. The singular event where Canadians of a certain age mark themselves – just as Americans of a certain age remember where they were when John F. Kennedy was shot – is September 28, 1972, when, at 19:26 of the third period, Paul Henderson scored the winning goal against the Soviet Union. "Hockey is Canada's game," Ken Dryden and I wrote many years ago in *Home Game*. "It may also be Canada's national theatre. . . . It is a place where the monumental themes of Canadian life are played out – English and French, East and West, Canada and the U.S., Canada and the world, the timeless tensions of commerce and culture, our struggle to survive and civilize winter."

Sidney Crosby might have been off to Pittsburgh to play, but he was really playing for Canada from the first drop of the puck. It was, everyone believed, certain to be a storybook year. He would be living and playing with Mario. The Penguins, once thought unsalvageable, had taken the new economic certainty and turned it into another sort of certainty – success in the new season. They would surround the youngster with some of the game's best veterans – defenceman Sergei Gonchar, goaltender Jocelyn Thibault, forwards Ziggy Palffy, John LeClair, and Mark Recchi – and the team would rise, like a phoenix from the ashes, back to the glory days of the early 1990s. Not only would Crosby win the Calder Trophy as rookie of the year, a given, but the Penguins might even make a run at the Stanley Cup.

With her storyline set, Shawna set off for Pittsburgh and the Penguins' training camp. It began as expected – he scored a point in his first game and looked not in the least like an eighteen-year-old – and the Penguins set off on a roll, but not the predicted one. And then it all unravelled. Gonchar couldn't find his game. Palffy couldn't find his passion and eventually quit. Lemieux couldn't find his health and retired. Recchi got traded. The Penguins were so terrible that soon the coach was fired and, once the season was over, the general manager was similarly dispatched.

So much for the obvious storyline.

As for Sidney Crosby himself, he was soon second in the rookie scoring race to twenty-year-old Alexander Ovechkin of the Washington Capitals, a Russian phenomenon with astounding speed and an absolute obsession for firing pucks at nets. It was, indeed, a season of remarkable rookies – Ovechkin in Washington, defenceman Dion Phaneuf in Calgary, Boston forward Brad Boyes, New York Rangers goaltender Henrik Lundqvist – and, at times, those who thought Sidney Crosby had already been given too much praise, and there were many who believed so, rather cavalierly dismissed him as just another gifted kid getting his predicted comeuppance in the big leagues. He wasn't even selected to the Canadian Olympic team that headed off to Turin, Italy, where the chosen players promptly fell flat on their collective faces.

Disaster? Hardly. The simple, obvious storyline now became complicated, far more intriguing, far more interesting. How would Sidney Crosby perform with all the best-laid plans collapsing? How would he handle the unexpected, targetted criticism? How would his year turn out when the Penguins' year was already, as they say in hockey circles, "in the toilet"?

I do not believe, in terms of a compelling book, Shawna Richer could have been more fortunate. What Crosby did, once Ovechkin moved far in front of him in the scoring race and Wayne Gretzky left him off the Olympic team, was decide to do it all on his own, if necessary. No Mario on the one wing, no Palffy on the other, no Gonchar playing as he had been expected – none of it mattered. Crosby simply took up with new linemates, younger and unknown, and went on a scoring spree – twenty-six points in his final thirteen games – that might well have seen him catch Ovechkin had the NHL season only gone on another week. He then headed off for the World Championships in Riga, Latvia, finally able to wear the Team Canada sweater he had hoped for in the Olympics. And though Canada failed to win a medal, the teenager led the tournament with eight goals and sixteen points and was chosen top forward.

The signal was simple and obvious: more to come.

Which means that Shawna Richer's marvellous book, *The Kid*, is instantly essential reading for the future of Canadian hockey. And the time may even come when we look back on both the player and the book as classics of their genre.

Roy MacGregor

ACKNOWLEDGEMENTS

The Kid, both as newspaper project and book, could not have happened without the complete and overwhelming support of the *Globe and Mail*, in particular editor-in-chief Ed Greenspon, who championed it from start to finish. Special thanks to executive editor Neil A. Campbell, who has always encouraged me to think big and who took my crazy, ambitious idea to Ed.

National editor Noreen Rasbach was the best project editor a writer could hope for. Her long-time friendship comforted me through a long season, and her editorial instinct was always right. Sports editor Steve Mcallister offered endless enthusiasm and a veteran's ideas and input. Special thanks to deputy editor Sylvia Stead and managing editor Colin MacKenzie for unselfishly allowing me to research and write this book while juggling my real job. I am lucky to work for a brave, smart newspaper that gets it;

for those of us who cherish writing, it is a wonderful place to call home.

Jackie Kaiser is the best in her business, as much supportive friend as literary agent. At McClelland & Stewart, Doug Pepper's enthusiasm and vision was infectious. It was a privilege to work with Chris Bucci, whose care with the manuscript improved it immensely. Trena White also has a superb eye.

A book of this nature is at the mercy of its principal character, and mine was tremendous on the ice and giving of his time away from it. Thank you to the Crosby family for their kindness and patience during a season that often felt surreal. Pat Brisson, whose blessing throughout the project, and Dee Rizzo, who made me feel welcome in Pittsburgh, made all the difference.

I am grateful to the Penguins organization for their day-to-day assistance, especially Tom McMillan, Keith Wehner, and Todd Lepovsky. Michel Therrien, Eddie Olczyk, Eddie Johnston, Mike Yeo, Stephane Dube, Steve Latin, and Scott Johnson were patient and helpful. Phil Bourque, Bob Grove, Mike Lange, Paul Steigerwald, Bob Erry, Jack Riley, Ray Walker, and Joe Sager offered help, insight, and humour and made me feel part of their extended family. Special thanks to Billy Wareham, for all of the above and for serving as photo editor. The team generously opened its photo archives to me, and the book is much better for it.

Thank you to the Penguins players, a band of brothers if ever there was one. Even in a tragically disappointing season, they managed many magical moments on the ice and great human ones away from it. If they ever tired of indulging me in talking about their teammate and my going concern, they never showed it.

I am blessed to have gifted colleagues, friends, and mentors – whose roles so often overlap – who generously offered advice both on hockey and writing, places to work, and rousing encouragement. Chief among them are Susanne Craig, Kim Honey, Roy MacGregor, Joe Lapointe, Robert MacLeod, Carolyn Abraham, Stephanie Nolen, Christie Blatchford, Julie Caswell, Andrew Gorham, Scott Burnside, Andrea Baillie, and Dave Feschuk. Joan Astley at the *Globe* always helped to make everything easier. Thank you to the Elizabeth Bishop Society of Nova Scotia for use of the poet's house. And to Marty Klinkenberg, who taught me to see the poetry in sports and inspired my love of sports writing so many years ago.

The Pittsburgh hockey beat writers adopted me and shared volumes of knowledge. Thanks to Dave Molinari and especially Karen Price and Robert Dvorchak, who made great company on the road, and *Pittsburgh Post-Gazette* editor David Shribman for his warm hospitality. Marc Lachappelle in Montreal offered important insights.

Most of all, I would like to thank my family – my mom and dad for encouraging my love of words and for nurturing my introspective side, and Darren, Rachel, Megan, and Emily, whom I love very much.

Shawna Richer
Chester, Nova Scotia
August 2006

THE KID

THE ARRIVAL

It was a great day for hockey.

THE NATIONAL Hockey League entry draft held July 30, 2005, on a warm summer afternoon in downtown Ottawa was the most celebrated and significant selection day held in several decades. At the same time, it was entirely anti-climactic.

Hastily arranged after the NHL owners and players reached a deal to end an acrimonious 310-day lockout that forced cancellation of the 2004-2005 season, the draft starred the most desirable young hockey player to come along since Mario Lemieux arrived on the scene in 1984. A teenaged boy from a small village on the eastern shore of Nova Scotia was a lock to be the number one pick.

His name was Sidney Crosby. He had tousled dark hair and an abundant cowlick, bee-stung lips, a generous, toothy grin, and in most lights he resembled exactly what he was – a boy still sixteen days shy of his eighteenth birthday. For someone who had not yet played a single shift of professional hockey, he was already remarkably famous.

Several seasons before the ugly labour dispute shut down Canada's beloved pastime, the 2005 NHL draft became billed as the Sidney Crosby Sweepstakes. For years, his childhood scoring prowess had been widely known throughout the Maritimes. He was thrust into the national spotlight at the age of fourteen after a remarkable MVP performance in what was then called the Air Canada Cup, the country's championship tournament for midget-aged players, in April 2002. Crosby went on to set records in the Quebec Major Junior Hockey League with the Rimouski Oceanic – his 135 points as a sixteen-year-old was the most by a player that age in the Quebec league's history and second in Canadian Hockey League history, behind only Wayne Gretzky's 182 points with Sault Ste. Marie in 1977-1978. In what had become the most often repeated tale of his young life so far, Crosby's reputation was bolstered even further when Gretzky himself told a sportswriter with the *Arizona Republic* that the Canadian youngster was the only player he had ever seen who had a shot at breaking his own numerous NHL scoring records.

The draft order had been set a week earlier, but even before that Crosby had eagerly promised to don the sweater of whichever team selected him. That he would play in the NHL was a highly anticipated certainty, one of the few things about the league's return to action that autumn that was predictable. Even more than the ratification of the collective bargaining agreement by the National Hockey League Players' Association and its subsequent unanimous acceptance by the league's thirty owners, this draft marked the return of hockey and the birth of the NHL's renaissance. Sidney's arrival in the NHL didn't just coincide with hockey's homecoming, it more or less launched it.

The league was desperately in need of a saviour, a gifted, gracious poster boy who could help repair the widespread damage caused by the previous season's strike and the flood of negative publicity that ensued. Crosby had already been christened the Next One, just as several other players, chiefly Eric Lindros and Joe Thornton, had been at one time. But already Crosby seemed different from those who had come before. The easy play on Gretzky's nickname, the Great One, came by both timing and Crosby's extraordinary hockey gifts – unarguably more profound than Lindros's or Thornton's – which were obvious at every previous level of competition. He had uncommon lower-body strength and an uncanny scoring touch, remarkable vision and playmaking abilities that channelled Gretzky himself. Crosby was also telegenic and almost unbelievably poised for a teenager; he wanted the responsibility the NHL had unofficially foisted upon him. Like so few up-and-coming hockey stars who had come this way before, Crosby wanted to be the guy, the game's next ambassador. The game needed a kid like him. With the lockout ending so suddenly a few weeks earlier – Crosby had given thought to playing in Europe if the dispute had continued into another season – there hadn't been time for much of a courtship. But it hardly seemed necessary. Shotgun or not, it was the perfect marriage.

In an irony that was irresistible to fans, the league, and the writers and broadcasters who covered the sport, Crosby was to be chosen by the Pittsburgh Penguins, just as Mario

Lemieux, the last young hockey player to cause so much fuss, had been twenty-one years earlier.

July 22, 2005, was a great day for the Penguins, and as their late Stanley Cup–winning coach "Badger" Bob Johnson used to declare, "It was a great day for hockey."

The Penguins, the NHL's worst franchise the last time the league played, had been blessed by, of all things, a simple, indiscriminate lottery ball.

I listened to the NHL draft lottery on the radio as I drove through a late afternoon nor'easter home to Halifax from the Miramichi region of New Brunswick, where I had been on assignment. It was compelling theatre. The lottery, with forty-eight balls in all, was weighted based on each team's record and draft order from previous seasons. It offered the Penguins, New York Rangers, Columbus Blue Jackets, and Buffalo Sabres the best chances of winning the right to draft Crosby with three balls each in the bin. Ten other teams had two balls each while the rest, including the Tampa Bay Lightning, Stanley Cup winners in 2004, each had just one ball to dream on.

The lottery was conducted in a closed room in a mid-town Manhattan hotel. As Deputy Commissioner Bill Daly watched over the lottery itself, Commissioner Gary Bettman addressed reporters and tidied up some official business on a small set nearby, announcing that the collective bargaining agreement had been accepted by the NHL board of governors and explaining some of the new rules. "When you look back in a year, five, ten, this era in history will be viewed as a pivotal point in time," Bettman said. "It's the time we could begin to move forward, finally in an effective way where the game could be as good as it could be. This will probably be a seminal moment." When the balls finished dropping, Bettman theatrically read the picks in descending order.

It was one of the most entertaining bits of live news drama I had witnessed in some time. Would Crosby, who grew up worshipping the Montreal Canadiens because they drafted his father, Troy, as a goaltender back in 1984, end up a Hab, his sentimental preference? Or would he be won by a struggling southern franchise that could use a charismatic star to sell the game in a non-traditional hockey market? Would he – heaven forbid – end up a Maple Leaf? Or would he land in New York, where it was felt by many league and marketing folks that he could have the greatest immediate impact on promoting the game in the United States?

In Canada, fans had been angered by the lockout – an Ipsos-Reid poll and mountains of anecdotal evidence found they blamed the stalemate and lost season on the players almost two-to-one over the owners. Truth be told, fans' dismay had been simmering for some time, thanks to escalating player salaries – the league lost $273 million in 2002-2003, according to a study commissioned by the NHL – enormously expensive ticket prices, and a dearth of entertaining play on the ice. The game had become dominated by clutching and grabbing and the deadly dull defensive trap. The NHL was slow and tedious, almost unbearable to watch, and fans were tuning out. The lockout was the last straw for some, even as it turned out to be the best thing to happen to the game. The lockout that hurt so many and destroyed so much may well have saved hockey.

In the months the NHL was gone, letters-to-the-editor pages in newspapers across Canada were filled with scorn, indifference, and pledges to ignore the great game should it ever return. Emotions ranged from disgust over what was seen as abject greed by rich players and even wealthier owners to ambivalence over the kind of product the NHL had on offer. Although it was the only professional sports league on the planet to lose an entire season to a labour dispute, that the NHL stopped playing for a year barely registered in most of the United States, where hockey had been a distant fourth professional sport in many cities, after baseball, football, and basketball, with only a fringe following in less traditional hockey markets, behind even NASCAR.

"At the end of the day, everybody lost," Wayne Gretzky, managing partner and coach of the Phoenix Coyotes, said at the time. "We almost crippled our industry. It was very disappointing what happened. For everyone to say 'all right, let's forgive and forget, let's move forward,' that's all fine and good but it's a lot easier said than done. It's going to take a long time. It's going to take a lot of hard work.

"We disappointed a lot of people and I don't mean the average fan. I'm talking about TV partnerships, corporate partnerships, the fan, the guy who goes to one or two games a year with his son. We've got a lot of work ahead of us. It's not going to all change and be nice overnight."

Yet in Canada, when the news broke on July 13 that the league and players' association had reached an agreement and the lockout was about to end, it felt as though an entire nation exhaled. For the most part, Canadians wanted the NHL back and were willing to give the new-look league, with its rule changes and salary cap and commitment to parity and the Olympics, the benefit of the doubt. If the new NHL was going to begin to succeed, the league needed fans' forgiveness. In Canada at least, it looked as though they would get it.

It was a brilliant marketing move on the NHL's part to broadcast the draft lottery on television and radio in Canada and via ESPN News on TV and satellite radio in the United States. The hour-long event turned out to be a harbinger of the captivating and entertaining season that ultimately unfolded. The NHL had not offered a show worth tuning in to since the Lightning beat the Calgary Flames in the seventh game of the Stanley Cup final on June 7, 2004.

With the Penguins, Rangers, Blue Jackets, and Sabres ahead of the game with the most balls in the lottery, Bettman began unsealing the envelopes.

As he announced the teams that would miss their chance to land the seventeen-year-old rising star, I held my breath a bit. I had written about Crosby during the World Junior tournament the previous winter. I spent an afternoon with his parents, Troy and Trina, at their home the weekend before Christmas 2004 for a story on his childhood that ran in the *Globe and Mail* during the tournament that was played in North Dakota and saw the Canadians win gold for the first time since 1997. And I had seen him play as a junior whenever the Rimouski Oceanic visited the Halifax Mooseheads; Crosby had six points on one of the nights I watched. It was impossible not to root for him to land somewhere that would be good for him and good for hockey. Not Toronto, where the daily scrutiny of the Maple Leafs rivalled that of the Prime Minister's Office and could crush a young player. And not Nashville, where his prodigious talents might not be appreciated. And not San José, where the four-hour time difference and revamped, unbalanced schedule meant his fellow Nova Scotians might never get to watch him play on television.

Anticipation grew as Bettman revealed the losers. In fitting fate, the Tampa Bay Lightning fell dead last. Then the Florida Panthers, Dallas Stars, Colorado Avalanche, Calgary Flames, Edmonton Oilers, St. Louis Blues, New Jersey Devils, Boston Bruins, and Toronto Maple Leafs, in twentieth place. Then the Philadelphia Flyers, Detroit Red Wings, Nashville Predators, Phoenix Coyotes, New York Rangers, New York Islanders, Washington Capitals, Buffalo Sabres, San José Sharks, and Los Angeles Kings, in tenth spot. Finally came the Vancouver Canucks, Ottawa Senators, Atlanta Thrashers, Chicago Blackhawks, Columbus Blue Jackets, Montreal Canadiens at fifth spot, Minnesota Wild, and Carolina Hurricanes.

As ten teams were ruled out, TSN, the national sports network reporting live from Cole Harbour, cut live to the Crosby family rec room for the young man's reaction. It was unprecedented coverage for a draft lottery. Satellite trucks and a half-dozen reporters idled on the Crosbys' quiet neighbourhood crescent.

On the radio the suspense played wonderfully. With the Pittsburgh Penguins and Anaheim Mighty Ducks the only two teams remaining, Bettman paused a few beats before divulging that the first overall pick would go to the Penguins, the team that, considering results, the standings, and general karma, certainly deserved it most.

Craig Patrick, the club's long-time general manager, who built consecutive Stanley Cup championship clubs around

Lemieux in 1991 and 1992, had stepped into St. Patrick's Cathedral, the storied midtown church, with a four-leaf clover in his pocket on the way to the lottery to pray for the Penguins' chances. Whether his appeals were heard by a higher power is impossible to say, but the pit stop certainly didn't hurt. The Penguins had landed Sidney Crosby.

In so many ways the team seemed the perfect destination. Crosby had already met and trained with owner and Hall of Fame centre Mario Lemieux the previous summer, and his parents had been charmed by both Lemieux and his mother, Pierrette.

It was a hockey coupling that had both league and media salivating – a seasoned lifelong member of the Penguins in the twilight of a legendary career on the same team and perhaps even the same line (and as it would turn out, the same house) alongside the fresh face of the new NHL, a kid who seemed destined for a tremendous, record-setting career of his own.

Pittsburgh was also an old-school hockey city with smart, knowledgeable fans, a funky, albeit dilapidated arena that was the oldest in the league, and a history, though fading with each passing season, of winning championships. Through recent years the Penguins had found it impossible to compete against richer and larger-market teams, and their desperate need to replace Mellon Arena – affectionately known as the Igloo for its domed shape and tenants – with a modern venue that would allow the team to increase revenues and ensure they remained in Pittsburgh made Crosby an almost necessary acquisition. The NHL hoped his arrival would jump-start interest in an entire league, helping to sell and transform the game, but the team was counting on

Crosby to have far-reaching repercussions that went beyond simply winning hockey games.

With the drop of a white lottery ball, a seismic shift occurred in the hockey universe. Several days after winning the rights to draft Crosby, Lemieux, who had put the Penguins up for sale, pulled the team off the market and kicked into high gear a campaign to build a new arena. It was a good day for hockey, to be sure. And if good things were to happen in this rust belt city with its NHL team on the brink, this season would be the time and Crosby would be the catalyst.

When the NHL last played in 2003-2004, the Penguins finished last in the standings with just twenty-three wins. They also ranked last overall in attendance, with an average of just 11,877 fans coming to each game. After winning two Stanley Cups in 1991 and 1992, the club had been in bankruptcy court. They saw their star player and owner, Lemieux, successfully battle Hodgkin's disease, save the franchise by converting twenty-six million dollars in owed salary to equity in the team, retire and un-retire, and jettison some of the team's top talent – including Czech stars Jaromir Jagr and Martin Straka – to slash payroll. Fan interest waned and so had Lemieux's interest. He had been ready to unload the team that had been his life's work, even if it meant new owners might uproot it from Pittsburgh. With Sidney Crosby in town, that was no longer the case. Lemieux's passion was rekindled. All the teenager had to do now was live up to the hype.

And all the NHL had to do was make good on its promise to put a better product on the ice. The league hoped this would come largely as a result of the rule changes. The players would have to do their part by embracing them and adapting.

Brendan Shanahan, the Detroit Red Wings veteran forward and an influential member of the competition committee that made over the game, was a long-time proponent of increasing hockey's flow and tempo. He promised things would be not just different, but also better. "In speaking to fans the one message I got from them is that they weren't interested in words of apology," he said. "The one thing I consistently heard was, 'We want a better product on the ice, that's the best way you can pay us back.'"

Two-line passes were now allowed – players could try home-run passes. Goaltending equipment, which had become ridiculously bulky over the years, would be trimmed to give shooters a wider view of the net. Shootouts would decide tie games through the regular season. There would be zero tolerance for obstruction – hooking, holding, and interference would be called consistently and without hesitation. The clutching and grabbing that had long hampered scoring sensations such as Mario Lemieux would no longer be permitted. Skill players would be encouraged to put on a show.

With the draft, everything was pretty much set. Crosby had a team to play for. He would wear the ornery, stick-wielding Penguin on his chest and carry the expectations for saving hockey on his shoulders. Unlike Lemieux, who refused to don his Penguins jersey because the team flinched at demands for a million-dollar contract (Pittsburgh general manager Eddie Johnston offered $760,000 and later added a $100,000 signing bonus plus performance bonuses), Crosby would eagerly pull the sweater over his head for the cameras on draft day. What had been little more than an unpleasant soap opera for the past eighteen months was back in business with a promise to compel and captivate. In the car, listening to the lottery that day, I was already hooked. It certainly seemed possible the NHL could evolve into a terrific show; could the game grow as well?

Crosby was revered by junior hockey fans in Rimouski and widely adored in the Maritimes. He had thrilled at the national midget championship in Bathurst, New Brunswick, three years earlier with a jaw-dropping, beyond-his-years effort as a member of the Dartmouth Subways. He was the only player in Canadian junior hockey history to be named best in the league for two consecutive seasons. He was also very much the boy-next-door, the sort of kid who might have come from any small town in Canada, someone who was easy to cheer for.

Since the rules had been overhauled with skilled players such as Crosby in mind, he was expected to do well right away. In many ways, the colossal fanfare didn't afford him much choice, given that he was expected to save the league, or at minimum resurrect it. But Crosby was nothing if not intelligent and self-aware. He was wholly alert to his place in the generally happy storm that was the return of the NHL. He was ready to be in the eye of it.

After an entire season without the NHL, but for sporadic updates on the cold war between players and owners, hockey's return was significant news, at least across Canada. With even the most embittered fans warming once again to the game, industries that had been hurt by the labour dispute could also begin getting back on their feet. The thirty clubs alone lost more than two billion dollars in ticket sales and sponsorships; team and league employees received layoff notices. The players lost one billion dollars in salaries. Associated economies, mostly in Canada, were damaged. Taverns that normally did brisk business on game nights laid off bartenders and wait staff and even the breweries noticed the slowdown. The hockey puck factory in Sherbrooke, Quebec, lost four million dollars and distributed pink slips.

But new rules, new stars, and a new schedule created to promote conference rivalries would complement the new labour agreement, the cornerstone of which was a cap tying player salaries to revenues that intended to make small-market teams – the Buffalo Sabres and Edmonton Oilers and Pittsburgh Penguins of the league – more competitive and financially viable. The pinched Penguins, who spent $23.4 million on player salaries in 2003-2004, twenty-ninth in the NHL, could now in theory build a team as worthy of the Cup as the rich Red Wings, who had the league's highest payroll at $77.8 million.

In this first year of the new six-year collective bargaining agreement, no team's payroll would exceed thirty-nine million dollars. For the first time in many years, the Penguins had the chance to be competitive, and with Crosby in their lineup, they would be the focus of the hockey world, for all the right reasons, at least to the start of the season.

Crosby would play hockey in the football-mad city of Pittsburgh and across an America where arenas in many markets, even an Original Six city such as Chicago, had difficulty drawing a crowd. He would make six rock star–sized appearances in Canada, where a country's affection for the game was returning, for the most part, with rapture. How would the U.S. – where the differences between the solitudes were in stark contrast when measured by hockey – react to him?

Symbolically, Sidney Crosby's first season was about so much more than hockey, and hockey, for Canadians, was so much more than the sum of its parts. Sticks and skates and pucks are cultural emblems, tokens of our national identity.

When I proposed shadowing Sidney as a means of exploring the return of the NHL and the impact this once-in-a-generation player might have on a league in transition to my editors at the *Globe and Mail*, I prayed he would live up to the expectations everyone had for him.

In the end, he was even better than I'd hoped for, even as the Penguins' season unfolded in no way that I had imagined. I came to it viewing Crosby as a touchstone for our cultural obsession, a happy, unaffected boy from small-town Canada who learned to skate shortly after he could walk, a boy who only ever dreamed of doing one thing for a living when he grew up, the very thing he had been doing since he was a toddler: playing a game with a stick and puck and playing it so much better than almost everyone else.

I arrived in Pittsburgh in the fall of 2005 unsure of what would unfold, and I left eight months later having witnessed much more than I could have anticipated. Over eighty-two games and a long season, I watched hockey both awful and wonderful, though none of the former was played by the kid I had followed to Pittsburgh to write about. I watched a young man who loved hockey in the most pure way imaginable, who possessed a desire to win, the likes of which I had never seen. He arrived game-ready for the NHL on his first day of training camp and found virtually instant success despite facing enormous challenges and, at times, serving as a public scapegoat for a nation's insecurities as they manifested in and around the game.

In *The Game of Our Lives*, his lovely book about a young Wayne Gretzky and the Edmonton Oilers' 1980-1981 season, the late Peter Gzowski wrote romantically and simply of Canada's relationship to hockey and the men who played the game.

> All that separated us from our true heroes was that they were better at something we had all done. They belonged to us, as no other kind of hero ever could, at once more celebrated and more approachable because of what we shared. They were of us, playing the game of our lives.

So too was Sidney Crosby.

The season began with many questions. Could he accomplish what so many rookies had struggled with and adjust to the NHL in his first season? Could he lift the Penguins from worst in the standings? Could his game, both graceful and gritty, lure fans to arenas in places such as Columbus, St. Louis, and Florida? Could he help generate enough excitement on the ice to convince politicians to support a new arena and ground the team in Pittsburgh? Could he help his sponsors Reebok and Gatorade sell shoes and T-shirts and sports drinks? Could he live up to the enormous and occasionally unfair expectations? Could he be better than them?

Before I left Canada, Ed Greenspon, editor of the *Globe and Mail*, recommended I read Gzowski's classic hockey book. Written a little before my time, it struck me as profoundly innocent even as it offered a close-up view – Gzowski enjoyed access sportswriters in this day could only dream about – into the NHL and the tricky and symbiotic relationship between failure and success. The book turned out to be an enormous inspiration, and as the season unfolded, I was struck by the numerous similarities between the experiences of Crosby and Gretzky as their youthful stars began to rise.

When I pitched the idea to my editors at the *Globe*, where I had been writing about Atlantic Canada since September 2002, they were enthusiastic. Ed said he imagined the continuing series as "a book in real time." Essentially, I would write the history of Crosby's first season as it happened, interwoven with the implications it held for the greater game.

So on the morning the Penguins opened their training camp at Mellon Arena, I woke up in a small studio apartment in the pretty Pittsburgh neighbourhood of Shadyside, a ten-minute drive from the Igloo.

The media frenzy that sparked at the lottery and grew through the draft exploded when training camp opened. Yet for all the cameras and microphones and notepads that were pointed at Crosby over eight months, there were many more moments that unfolded quietly in the day-to-day routine that paces a professional sports team through a long and grinding season. Many of them happened for only a handful of the regulars who were around every day.

For me, these times provided the subtlest but richest and

most insightful observations into the teenaged hockey wizard. For all the things he was – a playmaking savant and a study in humility – he was also an eighteen-year-old boy with a mischievous smile and irrepressible, high-pitched giggle who formed tight, all-for-one friendships with his young teammates, the kind only a brotherhood of boys chasing the same dream can form.

Seeing Crosby make José Théodore's water bottle leap from its resting place on top of the net while scoring a game-winning shootout goal against the Canadiens, watching him single-handedly embarrass the Philadelphia Flyers in an overtime win, looking down as he scored his 100th point, these were some of the best on-ice moments. But the others, the quiet ones, may well end up as my most treasured in the years to come.

From September 2005 to April 2006 I had a front row seat to the beginnings of what will almost surely unfold over the coming years as one of the most compelling chapters in hockey history. Crosby's was a coming-of-age story, with many rites of passage. Phil Bourque, the whip-smart former Penguins defenceman and two-time Stanley Cup champion, referred once to Sidney's tumultuous rookie season as his baptism. It was a sharp analogy. Often challenged but never overcome, Crosby rose above so much chaos. Even at the worst of times, when it seemed he wasn't having much fun, he never failed to excel and improve. As autumn became winter and winter turned into spring, you could see him growing up before your eyes.

He watched as Mario Lemieux, his mentor, childhood hero, and the legend who took him into his home as if he were a son, struggled with his health and was forced to leave the game for good. One season offered a young life's worth of lessons; the most painful and important was how to lose.

By the end of the season there were answers to many of the earlier questions. We knew how many points he scored, how few games the Penguins won. We saw how he fared in the big time. He stared from the covers of magazines on newsstands across an America that was, in many places, indifferent to hockey's return. But the best part of the season with Sidney Crosby was tagging along on a journey that saw a boy become the man.

He was just getting started. No matter what happened on the ice and away from it, I could never shake the feeling I was watching something special.

2
THE CROSBY SHOW

It feels like the nineties again.

He was different from the first day of training camp.

Sidney Crosby, the eighteen-year-old from Cole Harbour, Nova Scotia, stepped onto the ice at the Igloo in downtown Pittsburgh for the first time on the morning of September 14, 2005. It was just before eleven o'clock on a warm, late-summer day, and it marked an historic moment for the Penguins, one of the most beleaguered franchises in the NHL, and also for the league, which had been awfully beleaguered of late in its own right.

The number one pick in the NHL entry draft had drawn quite a crowd for his first public appearance among the sixty-seven other high-strung young hopefuls and veteran free agents in a scrimmage in which he was nearly unrecognizable.

Players abandoned their usual vanity sweater numbers during training camp, instead donning plain black, white, or mustard yellow team-issue sweaters with regular old

numbers and without their famous names. Crosby's number
87 – chosen for his birthday, August 7, 1987 (8/7/87) – was
replaced in his first NHL camp by number 12. He was easy
to follow on the ice initially, because unlike all the other
Penguins players, whose helmets were white, Sidney's was
black. The white one had not yet arrived from the supplier,
Reebok Hockey.

The best young prospect to land in the NHL in several
decades, filled with so much promise and expectation that
his arrival lured me to Pittsburgh for the entire eighty-two-
game season, sprinted around the ice to warm up, twisting
at the waist with his stick over his shoulders, looking like
almost everyone else but for the mismatched helmet, at
least for now.

It was the first time the Penguins held training camp at
Mellon Arena in their thirty-eight-year history. The team
announced it would throw open the doors for the first
week, and the public could watch for free. The first day,
about 400 fans and more than three dozen reporters – many
from Canada – turned out. Of the fans, some skipped work
and pulled on their Lemieux sweaters while others wore the
latest addition to the Penguins gift shop, Crosby's number
87 sweater, which was already selling briskly and was on
back order in some varieties. Some were hard core fans who
had desperately missed the NHL during the lockout and
were thrilled at its return. Others were casual fans, curios-
ity seekers who had heard so much about the teenager from
Canada and wanted to see him with their own eyes. They
wore digital cameras around their necks and pulled telephones from pockets, snapping his picture as he whizzed by
the boards or leaned on his stick waiting his turn in a drill.

Although Crosby arrived amid more noise than any player since Mario Lemieux, there was hardly a resident of Pittsburgh who had actually seen him play, on television or otherwise, before today.

No one in this football-crazed city of 2.3 million people – most of them still breathing fumes of four Steelers Super Bowl championships in the seventies – had witnessed what Canadian hockey fans had been hearing about and enjoying for years. In two seasons with the Rimouski Océanic of the Quebec Major Junior Hockey League, Crosby packed arenas from Cape Breton to Baie-Comeau, scored 303 points, and was the Canadian Junior Hockey Player of the Year in both seasons he played. His breathtaking breakaways, anticipatory passes, sleight of hand around the net, and explosive speed had all been highlight fodder on the sports channels across Canada. Here in Pittsburgh, people were seeing it for the first time. And everyone was on the edge of their seats, following the kid in the black helmet.

When the players hit the ice, thunderous applause echoed throughout the rink, just a few hundred fans making a din. Some shouted "Welcome back!" Many cheered appreciatively at Lemieux. They applauded Crosby each time he showed his agility and puck-handling skills.

About a half-hour into practice, in his first scrimmage on his first day in the NHL, Crosby scored one of the goals that he made his trademark in junior hockey, a beautiful backhand from down low. The crowd gasped as the puck floated, as if in slow motion, past young goaltender Marc-Andre Fleury.

What they had seen was familiar to the Canadian reporters here to cover Crosby's first week in the NHL. When he scored, some of them glanced at each other with slightly smug smiles, as if acknowledging membership in a secret club American hockey fans had not yet been invited to join. In Nova Scotia, where he grew up, in Bathurst, New Brunswick, where he was first introduced to a nation, in Rimouski, where he led the Oceanic to the Memorial Cup final, and in North Dakota, where he helped Canada to its first gold medal at the World Junior Championship in eight years, they had been familiar with his skills for some time. Now everyone else was about to see them too.

Even Eddie Johnston, the club's long-time assistant general manager and one of the best storytellers I've met in the NHL, only first glimpsed the future of the franchise when Crosby hit the ice that morning.

"When he arrived, everything changed," Johnston said in his chatty clip. "It was just like Mario. Suddenly everyone's a better player and there's excitement in the dressing room. The *players* are excited. You saw him; his first shift they dropped the puck and he skated through the whole team and scored. There's this kid playing against men. You look at him and it's just 'Wow.'"

Crosby was nervous on his first day in the NHL. Even if he hadn't conceded it at his post-practice press conference, you could see him slowly feeling his way in his new world, absorbing details and the faces of everyone around him, filing everything important away in his memory. He was eager to please everyone, answer every question and fulfill every request. He struck me as someone concentrating very hard on doing the right thing at every turn. He was acutely aware of the expectations of hockey fans not just in Pittsburgh, but across the league, and he wanted to be good. Others expected it of him; he expected it of himself.

"I know it means a lot to him to do well," Penguins president Ken Sawyer said. "He's looking forward to all the girls buying his jersey. It took Lafleur a few years to become great. He had a move I'll never forget. He'd come in, hit the brakes, and go laterally. This kid, I expect he'll have some moves."

With so much anticipation, it felt good to finally get out on the ice at the arena that would be his home for forty-two regular season games and skate around with the guys, some of whom would be his teammates. "I was a little nervous, but once I got out there and got playing, I settled down," he said.

The Penguins had a plan to rebuild as quickly as possible. They surrounded their young star with the best talent they could sign in the off-season, veterans with Stanley Cup rings such as forwards Mark Recchi and John LeClair, and Ziggy Palffy, one of the league's most consistent scorers over the past decade. And then there was Lemieux, a combination fans from Toronto to Tampa were dying to see.

With all the hype, all the expectations, and what seemed like endless possibilities, neither the Penguins' front office nor coach Eddie Olczyk wanted to overload the young player with too much too soon. The transition to the NHL from junior was truly staggering, and why so few rookies actually play for their NHL clubs in their draft year. Although Lemieux could claim of Crosby that "he was ready for the NHL last year," the big leagues could overwhelm a young star and often have. A new city, a new team, a tougher and longer schedule, against faster, stronger, more skilled opponents, some of whom were twice as old as the kids, frequently took several seasons –

and sometimes many more – to adjust to. And with the advent of ESPN, twenty-four-hour sports networks, all-sports radio, and the ever-proliferating Internet, Crosby was already dealing with more media attention than Gretzky and Lemieux had faced combined.

Crosby hoped that playing with Lemieux and LeClair and Recchi would push him to improve quickly in game situations, but he also loved practising with them. He closely watched everyone and asked a lot of questions.

After his first practice, the Penguins brought Crosby to a podium in the media workroom to address the more than three dozen print and broadcast journalists who had gathered there. He appeared awestruck as he gazed out over the room, but when he began to talk, he came off as anything but an overwhelmed kid. He was serious.

"Playing games with guys like that is great, but practising is where you're really going to benefit; seeing their habits is definitely going to help me. But you can't afford to go out there and watch too much," Crosby said of his teammates. "If you get caught watching, you're not going to get to the puck and not going to make good plays."

In the dressing room, Recchi was impressed with what he had seen so far. "He's going to be all right. He's pretty smooth out there. It's fun to watch him. His first couple of steps [are] incredible. He's making me feel young. I've got to try and keep up with him. It will be good for Johnny and I to have a young guy that enthusiastic around."

A day earlier, when players reported for medical tests and meetings, several dozen fans had gathered outside the chest-high chain link fence that surrounded the players' parking lot at the arena. They clutched sweaters and caps in black and gold and fresh Sharpies. They wanted a glimpse of Crosby, who they only knew from newspaper headlines and the sports talk shows. In a city dominated by the National Football League, sports fans across Pittsburgh were intrigued by a hockey player's arrival.

"There's a lot of rallying behind this kid," said lifelong Pittsburgher Jesse Long, who as a fifty-four-year-old African-American obsessed with the Steelers was not the typical hockey fan. He was curious to find out if Crosby was as good as advertised. "We're hoping he can do for the hockey team what Mario Lemieux did all those years ago. People have been down on hockey, with the ticket prices and no season last year, and Mario getting to be an old man. But this young man, Crosby, has generated a lot of excitement. The whole city is watching."

When the Penguins employees learned the news late that sleepy, summer Friday afternoon that the lottery ball had fallen in their favour, they shouted for joy. Almost immediately the telephones began to ring. They rang until midnight, and workers stayed to answer them until they stopped. The Penguins sold 486,961 tickets in the entire previous season, but they moved more than that in the first four weeks after the lottery. Craig Patrick said it felt "like the nineties again," a reference to the team's glory years when Lemieux was at the top of his game.

Add another layer to the expectation. Pittsburgh sports fans were over the moon about his arrival, even those who didn't count hockey among their preferred sports. The NHL was praying that Crosby's talents, poise, and matinee idol looks would elevate the league and recapture fan interest and imagination as it emerged from its nuclear winter and win over new fans such as Jesse Long. The league's rebirth wasn't solely on Crosby's shoulders, however. The NHL needed all its star players to shine in the game and away from it in order to make gains in the vast sporting land-scape of the United States, especially below the Mason-Dixon line, and even in plenty of spots above it.

One by-product of the NHL's new collective bargaining agreement, as both the league and players committed to win back fans, was a retooling of the rules in an attempt to open up the game, increase speed and offence, and let skilled players shine. With two-line passes now allowed, long feeder passes would create more breakaways. Goal-tender leg pads were reduced by one inch in width, and the rest of their equipment was tapered and made smaller. Regular season games would no longer end in ho-hum ties; shootouts would decide games. Holding and hooking would be a thing of the past. Gary Bettman said the rule changes were intended "to emphasize the beauty and skill in our remarkable game." In other words, they would hopefully turn a game that had grown painfully predictable into a thrilling spectacle once again.

The rule changes would allow Crosby, who was fast and physical and a skilled playmaker in the way of Bobby Orr, to excel at the NHL level almost immediately, if he was up to the challenge. The more quickly Sidney Crosby did well, the better it would be for all of hockey.

It had been universally assumed that Crosby would be the NHL's top draft pick. He had been talked up as such since he was fourteen years old, bettering kids two and three years older in midget hockey with the Dartmouth Subways.

After his performance at the national championship – Dartmouth lost a heart-breaker in the final to Tisdale, Saskatchewan – anyone who followed hockey suddenly knew something about Sidney Crosby.

"Sidney's performance was a little surreal there," Subways coach Brad Crossley remembered. "He was on another planet with the way he played at that event and to get us there as well. I saw a different level of drive and ambition at the national championship. He just felt it was his right to make things happen. Coming from a small town and being so talented, he wanted to prove he wasn't just a little guy from Nova Scotia. That was really the last year of Sidney truly being a kid."

Crosby went on to score seventy-two goals in fifty-seven games as a prep school sophomore at Shattuck-St. Mary's in Minnesota in 2002-2003. As the top junior player in Canada, he put up staggering statistics: 147 goals and 214 assists in 148 games. Of his draft class, no one was even close.

The week before training camp got underway, the Penguins held a press conference to announce that Crosby had signed a three-year contract that would pay him $850,000 a season plus bonuses. Reporters made the six-hour drive south from Toronto just to be there.

For the first time in NHL history, negotiating an up-and-coming superstar's contract had been relatively simple and straightforward. "I surrendered right away," Craig Patrick quipped to so much laughter. Crosby was earning the maximum allowed for a rookie under the new salary cap, but far less than he would have commanded before the new collective bargaining agreement. He had the potential, however, to earn an additional $850,000 in performance bonuses for hitting marks such as twenty goals, thirty-five assists, and sixty points. Up to two million dollars more could be his with league-wide achievements: finishing top ten in scoring, goals, assists, or points-per-game, or winning a major trophy.

The payroll range under the new collective bargaining agreement started at $21.5 million and was capped at $39 million. Players would earn a minimum of $450,000, but no one player could earn more than 20 per cent of the upper limit of their team's total payroll. In other words, no one could make more than $7.8 million. Even before he laced up his skates for them, the Penguins knew that Sidney Crosby would turn out to be a bargain; he would earn more from his endorsement deals with Reebok and Gatorade than from his hockey salary.

As he signed the final page of his contract for the cameras, he looked ready for his close-up in a midnight-blue pinstripe suit, open-necked peach-coloured shirt, and black, square-toed dress shoes. His dark, wavy hair was freshly clipped and shaped with gel. Every time he smiled, flashbulbs popped as if he were on the red carpet. He was just a month removed from his eighteenth birthday. I could already see his boyhood beginning to fade away.

Crosby had moved into his room on the third floor of the Lemieux household the previous day. A few hours after arriving, even before training camp formally opened, he sought out the one activity that made him feel at home wherever he was in the world. He went to play hockey. With some of his new teammates – LeClair and Recchi, Palffy, the Russian defenceman Sergei Gonchar, and workhorse veteran Lyle Odelein – he skated for the first time in over a week and finally felt like things were settling down. He was nothing if not pragmatic about his situation. He possessed plenty of perspective – more than some adults twice his age – and almost always wore it on his sleeve.

"I'm trying to learn as much as I can out there, but I'm confident in what I can do," he said. "I'm looking at this as short-term as possible. I'm going to push myself to raise my game as much as I can in camp. It's going to be a challenge to go from junior to the NHL. I feel very fortunate to be in this situation. A lot of guys who are drafted early go to a team that's maybe rebuilding, but that's not the case here."

That final sentiment would come to haunt him.

At the contract signing, after he finished doing an hour's worth of interviews, he found a quiet moment to eat lunch in a corner table away from the hum of the press. With Ken Sawyer, his father, Troy, agent Pat Brisson, the co-managing director of IMG Hockey, and Dee Rizzo, director of player development at IMG and a long-time friend who first brought Crosby to the attention of the world's largest sports representation agency, he tucked into roast chicken breast, Caesar salad, and bottled water. Soon the crowd began to disperse.

As the 2005-2006 season prepared to get underway, the Penguins found themselves a franchise at two extremes of the NHL spectrum.

At one end, they had a rich history in the city and the league and had won two Stanley Cups, consecutively in the springs of 1991 and 1992, creating a mini-dynasty of sorts. At the other end, their future in Pittsburgh was very much in doubt. They played in the oldest arena in the league, a forty-four-year-old building so worn down it was impossible for the team to turn a profit as long as they inhabited it.

Training camp wasn't even forty-eight hours old when Lemieux made it clear that even if the Penguins sold out almost every game and went two rounds in the playoffs, the season would see them lose about seven million dollars. They would lose millions even if they won the Stanley Cup. It was simply impossible to squeeze any more revenue out of the old barn, originally built as a symphony hall with a retractable roof that had long ago rusted shut.

The Penguins were in the middle of preparing a proposal to try and land a gaming licence that would allow them to generate revenue from slot machines that would fund a $290 million state-of-the-art arena. It was obvious to everyone that without a new building or the commitment for one made in the coming year or so, the Penguins would be forced to leave Pittsburgh, where they had been since joining the league in the 1967 expansion. It was not a threat, Lemieux would explain, sometimes coolly and occasionally with edge, many times throughout the season. It was simple economics.

But with opening night still three weeks off, Lemieux was energized by the revival Crosby had sparked. After taking the Penguins off the market in July, Lemieux claimed he was recommitted to finding a solution to the arena problem. He also thought the team they were assembling was going to be quite good.

"It feels a lot like the early nineties. It's a lot more fun to play the game this year than it has been the last four years. Five or six teams have a good chance to win the Stanley Cup, and we feel we're one of those teams."

For the second week of camp, the Penguins moved a three-hour drive east across state to Wilkes-Barre, Pennsylvania, a former coal mining town nestled in the foothills of the Pocono Mountains, home of the Baby Penguins, their American Hockey League farm team.

I was surprised that fewer than a hundred people showed up at the Wachovia Arena, a modern building that held 8,100 for hockey, for the Penguins' first practice. The ones who were there had one reason to be. A middle-aged man nearby said to his buddy, "Everyone is here to see the kid." Others spoke of the possibility of Crosby and Lemieux playing on the same line in the first pre-season game against the Bruins. The same guy piped up again: "Of *course* they will. If you got the best toy at Christmas, would you let your brothers play with it first?"

NBC and their high-profile broadcast crew – John Davidson, Mike Emrick, and Pierre McGuire – had come to shoot a promotional spot with Lemieux and Crosby and to film footage of the Stanley Cup, which was in the house. Crosby didn't glimpse it, and if he had, he said, he wouldn't have dared go near it. "Everyone knows it is bad luck to touch the Cup until you've won it," he said.

NBC's visit to Penguins training camp, along with all the other national U.S. media outlets that would drop in over the coming weeks, was considered a cause for celebration.

"That is unprecedented for a network in the U.S. to do something pre-season," said Tom McMillan, a former

Penguins beat writer who had worked for the club for more than a decade and was now their vice-president of communications. "It may be normal in Canada, but it's unheard of around here. That's a direct result of Sidney. It's incredible. In a very short period of time we've become the centre of the hockey world. It's been a challenge. We're still trying to give him enough space to be an eighteen-year-old hockey player. But it's exciting for us."

Even though it seemed the hockey world had descended on Wilkes-Barre, only 5,000 people showed up for that night's game against Boston, a small turnout considering Lemieux and Crosby would both be in the lineup.

Crosby had not scored competitively since May 28, when he had three goals and an assist in the semifinal game that saw the Oceanic beat the Ottawa 67s to advance to the Memorial Cup final. Although he was excited, he wasn't counting this contest as his first "real" NHL game. That he would reserve for the regular season opener. But if he was nervous, he didn't show it. He patiently answered dozens of questions after the morning skate before leaving with his teammates for the hotel, where he would take a two-hour nap and eat a pre-game meal of pasta.

That night, he played like a man possessed. He was all over the ice, working doggedly behind the net, getting the puck out in front. He showed his acceleration and strength, darting into position and fighting along the boards. He drew three penalties that yielded two goals. But he also over-passed the puck and got dumped on his rear trying to take on towering Bruins defenceman Hal Gill. He nearly scored in the first period after slipping through two defenders for a breakaway, but the puck rolled off his stick when he went to stuff it beneath the right pad of the goaltender. Mark Recchi buried the rebound. Crosby got the assist. The Penguins lost 5-4 in overtime. But everyone in the dressing room seemed pleased enough, especially with Sidney's first showing.

"His acceleration, his on-ice presence, finding the holes . . . I thought he performed well," Lemieux said. "He had some great chances. I'm happy with the way he played. I know he was nervous a little bit before the game. He had some almost breakaways and fought along the boards. He made some good plays and got to the net.

"He's good on his skates, strong on his skates. He's amazing what he can do at eighteen. He just turned eighteen. In a couple of years he could be scary."

Olczyk was happy with the way Crosby skated and saw the ice but thought he should have shot the puck more often. Even still, he thought his young star was coming along on schedule. "But the stakes are going up," Olczyk cautioned. "Two weeks from tonight, everything is on the line."

It had been Crosby's nature to look for the pass first, to be playmaker, but he agreed he should have taken the shot more often. He was surprised at how fast and strong most of the NHL players were. Everyone had more jump than in junior. There was no time to think, only to react. Everything was a few steps faster than he was used to. It took him a little while to settle down, but he thought it went pretty well. He was in a good mood, but he seemed slightly preoccupied. "I think I can play here and help the team," he said.

THE ICEBOX, PITTSON, PENNSYLVANIA, SEPTEMBER 23, 2005:
The Icebox was exactly as one might picture it, a dumpy, freezing cold rink on the outskirts of Wilkes-Barre with a

concrete lobby that smelled of stale popcorn. As the Penguins practised, fans gathered in the lobby and milled outside, waiting for the players to sign autographs on the way to their cars. Sidney's dad, Troy, leaned against the wall, watching from a distance. The crowd grew deeper.

Crosby had a superstition about signing a sweater for a team he hadn't yet made. Even though it was preposterous to think he wouldn't make the NHL roster, he wasn't making any exceptions. Before training camp, the Penguins held an autograph session with Crosby to raise money for Hurricane Katrina victims. It cost forty dollars, and fans began lining up at five-thirty in the morning for a ten o'clock event that would last just an hour. They posted a sign at the head of the queue that Crosby would not sign any Penguins sweaters.

Here in Wilkes-Barre, even though training camp was a formality when it came to him being named to the roster, he stuck to his rule, refusing even to sign a miniature sweater sized for a teddy bear. No matter, the mob had other tokens – photographs, pucks, and caps – for him to scrawl his name on.

With Penguins media relations manager Todd Lepovsky at his side, Crosby emerged from the dressing room and shuffled slowly through the crowd. Still in his equipment, sweaty nylon socks, and shower sandals, he scribbled as he inched ahead. Little boys screamed to get his attention, calling him by his last name. Some of the adults shoved photographs and cards tucked neatly in albums towards him. He always instinctively reached for children first. He loved signing for kids but was warier of adults who appeared to be collectors trying for autographed goods to list on eBay. Sometimes he noticed the same guys from city to city, trying at every opportunity – hotels, practices, and games – for signatures and even changing their clothes and donning hats to look different each time.

Here at the Icebox it was mostly children with their parents, eager teenaged boys, and giddy girls. The crowd shrunk by a body or two with each step Crosby took. In what would become a familiar scene throughout the season, it took him ten minutes to move as many feet. Outside the door, Mario idled in his white Escalade. Crosby finally emerged, autograph hounds still at his sides. "Come on, we've got to go," Lemieux barked like an impatient father. Sidney climbed in back with his real father and Lepovsky, who would serve as Sidney's helpful shadow on many occasions during the season, got in front before they pulled away.

The Penguins played their first home game of training camp on September 27 against the Columbus Blue Jackets. At the pre-game skate that morning, Crosby was excited but underscored his excitement with caution. He was still figuring things out. "I don't want to put a lot of pressure on myself," he said. "I'm still finding out what it's all about."

In what was becoming a normal part of his routine, he had already put in almost a full day's work doing interviews after practice. That morning, the usual Pittsburgh media crowd – a beat writer from each of the city's two newspapers – plus local newspaper columnists and correspondents with Fox Sports, ESPN, and the network affiliates were there. So were three Canadian television networks, OLN, Fox, the *New York Times*, *Newsday*, and *USA Today*. Crosby did the last one walking from the arena to the parking lot. He did one-on-one interviews with all the national reporters, one after another without a break, answering many of the same questions while the others waited their turns nearby. At one point, with a half-dozen interviews down and as many to go, it was the first of only a few times all season I saw Crosby overwhelmed. His normally sunny face grew weary at moments. He glanced a few times at Tom McMillan and Keith Wehner. Only two weeks into the pre-season, it felt as though the frenzy surrounding Crosby was actually picking up steam. To be the centre of so much attention must have felt slightly bewildering. But he finished up his obligations. Then he went home to take his pre-game nap.

Later that night, before about eight thousand fans, the Penguins' best players, including Lemieux, beat the Blue Jackets taxi squad 7-2. Crosby said later that he had "a few butterflies" because it was his first game on home ice. The crowd loved him, and even though he didn't score a goal, he got a standing ovation before a failed shootout attempt. (Shootouts were held after every pre-season game no matter the score, to acclimatize fans to the practice.)

"I could say I'm not trying to show anything, but that wouldn't be true," he said, trying to explain his nervousness.

"He'll be okay," Lemieux said.

Crosby was having fun watching Lemieux, whose posters had adorned the wall of his bedroom while growing up in Cole Harbour. "It's unbelievable just to watch him," he said, as if the fact that he was playing with, never mind living with, a legend still hadn't fully hit him. In just seven days the season would start for real in New Jersey.

The grand, green, rolling hills of Allegheny County are as dramatic and defining a part of the Pennsylvania landscape as the ocean and craggy seashore are to Nova Scotia. In both places, the citizens' humble manner extended from a history of reliance on natural resources and the toil it took to harvest them from the earth. The working class culture and all its charms continue in both places even though the coal mines and steel mills here and the fisheries there all suffered steep decline.

For years, this hard-labour culture in Pittsburgh and across the state bred football players the way Canada's small towns spit out hockey stars. Crosby had landed in one of this country's most passionate sports cities. Pittsburgh fans were particularly hard core and hell-bent. Though the Steel City had its sporting identity shaped almost entirely by football and four Super Bowl championships between 1974 and 1979, they also cheered the Pirates and Penguins and college football and basketball from Penn State to Pitt.

Joe Namath, one of the quarterbacking legends to spring from Pennsylvania coal mining country, once called the entire state "Great football country." In a city that has produced some of the most prolific football players in history – Hall of Famers Mike Ditka, Tony Dorsett, Dan Marino, and Joe Montana among them – hockey had occasionally struggled to be more than an afterthought, especially in recent years.

It took the Penguins a while to catch on. Part of the NHL's first expansion, they missed the playoffs in five of their first seven years. When Mario Lemieux was drafted in 1984, they boasted the league's worst record two years running. Better teams in the later part of the decade finally made the Penguins competitive, and soon they were winning division titles and Stanley Cups.

Team president Ken Sawyer, who said he felt as though he had "turned thirty again" when the Penguins won the lottery, walked on air throughout training camp. He believed the club was going to be "the team of the decade."

"We're not sure where it's headed, but this is a great moment to savour," he said. "We have a galaxy of stars."

Suddenly, in the heart of football country, hockey was making a comeback, mostly because of Crosby. "There's going to be a transition period," Olczyk said, cautioning anyone who expected the rookie to perform like an all-star right away. "If things go well or not, it's not going to be strictly on a young guy's shoulders."

Paul Yunt had lived in Pittsburgh all of his forty-seven years. He loved the Steelers and Pirates, but when it came to the Penguins, he was a Super Fan. He went to every day of training camp practice, shunning real-life commitments to check out Crosby and catch up on hockey. A clerk at a downtown law office, Yunt had been off work for the past five months, sidelined by depression, but he had skipped his counselling appointments the first week of camp because the Penguins' return had lifted his spirits so much.

"This makes me feel so good. We're very spoiled here. We got Lemieux twenty years ago, and now we've got Crosby. Mario scored on his first shot in the NHL, and I expect that Crosby is going to come out and play. The city is in a buzz right now."

Crosby was looking good but still hadn't quite found his NHL legs. He wasn't scoring the way he hoped to but had established an instant chemistry on a line with Mark Recchi and John LeClair. Lemieux was pleased with his progress. "It's always tough for a young kid to start his career. There's so much pressure on him. He's working hard on his game, working hard in the weight room. He does everything right."

He was also working hard in practice, turning his speed up a notch, fine-tuning his reaction, honing his timing. While hockey practice could seem routine to an outsider, and even like drudgery compared to the excitement of a game, Crosby just loved to be on the ice and play with the puck. He could do it with teammates, but he was just as happy to do it by himself.

Before almost every game during the season, Crosby and his friend the francophone centre Maxime Talbot would head onto the ice in sneakers and backward baseball caps an hour before the puck drop and play hockey's version of catch, passing back and forth, backhand, forehand. When Talbot broke away to shoot on the net, Crosby bounced the puck on the blade of his stick for minutes at a time. It was a calming ritual they did nightly at home and eventually performed for themselves on the road. When Talbot was sent down to the minors for good in January, instead of getting another partner, Crosby continued alone with his pre-game routine but eventually stopped doing it after the Olympic break.

Sometimes in practice when Crosby scored or did something nifty with the puck, he smiled to himself, as if he could amuse himself for hours with nothing but a puck, a stick, and a sheet of ice. He played hacky sack with the puck, bumping it off the back of his skate, balancing on one leg, kicking it into the air. He would bring a chair onto the ice and pass the puck between its legs in figure eights. He shovelled it up on the blade of his stick and bounced it endlessly as if it were on string. It was part entertainment, part skills practice, and sometimes part therapy.

"In Rimouski if I played bad, and back then I could still play bad and still get a couple points, they had outdoor rinks I'd go to," he said. "The coach might tell us we had the next day off, but I'd get the trainer to put pucks and skates in my car so the coach wouldn't see. And I'd go out and shoot pucks at night by myself."

It was his favourite time of the day, pure joy. "Oh, it was the best. I didn't have anyone telling me what to do. No one was telling me to dump pucks in or play the system. No one cared if I missed or scored. It was just me out there. That was probably one of the best therapies I'd ever done over those two years. That was my spot, my place."

One night, Yannick Dumais, the Oceanic's hockey operations assistant, was driving by at midnight and spotted Crosby out on the ice in the pitch dark. "I wasn't supposed to be there, but he never told my coach. I was just so competitive, and I didn't like not scoring. I'd go out there and work on things by myself."

The same work ethic kept him toiling harder than the others in NHL practice. One morning he fetched a white bucket full of pucks and shot repeatedly on Jocelyn Thibault for a half-hour after practice. He had been taking mental notes in the pre-season games after not scoring as much as he wanted. "I'm thinking about what I'm going to do too much. I don't like missing."

At the same time, he watched his veteran teammates closely. He was sandwiched between Mark Recchi and John LeClair in the dressing room, and he took notes on them too. What are their practice habits? When do they eat and sleep? When do they lift weights? How do they interact with the coach, the equipment manager, reporters?

"They're professionals when they come to the rink," Crosby said. "They're serious. It's contagious to be around guys like that. It's fun to have guys around who will give you feedback. There are questions to ask, but it's more observing. Sometimes it's best when you're just there watching."

The two were considered character guys in the dressing room – players long on steadying influence and short on anything that might steer a rookie in the wrong direction. LeClair, who proved to be a terrific mentor in the room for the young kids over the length of the season, quipped, "The last thing I want to do is tell him something that messes him up."

Recchi had seen a lot of first-year players land in the NHL overconfident and unwilling to ask questions. "If you're not afraid to ask questions, you can get a lot out of the older players. I was like Sid, a sponge. I took everything in from the veterans, how they handled things, how they prepared. You've got to use us. That's what we're here for.

"There are ups and downs. One day you feel like a world beater, and the next you think you're going back to the minors. Even someone with his talent will have good days and bad days. And that's why we're here, to bring him up and say 'This day is gone, get ready for tomorrow.' He's level-headed, but he's definitely going to have those moments."

In those moments during training camp, Crosby worked out his nerves in the weight room, on the bike, and on the ice. He went to a Steelers game, where he was recognized and cheered. He counted down the days until the season started.

"The dream won't be realized until October 5 in New Jersey," he said. "Until then, it's still a dream."

The day before the series I was writing began running in the *Globe*, I phoned Sidney's mother, Trina, to let her know about it. Troy was in Pittsburgh watching practices and pre-season games. His mom was about my age and that helped frame my perspective on Crosby. She was surprised, only half so, when I told her about my season-long commitment to documenting her son's rookie year. They had gotten used to the intense media interest in Sidney. She and Taylor, Sidney's nine-year-old sister, would join Troy in New Jersey for the first game and also attend the Penguins' home opener a few days later.

They were attempting to let Sidney ease into his big moment without interfering too much. "He's eighteen now. We're trying to give him his space but at the same time not miss anything," she said. "We want to let him develop his own life.

"Each time he'd go away and come home, he'd have grown up. Now he's eighteen, and he thinks he knows everything. Like everyone. He's a very normal kid in a very not normal situation. It's like he's gone to college and gotten his dream job. He just seems so happy. But he's not happy just to be there. He wants to prove to the guys he belongs."

He was doing just that. After thirteen days at training camp, Crosby had noticeably improved. He was faster and had fine-tuned his ability to anticipate passes and plays. He was fitting in. He also felt more at ease. The closest player to his age was Marc-Andre Fleury, who was twenty at the start of camp. Being the youngest kid in the room didn't bother Crosby, who had competed against older kids his whole life. He didn't think age had anything to do with ability.

"I have always had the attitude that age is just a number. I've always been the youngest one, the one learning, looking up, but eventually you want to be someone who is going to score that big goal and be out there in the last minute with the game on the line," he said. "I'm just trying to learn how to be that guy."

"Early on, it was be seen and not heard, and now I know his voice when he's around the corner," Olczyk said. "He's more comfortable, more outgoing. He's fitting in, learning."

Phil Bourque had a commentator's keen sense of observation and a player's sense for what was really going on. "Ed and Mario are careful about how much ice time he puts in, how many games he plays, how much media attention he can handle," Bourque said. "Everything is being controlled right now to put him in a safe place."

On October 2, after the Penguins' last exhibition game, Olczyk thought Crosby's confidence had grown measurably. He saw nothing but potential for his young star. "In a couple of years, he's going to do some damage."

3

BORN TO PLAY HOCKEY

He is the perfect hockey player.

IT WAS ENTIRELY possible that the only thing less than average about Sidney Crosby was his physical size and stature. At five foot eleven and 193 pounds, the natural centre was smaller than the average NHL player, who ranged closer to six foot one and 205 pounds. He was even smaller than the average Penguin, who was the same height but a couple of pounds heavier.

But perhaps the most standout feature that bolstered Crosby's on-ice talents, aside from a vision that bordered on sixth sense and the innate ability to make creative plays in difficult situations, was his impressive lower body strength.

The NHL draft guide from 2005 is a collection of player biographies and notes from scouts on the potential picks. Crosby's read like a report card from an honour roll student headed for Harvard on full scholarship.

An exceptional skater with a smooth stride, tremendous balance and agility . . . he has great speed to the outside and can also split the defense carrying the puck or receiving passes for clear breakaways . . . very quick off the mark with tremendous acceleration . . . his vision is unparalleled . . . can feed wings from anywhere in the offensive zone both forehand and backhand and set them up for scoring chances . . . uses the hard crisp pass and puts it on the tape every time . . . can also use the soft flip pass effectively . . . his leg strength and stamina allows him to be first on the puck and many times be the first guy back to help the defense on transition. . . . Blessed with natural scoring instincts, he can score many ways and always seem to be in the clear to receive passes and turn them into scoring chances . . . needless to say he has great hockey sense; can play any position . . . can control the power play . . . good on faceoffs . . . very accurate wrist shot . . . his backhand is as good as the forehand . . . competes every shift, works hard but makes it look easy and plays with discipline . . . not adversely affected by physical play . . . takes many hits to make a play and will retaliate, which he has to do often because of the close checking and makes it look easy sometimes. Unselfish player who plays all game situations . . . logs a lot of ice time . . . at home or on the road, does not matter to him; plays with great poise . . . possesses great leadership qualities, desire and determination . . . will strip opponents of the puck rather than punish with the body.

The thing I noticed immediately about Crosby the first time I saw him in the Penguins' dressing room that September was his thighs. They were the circumference of good-sized tree trunks. His quadriceps were wide and sturdy, and they tapered into a bow-legged stance.

It was the same with his glutes, substantial and strong and set high to power what often appeared to be an effortless skating stride. His upper body was compact, with lean, ropey muscle. He was strong but sleek, aerodynamic, with about 7 per cent body fat and was as pliable and limber as a gymnast.

"He's stretching all the time," said Penguins forward Colby Armstrong, another rookie and Crosby's roommate on the road. "If he's not sleeping, he can't sit still."

Crosby came in a package that, because he was only eighteen, left all kinds of room for potential. He was, in the words of Stephane Dube, the Penguins' strength and conditioning coach, built for hockey.

"Physically, when I first saw him I thought, 'Wow,'" Dube said. "You can see he's built for speed. The guy was born to play hockey. Physically, he is something else. The way he skates, the way he handles himself positionally, the way he puts his legs, you can see the kid is very strong.

"Before I even saw him in shorts, I knew his legs would probably be like tree trunks. When I finally saw them, I was like, 'Whoa!' His legs are so strong and he's only eighteen. He won't hit his full potential until he's like, twenty-four or twenty-five."

Dube, who is from Montreal and has been training professional hockey players for almost two decades, first saw

Crosby play as a junior in Quebec. He never imagined having the chance to actually work with him.

"For me, it's a really fun thing. I feel blessed that the kid has come into my life. You could see even as a kid he was gifted," Dube said. "But even though Sid is gifted physically, he works like Rudy."

It was a reference to the 1993 film of the same name, the true story of Dan "Rudy" Ruettiger, a five-foot-six Notre Dame football player who warmed the bench but practised as if he were a starter and finally got a chance to prove himself in the last game of the season.

"There's the kid who doesn't have talent but works like his life depends on it. But Sid, he's got more talent than anyone and still works like a guy who doesn't have any. He doesn't rely on the fact he's gifted physically. He wants to be the best, in the weight room, on the ice, everywhere. He never takes a day off."

When Sidney was a young boy, all he wanted to do was play hockey. His parents remembered him in the basement, shooting on a net set up in front of the washing machine and dryer, where the puck often missed its intended target and left the dryer so infamously scuffed with black marks that the Penguins designed a between-periods promotion around fans shooting into a dryer they wheeled onto the ice. Even Jay Leno brought one out for Crosby to shoot at during his *Tonight Show* appearance after the draft.

He shot on his grandmother Linda Crosby while she played goal on a chair in the living room. He shot on anything that would remain still. He started skating when he was just two and a half years old, and was playing Timbits hockey with Dartmouth at the first opportunity, when he turned five. He always played against older kids.

"He always was more advanced than the other kids," Troy said. "Everyone else would be skating on their ankles, and he was skating and passing the puck. He even had a natural wrist shot."

In 1994, when he was seven years old, Crosby began attending a Halifax hockey camp for the top players in the Maritimes. One of the older boys who taught at the camp was Brad Richards, the Tampa Bay Lightning forward who grew up not far away in Murray Harbour, Prince Edward Island. He saw Crosby four or five summers in a row.

"You see a lot from a lot of kids early, but he was different. Even the way he put his equipment on was different. He was already professional in the way he carried himself. Even at that early age, you could tell he was special, head and shoulders above everyone else his age. He never stopped learning, he just kept going. Kids usually peak. He never did."

Crosby followed Richards in Rimouski, and Richards kept tabs on Crosby as he progressed through the junior ranks. He was constantly impressed. "I'd never seen a junior player play a pro-style game like he does," Richards said. "You don't see kids using their bodies the way he does. That's why he'll adapt so well to the NHL. He has all the moves, but that's what's put him ahead of everyone else his age."

Crosby got an earlier start than most kids in every respect, taking on a personal trainer when he was just thirteen years old. Playing against older, bigger kids meant he took a lot of abuse on the ice, so Troy and Trina began looking into the benefits of getting Sidney a personal trainer. That's how they discovered Andy O'Brien.

"They were looking to find someone to work with him and develop him physically," said O'Brien, who also worked full-time for the Florida Panthers but trained Crosby for the past five years in the off-season.

"He was a thirteen-year-old playing against sixteen-year-olds, and they wanted someone who could develop his mind and body so he could continue to compete against older players who were running him. They had identified their kid had a special talent and were willing to do whatever it took to develop it. And Sidney had a determination about wanting to develop as well. It just seemed to come very naturally to him."

At the time he met the Crosbys, O'Brien was based in Prince Edward Island. The family briefly contemplated moving to the Island, but the twenty-two-year-old O'Brien was finishing school and wanted to expand his business to Halifax. That summer, he relocated and began working with the young phenom.

"The minute I met him, I was impressed with his maturity," O'Brien said. "When he walked into a weight room at thirteen, he knew exactly what he was doing and what he was there for. He reminded me of a lawyer entering a court room. He was polished and focussed and had this gift of vision. He was able to free himself from distractions. He had the greatest amount of maturity of anyone I'd ever worked with. It made me want to work with him.

"So many times you hear about a great young player and then you never hear about them again, but he was very unusual."

Crosby grew up adoring the *Rocky* films and identified with the pugilist protagonist. When he left for the Minnesota prep school Shattuck-St. Mary's at fifteen to pursue hockey at a higher level, his parents gave him a poster of a runner taking on a steep flight of stairs. The message was that persistence led to excellence. He hung it in his room. "I loved that, and I identified with that image, those movies," Crosby said. "They said it reminded them of how much I loved those movies. But I got a lot out of them. I loved how they portrayed hard work translating into winning."

O'Brien even found the kid was inspiring him, and as the years went by, the pair became friends. "Because he was so serious and passionate, it set my mentality with what I was doing. And suddenly there I was, learning things from a thirteen-year-old."

They began working four hours a day through the summer, mostly at St. Mary's University in Halifax. As Crosby matured physically, they increased the workload, training three times a day, beginning at 8 a.m. and not knocking off until early afternoon. Speed work and lower body and then upper body workouts were punctuated by meal breaks to refuel.

Even though he grew up not far from Citadel Hill in Halifax, Crosby became intimately familiar with the city's natural centrepiece. The former military fortress and national historic site sits atop steep slopes and offers uneven footing and inspirational views of the Atlantic Ocean – Mother Nature's treadmill.

"It was a great way to throw off his balance and make him aware of his environment," O'Brien said. "We did a lot of agility work there, a lot of stops and starts. He ran up the hill with a medicine ball, up and down and laterally. It was a big part of his training. We *love* that hill."

For O'Brien, the best thing about Crosby besides his God-given talents was that he was too young to have picked up any bad habits. O'Brien was used to undoing the mistakes some pros had spent years practising. "Here was a kid who was a blank piece of paper."

Hockey is a highly technical sport when well executed. They did speed work, plyometrics – performing explosive resistance moves to improve power – weight lifting, and body movement geared to refine Sidney's moves on the ice so he could get the most from every stride.

"Most hockey players, when they run they're bad runners, when they lift weights they do it wrong, they are very sloppy in the way they control their bodies," O'Brien said. "So with Sidney, before we did any running we taught him how to run. We taught him how to jump and stabilize his body. When you move improperly and engage in exercise, all you're doing is breaking your body down and setting it up for injuries. But if you move correctly, you are moving for power every single time."

Crosby's strong, sturdy haunches made for a smooth and powerful pace. All his hard work looked easier because he had learned to move his body efficiently. His first few steps were explosive and then the economy of motion drove him.

Dube, who shared O'Brien's training philosophies, believed many of Crosby's on-ice skills sprang from mechanics honed from starting workouts at such an early age. Teaching young Sidney the fundamentals of human movement amplified his abilities.

"He got the right exercises and the proper environment at the right age," Dube said. "I've seen so many guys who don't start working out until junior and then they think they can change the world. But it's a process. They are most influential from ten to sixteen years old. I'm not saying a little kid needs a personal trainer, but if you work on co-ordination, movement, balance, and agility, work on building an athlete rather than a hockey player, you develop good habits and form early, and it makes all the difference."

Sidney, Dube said, was physically ready to play in the NHL a year before he actually did. "Not only because of his talent, but the way he thinks about the game. A lot of guys have had talent in the past, but to put the mind that he has to that talent is special."

In training camp, Phil Bourque predicted Crosby would take ten to fifteen games to adjust to the NHL. That's exactly how long Crosby needed to look completely comfortable as a boy among men.

"He's a sponge. His eyes are wide open. You can see him absorbing his surroundings, feeding off everything that's going on. No matter how good you get, you can never stop learning. He gets that. It's rare in this day and age of athletes. Maybe some get caught up in the money or the accolades and come in on their own page doing their own thing. But this kid seems to have a great feel for exactly what he has to be doing."

Even with all the elite level training in the world, Crosby's commitment to the process was highly unusual for his age. He carefully watched what he ate, read food labels, eschewed junk food and soda pop.

"He took an interest in a really high-performance approach not only in his workouts, but also his lifestyle," O'Brien said. "I give him high marks for being about to commit to that at such a young age, because it's not an easy thing at any age.

"He doesn't go to parties. He doesn't go to bars. He doesn't have the same lifestyle a normal teenager would. He's just not interested in that. He's very seriously committed to being a professional athlete and doesn't see it as a sacrifice. There's just no attraction."

The previous summer, O'Brien accompanied Crosby to Prince Edward Island, where he was playing in the Brad Richards Celebrity Golf Tournament. Crosby had to be at the tee at 9 a.m., but he got up at six o'clock and went running on the beach – where jogging on the sand dunes improved strength and balance for skating – for two hours with his trainer. He was the only player at the tournament to bring his strength coach.

"For him, it would have been unacceptable to do anything less," O'Brien said. "Everyone has a choice of lifestyle. And even though some commit to occasionally take it easy or commit just partway, he's never influenced by people around him. He never loses his vision. He's not swayed by peer pressure. He's got a confidence in what he's doing most people his age don't have."

The result of his dedication is what has allowed Crosby to excel at every level of hockey he has played.

He can barrel down the ice at top speed and look as though he is hardly working. He can burst into open ice before a defender even notices he has lifted his lead leg.

His legs are so strong that he can protect the puck better than most. He charges down the ice and sets up like a human tripod, legs wide out with his stick in the middle and the puck protected in the expanse between. Defenders have a difficult time getting to him and the puck as he approaches the opposing net.

He reminded silver-haired Penguins president Ken Sawyer of a young Guy Lafleur. "He's one of those players you notice every shift he's on the ice. His creativeness, he has incredible speed, just incredible. He's much more physically impressive than Wayne Gretzky was."

In the fall of 2005, there was little doubt in anyone's mind that Crosby still had some growing left to do. He was listed at what I thought was just an ever-so-generous five foot eleven in the Penguins media guide. He had been noted as a full inch shorter in the World Junior team guide the previous December. He said earnestly that he had been "rounded down." He had grown a good inch over the summer. But he still couldn't sprout a full chin of whiskers or even a half-decent moustache.

Dube estimated Crosby could add up to ten pounds of muscle by the beginning of his second season. "His muscles are not mature," he said. "He's going to accumulate a lot of strength over the next year. And even then he's far from his peak. He won't hit that until between twenty-three and twenty-seven. This kid is going to be even stronger and faster. The sky's the limit for him."

Though Dube's primary job was to concern himself with Crosby's physicality, he loved the kid's personality even more. He was raised right and it showed.

"As talented as the hockey player is, the human being is

even better," Dube said. "He's not pretentious. He never makes you feel like he's the big deal. He talks to everyone and remembers people's names, remembers everything, pays attention to so many things."

Indeed, on the day after the final game of the season, Dube stopped by to gently remind Crosby that he had a few things he wanted him to sign before he took off for the summer.

"Definitely," Crosby said without missing a beat. "I won't forget. I'm keeping a mental list." And it was easy to believe he was.

Mark Koelfgen, a writer for the New York agency McGarry Bowen, which came up with Crosby's Reebok ad, attempted to tap into his childhood for the television spot that began airing in November and featured a montage of the rinks he had played in as a kid set to a sentimental voiceover. It didn't take Koelfgen long to figure out that where Crosby came from – a good family and the blue collar Maritimes – defined him more than anything else.

"I could tell that for him it was all about sacrifice and devotion to the sport. He's one of those people who was, at a very young age, capable of sacrifice and control, very rare for a kid. He wasn't hanging out at the mall wolfing down pizza. When he wasn't playing hockey, he was playing hockey.

"My sense of Sidney is that he comes from a working class background and gave up a lot for his sport. Well, now you see the consequences of that."

"I think he understands what he represents," Dube said. "He never turns down a single autograph. One day I had two jerseys from Rimouski for him to sign. He came in and he said, 'Steph, I could sign the Oceanic jersey all day long.' It was important to him that those people were there from the first day. It means so much to him to give back."

Dube paused and his face grew meditative.

"So often you don't realize the impact you have in a person's life. It's really serious. You can't imagine the magnitude, but I know he gets that."

Early in training camp and many times throughout the season, Crosby often said he felt lucky to be where he was, on the cusp of his National Hockey League career. He often reminded me of the cliché that luck is what happens when opportunity meets preparation. In October 2005, the talent and training, sacrifice and preparation, all of it was about to pay off when it met finally with the opportunity he had been waiting for his whole life.

4

UNDER A PENGUIN'S WING

I've been waiting a long time for this.

ONE OF THE MOST compelling storylines to emerge immediately after the draft lottery and hold interest through the first few months of the season was the relationship between Sidney Crosby and Mario Lemieux.

They had been introduced the previous summer by Crosby's agent, Pat Brisson, and had skated together and gotten to know each other.

More than two decades earlier, Lemieux held the Quebec Major Junior League scoring records that Crosby finished just shy of. Lemieux was such a highly coveted top draft pick that Eddie Johnston, then the Penguins' general manager, traded the team's top defencemen and sent their goaltender to the minors so as not to finish out of last place in the 1983-1984 season standings.

When the Penguins won the right to draft Crosby, it was eerily similar to what had happened two decades ago. In his final year of junior with Laval, Lemieux scored 133 goals and had 149 assists to break Guy Lafleur's long-standing record for goals and Pierre Larouche's for total points. Crosby led the league in both his seasons to earn its top honours. But the eras in which they arrived could not have been more different. For one thing, Lemieux's draft selection wasn't broadcast on television. For another, Crosby proudly pulled on his Penguins sweater before the cameras. Even if he had *wanted* more money in the way Lemieux did, under the new collective bargaining agreement it wasn't possible for a rookie to earn more than $850,000 in salary.

On the afternoon of the draft lottery, Lemieux was at the doctor's office in Pittsburgh with his daughter when he learned the Penguins would select first. He immediately called Brisson, who was at the Crosby's house watching it on television. Brisson handed his cellphone to Sidney, and Mario offered congratulations and told him that Pittsburgh would be happily taking him first overall with their pick. Crosby assured Lemieux he would be delighted to become a Pittsburgh Penguin.

Later, it was Brisson who gently broached the subject of Crosby living with Lemieux, suggesting that perhaps it would be nice if the kid could live with the family while he adjusted to life in the NHL. Mario had stayed with a local family when he first arrived in Pittsburgh, and the living arrangements smoothed his first season. "Mario liked Sidney as a person," Brisson said. "When they met, they immediately hit it off. Sidney was laughing and telling stories and felt very comfortable around Mario, so it was a good fit for both."

Lemieux liked the idea. His wife, Nathalie, and four kids, Lauren, twelve, Stephanie, ten, Austin, nine, and Alexa, eight, were excited to have another youngster, not all that much older than them, join the family.

The day Crosby arrived at the house in Sewickley, a stately suburb about a half-hour drive outside of the city, Austin and Stephanie, who both played organized hockey, had a game of ball hockey going in the driveway while they waited for him. They saw him as a new playmate, an addition to the brood rather than a house guest. Crosby laughed when he saw the game and joined in immediately.

"Sidney liked that a lot," Lemieux said. "It made him feel more comfortable. He's adjusted very well. He plays with the kids a lot, and he's very chatty. He talks all the time. The kids love him. We talk a lot, have dinner together every night."

During training camp they would get up early, around 6:30 a.m., work out and skate, and then return home to relax. "We do our own thing until the kids get home from school and start bothering him," Lemieux said. Often Crosby would head out into the backyard "to goof around" or play video games and sing karaoke with them. The kids were always trying to wrestle with him. But Crosby loved it. "I like a busy house," he said. It also gave his life, which could feel surreal and hectic with so much travel and so many commitments, a normal sensibility.

Early in the season Lemieux joked, "We have no rules," and said Sidney was allowed to have girls visit but not overnight. When Sidney was asked about it later, his cheeks turned red and he quipped, "No comment."

Their relationship, despite the twenty-two-year age difference, was more buddy-buddy than father-son. The living situation was seen as a real boon for Crosby as he got used to the NHL.

"I think just being around him is going to help me," he said. "I can ask him little questions, even about things in town, where things are, and he's just going to make me feel comfortable right away and familiarize me with what's here. That's the main thing, being around him and seeing how he goes about things in his day."

"He got lucky," Brad Richards observed. "He's with one of the best to ever play the game. To have that to learn from is amazing. Mario will protect him. He's got people watching him every shift, every step. It's tough on a thirty-year-old man, never mind an eighteen-year-old kid."

Ryan Malone was a native Pittsburgher who was the Penguins' best rookie the previous season. His father, Greg Malone, had played for the club and was now a scout. Even though he had grown up around the Penguins, he knew it could be jarring to look up in the dressing room and see one of your teammates and one of the greatest players of all time.

"When you're lining up alongside Mario Lemieux, and you've looked up to him your whole life, that's intimidating," Malone said. "But you eventually realize that you're on the team, and in that regard you're all the same. It doesn't matter how old or young you are."

Still, seeing Lemieux at the breakfast table had to be odd, at least at first, but Crosby seemed to settle in quickly. They drove to practice and games together until Crosby bought his own car a few months into the season. Lemieux tried to balance being a steadying influence with giving the kid his space, and Crosby was naturally drawn to his younger teammates, guys such as young forwards Malone, Maxime Talbot, and Matt Murley.

In the end, the experiment had gone well enough that

Crosby would decide to stay on at the Lemieux house for at least another season. The kids had been pestering him to stay, and he let them know he would return in late August.

"They were just great for me," he said. "The whole atmosphere, the environment was perfect. I'm away from things a little bit there. I don't have to worry about cooking or cleaning. When you have so much going on, it's nice to come home and not have to worry about stuff like that." He paused and chuckled. "I'm trying to get as many years as I can in with that."

He felt it was a good, stabilizing influence to be there.

"It's like a second family for me now, though sometimes it's tough to think of it that way. I mean, it's Mario Lemieux, a guy I grew up watching, but they've treated me really good and it's like relatives. It's not like I'm just staying there. My sister gets along with the kids, and they always ask about each other. It's a great environment and it couldn't have worked out better."

Lemieux's wife, his teenage sweetheart, Nathalie, took care of Crosby and treated him like a fifth child. She cooked him special meals and repeated them if he had played well after eating something specific.

"One night she made a certain spaghetti sauce, and I had it and had a four-point game. Then we played the next night and she had run out, so when I got home all this stuff was laid out on the counter and she was trying to make it from scratch. All the kids were helping. I was like, 'Oh my God.' I was blown away that she'd actually do this for me, go to that length to make sure I was comfortable and happy. I'm spoiled there in a way, but I really appreciate it."

On October 11, 1984, Mario Lemieux scored on the first shot of his first shift on the first night of his NHL career. He finished the season with 100 points – forty-three goals and fifty-seven assists in seventy-three games. Olczyk was drafted the same year, as was Crosby's father, Troy, who was a goaltender with the Verdun Junior Canadiens of the Quebec Major Junior Hockey League.

While playing with Laval, Lemieux once beat Troy Crosby with a slapshot from centre ice. Eddie Olczyk, who was the number three pick that same year – he went to the Chicago Blackhawks – knew how long a shadow his captain cast.

"I was intimidated when I first came into the room," Olczyk said of his first days as the Penguins coach the previous season. "It's hard not to be intimidated by a player like him. But what better a player to learn from, because he lived it. When Mario came here in 1984, he was the guy. But now we have six or seven other players who will share the limelight."

When Lemieux arrived in Pittsburgh, he barely spoke a word of English. But Crosby spoke better than just decent French. He had learned over two seasons in Rimouski and continued to practise it in Pittsburgh when he had the chance. Lemieux acknowledged that he wasn't nearly as mature at the same age. He didn't have the same training habits, smoked, and loved junk food. But he had much to share from seventeen seasons.

"He's always asking questions. I'm here to give him some confidence and encouragement and look out for him, make sure he's holding up with everything that's going on. It's going to be a lot easier for him to start his career."

Crosby had already formed a plan for how he would approach the season and what he wanted to accomplish other than winning. "I just want to be a good role model, an honest worker on the ice, and a good person off it. You can't be putting in time."

He figured Lemieux would be a big part of refining that character at the NHL level. "It's a matter of getting good habits," Crosby said. "A lot of guys start out and don't have someone to point them in the right direction. I feel fortunate to have that."

Lemieux felt just as fortunate to have Sidney in his life as a player and adopted son. He was committed to keeping the Penguins in Pittsburgh and was willing to lose roughly seven million dollars a season for the next few years if a new building was on the horizon. In the early weeks of training camp, Lemieux was in the best mood many remembered ever seeing him in. "I can't remember when I have seen him so excited and smiling so much," Craig Patrick noted.

Given everything Crosby had already accomplished, one of the most remarkable things was making Lemieux, who would turn forty years old on opening night, October 5, feel like a young man again. For his part, Lemieux hoped to turn that spark into twenty to twenty-five minutes a night on the ice.

"It's difficult to play when the building is half full, but Sidney is allowing us to start turning things around," Lemieux said. "Drafting him allowed us to put a good team on the ice this year."

The day before Crosby signed his contract, Lemieux inked a one-year deal worth three million dollars, a 43 per cent pay cut from his 2003-2004 earnings of $5.25 million.

He had been playing professional hockey almost as long as his young protegé had been on the earth. Lately, it was rare to see him without a grin on his slim face. He even felt upbeat about seeing an arena built. "Optimistically," he said, "we'll be here forever."

In a pre-season game against Columbus, Lemieux had shown signs of his old self. He scored once and set up three other goals in the meaningless 7-2 win. He was having a terrific training camp. It took him about a week to get comfortable; after that, he didn't look nearly his age.

"I felt better," Lemieux said after his four-point night. "The first couple of games, I didn't feel good at all, especially handling the puck and making plays. But tonight I felt good on my skates, making good plays and seeing the ice. When I'm able to see the ice ahead of time when I get the puck, I'm able to make some pretty good plays."

CONTINENTAL AIRLINES ARENA, EAST RUTHERFORD, N.J., OCTOBER 5, 2005: At the morning skate on the day of his first game in the NHL, Crosby emerged from the tunnel between the dressing room and the ice. He looked up at the seats behind one of the nets and saw his parents and his agent, Pat Brisson of IMG, surrounded by a cadre of reporters.

He shook his head in disbelief and half-chuckled. "Oh my God," he said. The *New York Times* was lined up to talk to his mom and dad.

It was a big day for Crosby, but it was also a huge day for the new NHL, which had not seen hockey played since the Tampa Bay Lightning hoisted the Stanley Cup. For the first time in history, opening night featured all thirty teams in action.

But most of the action and the attention seemed to be right here in the swamps of Jersey, focussed on the kid who had been called, in only slight exaggeration, hockey's saviour. "It's going to be a long day for him," Eddie Olczyk said. "Seven-thirty is not going to come soon enough."

I left the team hotel on my way to the morning skate and spotted four gentlemen waiting in the parking lot where the team bus was parked. One of them was wearing a T-shirt with the words Cole Harbour printed on the chest.

Dan Gillis ran a barbershop in Cole Harbour. He and three buddies were on a trip to see seven NHL games in as many days, starting with Crosby's debut.

They would also travel to North Carolina, Buffalo, New York, Philadelphia, Detroit, and Toronto. He wanted to see what the new league had to offer, but mostly he was here to see the kid.

"He's going to be a star in this league, a superstar is more like it," Gillis said. "And it's all going to start tonight, when he steps out on the ice. This is a once-in-a-lifetime event. I wouldn't have missed it for anything."

At practice, Crosby felt precisely the same way, minus the superstar predictions. "It's going to be a good feeling, stepping out onto that ice. I am ready for it. I've been waiting a long time for this.

"It's something I've been imagining, and I want to enjoy it. I'm nervous, but anyone in this position, doing it for the first time, would be. But I don't want to get it over with. I want to enjoy it."

The past few days, he had been thinking a lot about his family, the sacrifices they had made to get him here, the extra jobs delivering flyers they all took to pay for the best equipment they could afford and hockey trips that doubled as family vacations. "I've been thinking about all the people that helped me along the way. I've been thinking about my family. But I'm always thinking about them."

The previous day, before the team left for New Jersey on their charter flight, he woke up at six o'clock in the morning, an hour and a half earlier than normal. He felt anxious. His stomach was jitterbugging, and he wanted to make sure he picked out a nice suit and didn't forget to pack anything he needed, so he could concentrate on playing hockey.

After arriving in New Jersey, the Penguins held a press conference in a hotel ballroom, an unprecedented move before the first game of the season. They put Crosby and Lemieux before the microphones and cameras to answer questions from dozens of reporters from the U.S. and Canada. The Devils had allowed for about 150 media members for the game, the sort of numbers usually reserved for Stanley Cup final games. McMillan was even asked if Crosby's parents and little sister would be made available to the press.

"When [former number one pick] Eric Lindros played his first game, it was a sidebar," he said. "This is unprecedented."

Even though the attention focussed on Crosby had grown extreme over the past week, recent days had also unfolded in a routine: practice, team meetings, workouts in the weight room, more practice, plenty of sleeping, the last-minute fine-tuning of plays and systems.

On game day he woke up in the team hotel, a nice but

unremarkable Embassy Suites tucked away in a mall in Secaucus, N.J., a ten-minute drive from the arena. He showered and dressed in a dark suit and dress shoes and went down for breakfast shortly before 9:30 a.m. He ate an omelette and yogurt, drank orange juice and bottled water, and talked quietly with some of his teammates. Lemieux sat across the dining area by himself, reading *USA Today*.

Crosby was anxious before practice, but getting onto the ice, stretching and skating and working on drills helped him relax. Near the end, as his teammates began heading off, he stayed out, drifting around in lazy figure eights, making backhand and forehand passes, bouncing the puck off his skates and dribbling it between them.

When he got inside the cramped visitors' locker room, with its scuffed blue floor, cold concrete walls, and un-comfortable folding chairs, Crosby removed his helmet, sat down, and stripped off his jersey. Three television cameras filmed his every move. They shot him removing his elbow pads, and unlacing his skates, and dropping his sweaty hockey socks in a pile.

"Oh my God," Kara Yorio, the NHL writer for the *Sporting News*, said as she looked on. "Is it *always* like this?"

I had gotten used to the circus, but it had reached another level with the first game just seven hours away.

Crosby felt a thousand emotions throughout the day. He was eager and excited, nervous and tense, anxious and awestruck, expectant and happy. It was the biggest day of his life so far, and once it was over, he would be able to say that, finally, he was an NHL player.

"There's no doubt in my mind that I've done all I can to prepare myself; I have to go out there with confidence," he said. "You can't have any doubt. I am going to play hockey in the NHL."

During warm-ups he skated furiously, head down, concentrating, an action he said later made him "feel comfortable."

Shortly before the player introductions, he stood among his teammates in the blue carpeted hallway outside the visitors' dressing room, his head bowed in meditation. He was nervous. He teetered ever so slightly from side to side on his skates with the fretfulness of a teenaged boy waiting for his prom date to descend the staircase.

The lights in the arena dimmed and the Penguins skated onto the ice. The crowd booed. It was just a few minutes after 7:30 p.m. It was Mario Lemieux's fortieth birthday.

After the red carpet was rolled up and tucked away, and "The Star-Spangled Banner" sung in lung-busting glory, the puck dropped. And after Malone, Lemieux, and Palffy had taken the first shift, Crosby vaulted over the boards like an anxious colt kicking at a barn stall door. The time in the first period was 19:28. His linemates, Mark Recchi and John LeClair, were his tutors. Sidney Crosby's NHL career was underway.

On his first shift, he made a nice interception near centre ice and had a decent scoring chance almost immediately. He swooped in on Martin Brodeur's stick side and tried to tuck the puck past him with a backhand, but the veteran goaltender brushed it aside. After the game, Crosby would ask Brodeur if he could have the stick as a keepsake. Brodeur happily gave it to him.

In the second period, he hit the crossbar, and the fans chanted in singsong, "Overrated!" and "Parise's better!"

Zach Parise was the Devils' own top rookie prospect, a cheerful centre from Minnesota who was a first-round pick in 2003. His father, J.P. Parise, had coached Crosby at Shattuck-St. Mary's.

In the third period, with the Penguins on a power play, Crosby found himself behind the Devils' net. He corralled the puck and made a tight, tidy pass to Recchi, who scored. Crosby raised his stick and pumped his fist, but not too emphatically. The Penguins were losing 4-1, and the game looked out of reach. Muted celebration, even for the first NHL point, seemed more appropriate. The taunts rained down again when Crosby, on a frantic breakaway, tried to go upstairs on Brodeur, but his shot sailed wide. The Penguins lost 5-1.

Crosby played fifteen minutes fifty seconds, twenty-three shifts in all, for an average of forty-one seconds each time. He spent six minutes thirty-three seconds on the power play and had three shots on goal, one in each period. He lost ten of sixteen faceoffs. He turned the puck over once. He finished minus two, caught on the ice for two Devils goals. His one assist came on the power play, which didn't reduce his plus-minus.

His numbers were just fine, but they couldn't quantify the most telling thing, which is that he looked like he belonged.

"When you're a young player, you come into the league with expectations, some from what you've seen on TV and how you imagine it will be," Olczyk said. "I was happy with the way he played. He made a great pass to Rex. Not many players, think of all the kids in Canada and the U.S., get a chance to play in the NHL. Sidney will never forget this night."

When he emerged from the dressing room for his post-game press conference, his face was drawn and his body drenched in sweat. He looked exhausted, emotionally spent.

"I was a little bit nervous in the warm-up, but after I got out there skating around, I started feeling more comfortable," he said. "It wasn't too bad. I just tried to do what I was told on the ice. Coach said to enjoy it, because it only happens once, and I tried to do that.

"It was nice to get that point. It's nice to be a playmaker, I won't complain. But you play to win, and I don't think that ever changes."

When someone brought up his faceoff statistic, he immediately agreed that it wasn't great. "That's not very good," he said, with a self-effacing chuckle. "That's something I tried to work on in camp and I'll continue to work on."

"He did pretty well," Lemieux said. "It's always tough to start your career in the NHL. He's only eighteen. He made some pretty good plays and he skated well. It's going to take a few games, but he didn't look out of place at all. I know he was nervous, but before the game, he was talking and joking around. We told him to enjoy it."

MELLON ARENA, PITTSBURGH, PENNSYLVANIA, OCTOBER 8, 2005:
Trina Crosby emerged from the Pittsburgh Penguins locker room clutching a sweaty, neatly folded hockey jersey to her chest. Troy followed behind, in his right hand a stick, a black Sherwood Momentum model that would never score another goal. The stick's work was done. Its owner's was just beginning. She held out the black Penguins home sweater to show me. On the bird's chubby belly in black

Sharpie, Sidney had written: To Dad, Thanks for helping me live my dream! Love, Sidney Crosby 87.

"Isn't this wonderful," she said proudly. "What an incredible night for him. He is *here*."

Crosby scored his first NHL goal in his third NHL game, at 18:36 of the second period of the Penguins' home opener in front of a sellout crowd of 17,132 fans, among them his parents and sister. Gary Bettman saw it too.

Pittsburgh led 5-4 on the power play late in the second period when Crosby slapped the puck towards the net and then skated in to fetch his own rebound. Mark Recchi and Ziggy Palffy tried to score, but Crosby found an opening and swept the puck high on the right side through traffic and into the goal. "There was a big crowd, so I just tried to stay off and hope the puck came my way," he said afterwards. "It bounced to me and I had an open net."

He did not know exactly where the puck had come from. "It just was in front and guys were battling for it. It came my way and bounced into the net. I was lucky."

When the red light flashed, he pumped his stick in the air and charged towards the boards. He hurled himself aggressively three feet into the air, backwards into the glass. His screams were primal. "Yeah! Yeah! Yeah!"

Palffy and Recchi stormed their teammate and embraced him. On the Penguins bench, the others, on their feet even before Crosby touched the puck, shouted through smiles. "We were excited for him," Lemieux said. "But he was pretty excited too."

The crowd stood and gave him two ovations and chanted his name. "Craws-bee! Craws-bee!"

Troy and Trina and Taylor watched the game from Section 32, with Pat Brisson and Dee Rizzo. They were near the net being minded by Boston Bruins goaltender Hannu Toivonen when Sidney scored.

"I cried," Trina said. "So did Troy. Not big sobs, just happy, emotional tears."

"I'm pretty proud of him," Troy said. "We both are happy for him."

The Penguins had two two-goal leads and Lemieux had his first two-goal game since February 2003, but the Penguins still lost, 7-6 in overtime.

In the dressing room afterwards, Crosby was upset they hadn't won, but the happiness of scoring his first NHL goal prevailed. "I looked forward to it for a long time. It feels awesome. I was happy. It's something you dream of, scoring in the NHL, and you only do it the first time once. It was big. There's a lot of emotion. The fans were great. It was so loud. I never expected to hear them chanting my name. You never expect that."

His mother was right; he looked as though he belonged. More than occasionally, Crosby found himself in the right place at the right time. He had made a reputation on timing like that, and he was exhibiting it at this level. He already looked like the best player on the ice for the Penguins.

His prettiest play of the night set up Brooks Orpik, the Penguins defenceman who had one goal in his last eighty-six games. Crosby charged along the right wing with the puck, fought off Boston blueliner Hal Gill, who was eight inches taller, fifty-five pounds heavier, and who had dumped Crosby on his butt during training camp. He used a crafty backhand pass to feed Orpik in the left circle, putting the puck right on his stick so he could score. "I couldn't believe he saw me," Orpik said later. Crosby also set up a goal by defenceman Ric Jackman.

"Those two passes he made were as good as it gets," Olczyk said. "It was quite a way to kick off your home debut. He'll never forget it, that's for sure. You never forget your first one."

Crosby was named the game's second star. He skated out and saluted the cheering crowd with his stick. The Penguins had lost their first three games – they'd fallen 3-2 in a shootout loss to Carolina the previous night – but Crosby already led the team with five points in three games and was out to a one-point scoring lead ahead of Russian rookie Alexander Ovechkin, who was considered Crosby's main challenger to be rookie of the year.

"Look at him," Trina said as she watched Sidney sign autographs for fans who waited hours after the game had ended. "He is going to be fine. He belongs here. [Losing] doesn't take away from it at all. When he scored the goal, he was so happy. I could see his face from where I was sitting. He was just so excited. And to hear the fans chanting his name was just incredible. They love him."

In the dressing room, Crosby posed for photographers from the team and the *Pittsburgh Post-Gazette*, grinning and holding the precious puck. It was marked with a piece of tape on which team trainer Steve Latin had written "First NHL goal, October 8, 2005."

The other Penguins, especially the veterans LeClair, Lemieux, Palffy, and Recchi, said they were proud of him. But they were also, as Crosby was, bothered by a third consecutive loss. They were bothered by their inability to win faceoffs and those mistakes that often saw them so far out of position it looked as though they didn't quite know where they were supposed to be. LeClair, who was thirty-six years old and coming off back surgery but who managed twenty-three goals and fifty-five points for the Flyers in 2003-2004, had just two assists and was obviously struggling to adjust to the new rules. Olczyk had moved Palffy into his spot on Crosby's line with Recchi in the Carolina game.

After the game, Crosby, freshly showered and dressed in a dark pinstripe suit, pale blue shirt, and patterned blue tie, emerged from the locker room with his parents, who were clutching the tools of their son's trade. The sweater, the stick, and the puck would find a home in the Crosby family recreation room, which boasted a museum-like collection of memorabilia.

After he talked to some friends from Montreal and signed some jerseys, he and his parents and his agents rode the arena elevator upstairs to the Igloo Club for a private reception with city dignitaries, sponsors, and club investors to celebrate the return of Penguins hockey, Lemieux's recent fortieth birthday, and Crosby's debut and first goal.

Outside the arena, shortly before midnight, a black stretch limousine idled in the players' parking lot, now mostly empty, waiting to take him home.

ROUGH START

We're not playing as a team.

THE DAY FOLLOWING the Penguins' first home game and Sidney Crosby's first goal, a US Airways baggage handler working at Pittsburgh International Airport swiped the white sweater he had worn in his first game in New Jersey from his father's checked luggage. It was a sign of how far and fast Crosby's hockey stardom was spreading.

When the red Team Canada sweater he wore in the junior gold medal game against Russia in January 2005 was stolen by an Air Canada employee, it made the national news. That sweater was removed from his hockey bag while the luggage was being transferred in Montreal between flights from Winnipeg to Rimouski, taken by baggage handler Jacques Lamoureux, who told police he wanted it for his daughter. A week later, it turned up, after Lamoureux got nervous and stuffed it in a mailbox in Lachute, Quebec. He lost his job and was forced to apologize to the Crosby family and donate $300 to crime victims to keep from having a criminal record. The wayward jersey was auctioned off and raised $22,100 for youth hockey charities and tsunami relief.

It wasn't the kind of thing anyone imagined could happen twice. The day after the home opener, Trina and Taylor returned to Halifax, and Troy travelled to Buffalo, where the Penguins would play Monday night. He took a late-afternoon US Airways flight and checked his luggage. The black sweater from Saturday night was packed in his carry-on bag. Trina had taken home the stick.

When Troy arrived in Buffalo, he collected his luggage and noticed the zipper on his black Penguins duffle bag was slightly agape. He felt sick. The jersey was gone. His son's jersey had been stolen again. He notified the airline, which promptly began a search. Employees were questioned. The police were called in. Two days later, the sweater was found by an airline employee, stuffed between some equipment, still in the plastic bag Troy had packed it in. The thief's name, was never made public. Sidney decided not to pursue charges against anyone. "He just wanted it back," Troy said.

"It does seem a little weird, a little odd for it to be taken out of the bag, only to turn up again," Trina said. "We're not sure what happened. We're just so happy we got it back. It was very special. Troy's a real stickler for zippers. Anytime we go anywhere, he's always zipping up everyone's bags, especially after what happened the last time."

Trina had called Sidney before his game against the Sabres to tell him about the missing hockey sweater.

"He was okay, he didn't really say a lot," she said. "I think he was like, 'Geez, not again.' But when I told him it had been found, he was really happy. It's nice to have it back. It was less painful than last time."

Crosby is deeply sentimental about the sticks, sweaters, pucks, and photographs that have marked significant moments in his career, going as far back as his peewee days. The stick made it to Halifax without incident. Trina was reluctant to check it, but Air Canada, which regards hockey sticks as weapons, forced her. "I didn't make any bones about it," she said. "I told them, 'If I get to Halifax and this stick isn't on the plane, I'm going to pop a gasket.' I told them it had a lot of sentimental value."

It was not the start anyone had in mind on several fronts. The Penguins left Buffalo still looking for their first victory. Crosby had an assist against the Sabres, but the Penguins lost 3-2 in overtime. With that, they were the only team in the NHL that had yet to win a game.

WACHOVIA CENTER, PHILADELPHIA, PENNSYLVANIA, OCTOBER 14, 2005: The Penguins' fifth game of the season brought the first round of the battle of Pennsylvania, and it didn't take long for the Flyers to assert their dominance.

In the first period, Flyers centre Keith Primeau scored on the power play by wrapping his stick around Marc-Andre Fleury's crouched body in the crease to give his team an early lead. About halfway through the period, Crosby picked up the puck at centre ice and started into the Flyers zone, where defenceman Kim Johnsson tried to take it away from him. In a move that would become familiar, the rookie pushed the puck between Johnsson's legs, darted past the big blueliner, and picked up the puck again on the other side, deep in the Flyers zone. Crosby tried to drop a pass behind him, but no one was there to receive it.

The Flyers' second goal, scored by Joni Pitkanen, was challenged by the Penguins, because Peter Forsberg was in the net when the Flyers scored. Crosby and LeClair both argued vehemently with the officials, but the Flyers countered that it was Crosby who shoved Forsberg into the goal, and the officials ruled the score good. Suddenly, the Penguins were down 2-0.

With just 2.5 seconds left in the period, Crosby displayed a brand of determination that would show up often throughout the year. Rushing after the puck all over the Flyers zone, he finally corralled it on his stick and fed a cross-ice pass to defenceman Ric Jackman. The puck glanced off Jackman's stick and then LeClair's and went in. It was 2-1 even though the Flyers had outshot the Penguins 13-5. It wasn't a pretty game. But now it was close.

In the second period, it took Simon Gagné just ninety seconds to put the Flyers up 3-1. Then Gagné struck again, beating Fleury high from a sharp angle to make the score 4-1. It was Gagné's sixth goal of the young season. The Flyers were rolling. The Penguins called a thirty-second time out as Olczyk yanked Fleury and sent in Sebastien Caron, a third-year backup goaltender who, like Crosby, had played his junior hockey in Rimouski and won a Memorial Cup with them.

Halfway through the period, Pittsburgh got a desperately needed power play when Johnsson received a double minor for high-sticking Matt Murley in the nose behind the Philly net. But the Penguins' bad luck continued. Derian Hatcher was credited with a short-handed goal when the puck deflected in off Ric Jackman's skate. It was 5-1 and there was still half the game to play.

Then the Penguins, as if sick of being embarrassed, started pressing. Mario Lemieux hovered low outside the faceoff circle and picked up a rebound from Jackman. He waited for what seemed like a beat too long, but his timing, like old-school Lemieux, was perfect and his pass across the goalmouth found Ryan Malone's stick. It was Malone's second goal of the season. Suddenly, the Penguins looked like a different team. Even though they were still down by three goals, they were energized.

Crosby beat Jeff Carter on a faceoff in the Flyers zone and the puck sailed back to Lyle Odelein, who put a slapshot to the net. The puck grazed Crosby's stick and went in. It was his second goal of the season and the score was now 5-3.

On the bench moments later, Crosby and Odelein talked. Crosby said the journeyman defenceman should have been credited for the goal. Odelein didn't seem to care.

In the old NHL, a two-goal lead was almost always secure. Teams would just slip into a defensive style and protect the puck the rest of the way. But the Penguins had already seen three two-goal leads evaporate on them this season, the result of more wide open offence, and they felt confident they could chip away at the Flyers' advantage.

Crosby tried to set up Recchi with a nice backhand pass in the slot, but Recchi wasn't looking for it, and the puck sailed past him. Late in the period, the Flyers got a power play. When the score is so close and it's late in the game, the penalty kill always seems to unfold in slow motion, which makes it appear agonizing for the team that is trailing. The Penguins effectively shut the Flyers down, but just as the penalty expired, Maxime Talbot was caught slashing and the Penguins had to do it all over again.

In the third period, Gagné fired a clear shot on Caron, who made a snappy glove save. A few minutes later, Penguins forward Rico Fata lugged the puck down the right wing, pushed past the defender, and took it to the Philadelphia crease. It appeared to roll in during the goal-mouth scramble, but veteran referee Paul Devorski wanted a review. He wasn't convinced the puck had broken the goal line. Television replays showed the puck coming to rest on the line. On the Penguins bench, Eddie Olczyk held his head in his hands.

A cheer rose from the crowd. The goal was waved off. The puck had not gone in. Would the decision kill the Penguins' momentum or stir it up? It was tough to say. They still hadn't won a game and had lost their last three after being tied at the end of regulation.

With about thirteen minutes left in the game, Pittsburgh got a precious five-on-three power play when the Flyers hooked Recchi and Malone a minute apart. It only took Lemieux and Recchi twenty seconds to set up Dick Tarnstrom for a slapshot from the top of the faceoff circle. There was 12:34 left in the game, and the Penguins had taken control. The Flyers had their best shooters come at Caron – Gagné, Forsberg, and Gagné once again. But their shots flew wide, hit the crossbar, or were sharply turned away by the backup goaltender.

Then something occurred that suggested Pittsburgh's luck had really turned. Talbot won a faceoff and flipped a shot from beyond centre ice into the Flyers zone. Antero Niittymaki was in his net taking a long drink from his water bottle and wasn't paying attention. The puck drifted slowly past him into the net and he didn't even notice. The Penguins on the bench frantically jumped up and down shouting "It's in! It's in!" The game was tied. Talbot and LeClair fell into each other's arms laughing.

The last four minutes of the game were frenetic. Mike Richards held Brooks Orpik down behind the net, and the Penguins defenceman retaliated with a shove against the boards, only to be called for roughing. A gutsy effort by Malone, Recchi, and Fata killed the penalty. Then Malone, trying to clear the puck, accidentally pushed it towards Caron, but he was able to slap his glove over it in the crease.

Finally, Forsberg thought he scored with 1:11 left, but a review showed that Caron had stopped the puck at the line. In overtime, towering defenceman Mike Rathje scored for the Flyers to end the game, and despite a heroic comeback attempt, the Penguins were left still searching for their first victory after five games.

After a 3-1 loss the next night to Stanley Cup champions the Tampa Bay Lightning that saw Crosby set up Ziggy Palffy for the Penguins' only goal, Lemieux was pissed off. He tersely blamed "sloppy execution" for the team's worsening struggles. "We just have to put in the effort and make sure we do the right things on the ice and play as a team. Right now we're not. It's not the start we want. I think everyone's surprised. The expectation level was pretty high here. We made a lot of changes this summer to put a good product on the ice. We just have to pull out of it, quickly."

Crosby believed every night that they were close to turning things around. He had never known any different.

Winning had always been within reach. "We know we're right there," he said, using his hands to suggest the space between winning and losing was not so far at all. "We're confident in ourselves."

They ran long practices, watched game video, talked about their struggles, and tried to find solutions before they met the New Jersey Devils later in the week. With four days between games, Crosby filmed his Reebok commercial at the Igloo, calling on Maxime Talbot, Andre Roy, and Marc-Andre Fleury to join him as extras in the ten-hour shoot. Right after Fleury had finished filming his part, he gathered his things to go back to Wilkes-Barre. He had been sent down again. Crosby gave him a bear hug.

The following day, the Penguins went to a local shopping mall for an annual charity event. The Salvation Army gave each player $100 and they took a child shopping for winter clothes. Mark Recchi chaperoned two little girls and lugged an armload of pink clothing. When one girl was afraid to come down the escalator, Recchi raced back up it to carry her down. Jocelyn Thibault pushed a cart over-flowing with Steelers shirts and caps. Ric Jackman weighed the pros and cons of pink or blue mittens. A clever, blond-haired fourth-grader named Damen McDermott got Sidney as his shopping pal. They picked out boots, a coat, ski gloves, and a Pittsburgh Steelers jersey. Crosby suggested he also pick up a toque. McDermott didn't know what he was talking about. "What the heck's a too-k?" he asked. "You know, a toque, a winter hat," Sidney said, dangling the wool cap in front of the puzzled nine-year-old. "That's a *tossle* cap," Damen said matter-of-factly, lecturing Crosby on the Pennsylvania word for toque. "He was nice," McDermott said at the end of the afternoon. "He has a Canadian accent. I think he needs a haircut though. But he taught me a new word. It's kind of a funny word. I might have to run it by my English teacher."

Crosby had fun at the mall. It was a lighthearted few hours that took his mind off the fact that he was six games into his NHL career and still didn't know victory.

Two nights later, the Penguins failed again, falling 6-3 to the Devils. Crosby played well but was held pointless. His lip bloody and cheek cut from an errant stick, he stayed in his equipment long after all his teammates had tossed their jerseys in the laundry bin and headed for the showers. He stared at the carpet, lost in thought. "I just want to win," he said softly. "I'm not worried about points right now. Team points, that's my focus. Every team goes through a tough point in a season, and we have to look at it right now as a hump we have to get over. We can't give up. Because that first win is going to be even tougher the way things are going right now."

TD BANKNORTH GARDEN, BOSTON, OCTOBER 22, 2005:

It was Saturday night, the Penguins' eighth game of the season. They had lost three games in regulation, were out-scored 14-5, and lost four others in overtime or shoot-outs. The frustration was growing obvious in the tense dressing room.

They got blown out in Boston. Trailing 5-1 in the third period, Crosby finished another frustrating shift. But instead of just taking a seat on the bench, he stopped in front of it, dropped his stick over his right shoulder, and then brought it down with all his might, like a six-foot samurai sword against the top of the boards.

The stick shattered, its pieces flying in all directions. He slammed the bench door closed so loudly it cracked like a gunshot in the near sold-out arena. Then he sat down, tidied up the shards of his broken stick, and helped himself to a fresh one. The chronic losing had made him angry. Would the Penguins *ever* win a game?

How could a team that looked so talented on paper – with veterans who had scored 1,987 career goals between them – be mired at the bottom of the standings? Before the season began, expectations were ridiculously high, inside the Penguins' dressing room and outside of it. How could they not be, with that lineup? Fine, if they weren't going to be *that* good, but how could they be so bad? No one had any answers.

It was the worst start in the thirty-eight-year history of the franchise. They had lost four of those games outright, and four others in overtime. They had scored just twenty-three goals against opponents and allowed thirty-nine, second worst in the league, ahead of the Washington Capitals.

Even casual fans had started to speculate, mostly on the sports call-in shows, that soon Olczyk would be fired and underachieving players traded.

After they lost 6-3, Crosby was worn down. He had enjoyed a pretty good game, but it hadn't translated into a win. The Penguins had eight penalties in the second period and the Bruins scored four goals in ten minutes. Crosby had two assists in the game and hit the post on a breakaway. He had levelled Bruins winger P.J. Axelsson with a vigorous check that knocked him down and allowed Crosby to steal the puck and set up Ryan Malone for a goal.

"The first few games, I was just happy to be in the NHL and I didn't think much about [losing] because I was just happy to be here. But now that I'm here and working hard and we haven't got a win yet, it's tough. Winning is fun. Losing isn't. This hasn't been a fun time lately. That's for sure. We dig ourselves in a hole and can't deal with it."

The mood was grim in the dressing room. When Jocelyn Thibault came out to talk to reporters, he was at a loss for words. He had struggled against forty-seven shots, but the loss was hardly all his doing. The Penguins had managed only twenty-one shots of their own, hardly enough in the new-style NHL to win, and the defence had been sloppy. In eight games they had scored the first goal only once, in their home opener against Boston.

For the first time in his career, Crosby was playing on a losing team. In junior the previous season, the Oceanic had gone on a thirty-five-game unbeaten streak. He had never experienced a slump like this, though the Penguins who had been around last season suffered through an eighteen-game losing stretch.

"It's no secret," Crosby said with a shake of his head. "We get down and dig ourselves in holes. We have to play with the lead; enough of chasing and falling behind."

After the game, Crosby visited in the hallway outside the dressing room with Bruins forward Patrice Bergeron, a teammate from the World Juniors and a close friend. And the Penguins went back to Pittsburgh, where they would lose yet again a couple of nights later, 4-3 in overtime, to the Florida Panthers. Lemieux took a questionable interference penalty that allowed the winning goal. He was so angry about the call he charged out of the penalty box and shouted at the referee. He was so angry about everything else he stayed in the treatment room for almost an hour after the game and didn't come out to talk to reporters. Crosby was the only Penguin in the room who answered questions. Lemieux was at wit's end. And no one had any answers.

Two nights later brought the Penguins' tenth game of the season and offered a desperately needed reprieve: the Atlanta Thrashers, losers of six of their last seven games. Olczyk, desperate now, juggled his lines, pairing Lemieux with Crosby and Recchi; and Rico Fata with Ryan Malone and Palffy.

At first, they looked like the same old Penguins as the Thrashers scored four goals in the first ten minutes of the game. Olczyk called a time out, and the veteran leader LeClair gave a quiet speech by the bench, telling his team-mates that everyone had to play smarter and better.

"Out of that whole stretch of games," Ryan Malone said later, "that was the worst of the worst. Four-nothing was the bottom of the barrel."

Almost magically, LeClair's words inspired. The Penguins frantically scored to win the game 7-5. Crosby had two assists, and while he didn't score, the veteran Penguins showed an honest and collective leadership they had lacked since the season began.

Lemieux, LeClair, and defenceman Sergei Gonchar scored two power play goals each. Lemieux loved playing with Crosby, and everyone felt the weight of the mounting losses lift just a little.

"It feels good," Malone said. "We can breathe a little bit now."

Not that it started the Penguins on a roll or anything. They lost their next game 5-3 to the Hurricanes, blowing a two-goal lead with nine minutes left in the third period. Olczyk called it "a kick in the teeth." And dismal October mercifully came to an end.

Crosby, who had two goals and twelve assists in eleven games, was named the league's rookie of the month, edging out his twenty-year-old rival Alexander Ovechkin, who had eight goals and five assists in eleven games, by a single point. That upset the Capitals' front office, who thought that Ovechkin's numbers were more worthy, especially given the fact that he wasn't playing with the kind of high-priced, free-agent talent Sidney was. But there was no doubt which of the two rookies had more to deal with beyond playing hockey in the first month of their NHL careers.

That week Crosby made the cover of the *Sporting News.* His NHL career was off to a tremendous start. As for the Penguins, they were another matter altogether.

A DREAM COME TRUE

To do the things he does on the ice, and he's only eighteen.

EVEN BEFORE THE first puck dropped to open the National Hockey League's eighty-eighth season, the league was selling Sidney Crosby. With the exception of Wayne Gretzky and Mario Lemieux, no professional hockey players had ever transcended the sport itself. They were the only ones who had a chance of being recognized on a street corner that wasn't in Canada and outside their markets, on the cover of a mainstream magazine, or on a television show not associated with sports.

Crosby's profile was quickly rising. While the rest of the Penguins each had mail slots in the players' lounge outside the dressing room, Crosby had his own mail closet that overflowed with packages and boxes of letters.

Ed Horne, the president of NHL Enterprises, the marketing arm of the league, thought the timing of the young player's arrival alongside the new NHL was "something really special."

Sports marketers saw it too. "This kid absolutely has the potential to be it," said Dean Bonham, president of the Bonham Group, a sports marketing firm based in Chicago. "He's the real deal, not only on the ice, but off. He could be the Michael Jordan of the NHL. There's more buzz about him than anybody since Gretzky. There's always buzz about the number one draft pick, but he is different, and it's a combination of some extraordinary on-ice skills and some incredible characteristics he displays off the ice."

He had been featured prominently in ESPN *Magazine* and *Sports Illustrated*. But it was going to take more than just Crosby to relaunch the NHL. When the lockout ended, Brendan Shanahan had encouraged his fellow players to "become more famous in more markets."

Historically, hockey players have made less flashy celebrities than athletes in other sports. All that equipment is partly to blame. NFL players wear skin-tight pants and are often seen on the sidelines with their helmets off. NBA players ply their trade in skimpy singlet jerseys and shorts. Fans can see their faces and how athletic their bodies are. Hockey players go to work in layers of padding and helmets and pants baggy in the butt. The NHL was working with NBC and their new broadcast partner, OLN, to emphasize more "life stories" and show players out of their helmets more often. It wasn't going to help that the NHL was no longer on ESPN, which meant games were going to be available in about twenty-five million fewer households at the start of the season compared to the previous arrangement with ESPN. OLN, however, had offered more prominent placement and coverage of the NHL, and the league was banking on more exposure in fewer households.

"We've got some amazing people, some amazing human beings in this league, and we need to show them, show their stories and get viewers acquainted with them," said the former goaltender and TV analyst John Davidson.

"Our guys are such great and humble individuals who haven't wanted to be out in the spotlight as much," Horne said. "But the good-looking and articulate athletes we have, combined with more exposure on NBC, will help us eliminate some of those hurdles that have existed in the past."

With the exception of a thick-headed sports reporter in Raleigh, North Carolina, who wandered into a post-game scrum with Lemieux and asked loudly of no one in particular, "Who is *that*?", Lemieux was the only active player whose celebrity reached past hockey.

The NHL was pleased Crosby was attracting so much attention. He had performed well enough on the ice in the early weeks, despite playing on a terrible team in a smaller market. And he had done his part to draw casual attention to hockey in the U.S. After the draft, he went on the *Tonight Show with Jay Leno*. He posed for the October issue of *Vanity Fair* with his Dolce & Gabbana shirt off and Gap jeans low on his hips – not, he said, "your typical hockey player pose."

The November issue of *Gentleman's Quarterly* featured Crosby over two shirtless pages and called him Hockey's LeBron James, a reference to the NBA's new Michael Jordan. "It's good for hockey if you can get it out there in a different way," Crosby said. "I don't want to do too many of those things, but if there's time and it helps promote the game a little bit, I will."

Privately, he worried about becoming over-exposed. Before he had even played a game in the NHL, he was treading some of the same places the world's biggest celebrities did. What would an established NHL star like Steve Yzerman, one of Crosby's boyhood favourites, think?

He did the *GQ* shoot in the Penguins' dressing room when his teammates weren't around to tease him.

"Has your mom seen the magazine?" I asked him one afternoon. "What did she think?" He said modestly, "She thought I looked good."

"Have your teammates seen it?" He blushed. "I don't think so. You don't have to show it to them."

Bonham figured on what he called a magical three-part formula that would determine an athlete's star power: they must perform at an extraordinary level and win, they have to be charismatic and media friendly, and they must have a compelling story or endure an ordeal of fire and water. "When you have these three things, you get a Tiger Woods or a Michael Jordan."

Crosby already had lucrative deals with Reebok Hockey signed in November 2004 (worth $2.5 million) and Gatorade (reportedly worth $500,000). He would make more money in endorsements in his first season than from his NHL salary.

Now he was going through his ordeal of fire and water. The Penguins had only won one game by the time November 1, the start of their longest road trip of the season, came around. They would play five opponents in nine days, opening in New Jersey against the Devils before facing the New York Islanders, Boston Bruins, New York Rangers, and wrapping up in Atlanta against the Thrashers, the only team worse off in the standings than the Penguins, who had lost ten games.

Even though losing had not yet started to erode their attendance at home, the road could be a good place to try and turn things around. Crosby was excited by several things. He was eager to return to Continental Airlines Arena in New Jersey, a road rink at which he had already played. It would be less nerve-wracking the second time around, and the distractions he faced during his first NHL game would be gone. "The first time, I was a little nervous. When you've already been somewhere, it's easier. Now it's just a matter of playing my game."

He was also looking forward to playing in Madison Square Garden, the rotund venue in the heart of Manhattan where the Rangers and Knicks had won titles and the site of some of the most storied events in sporting history.

And just a few days before they left, he had picked up his new car, a silver Range Rover. He would start driving himself to practice. Lemieux would no longer have to wait for him. As well, the Penguins arranged for Sidney to open a bank account in Pittsburgh. He had been keeping his NHL paycheques in his sock drawer.

Crosby had never been to New York and had only seen the Garden on television. At eighteen he had already played hockey in tournaments across the world, but finally he would get to play hockey in the centre of the universe, where images are made, approved, and projected around the planet. It was good timing. His Reebok television ad, filmed last month at Mellon Arena, was set to start airing in a week.

The thirty-second ad was one of Reebok's landmark,

edgy *I Am What I Am* spots that had previously featured athletes Allen Iverson, Curt Schilling, Donovan McNabb, and hip-hop artist Jay-Z, among others. Crosby was the first hockey player and a different kind of pitchman than the campaign was used to.

"He has no attitude," said Yan Martin, marketing director of Reebok Hockey. "He's not out there saying he's going to break Mario Lemieux's or Wayne Gretzky's records. He's got his own standards. We wanted the spot to say that, to show his personality and individuality. His talents speak for themselves. We wanted someone relevant to youth culture and individualistic. He has a chance to be more than just a hockey player. To be accepted outside hockey you need that aura, and Sidney has it around him."

In a world where not a single hockey player has appeared on the *Forbes* list of highest paid athletes since Wayne Gretzky made number fourteen in 1998, hockey players have traditionally been the least marketed athletes of all four professional sports. Over the years, Gretzky endorsed Campbell's Soup, Tylenol, McDonald's, Hespeler sports equipment, and CIBC; he had restaurants and a line of clothing at the Hudson's Bay Company. Crosby, who had also developed a limited line of casual clothing – T-shirts, hoodies, and sweatpants for Reebok – had decided to take things more slowly. He didn't want to be a walking billboard. "He has what it takes to do all kinds of things," Brisson said. "He has so many options in front of him, and he always takes his time and makes the right decisions."

Crosby was a sharp kid with naturally good instincts. They guided not only what products he chose to endorse, but also his personal relationships and how he ultimately dealt with the rollercoaster season. He credited his parents. "I got a little bit from each; they have strong senses about things. My mom, she's really sharp. On people, she always has the right sense. It's important, especially in my situation. You have to pick your friends carefully. Not that I care how people judge me, but you want to surround yourself with good people who are going to make you better. My parents worry, but that's natural for any parents. Mine probably worry ten times more because of my situation. They definitely lead me in the right direction. I still have a lot to learn, but I won't be eighteen forever. I've learned a lot about myself this year . . . mostly not to have a lot of expectations. If I do something well, I don't need someone to tell me I did it right. And when I do something wrong, I'm going to be my own hardest critic. I don't get too high or too low. It's a cliché but it works."

A few days before the road trip, the Penguins recalled rangy, second-line centre Erik Christensen and big, offensive defenceman Ryan Whitney, who were playing well for the Baby Penguins. Both seemed more surprised about the state of the Penguins than their actual call-ups.

Olczyk continued to say he believed the core personnel would eventually gel, but Lemieux and Craig Patrick were clearly getting anxious, spending a lot of time on the telephone trying to tinker with the chemistry of the team to find something that might work. "It wouldn't surprise me to see anything happen," Olczyk said. But his firing didn't seem a possibility. Not yet, anyway. Both Lemieux and Patrick publicly said Olczyk's job was safe. He was not viewed as the problem.

"I believe they have confidence in me," Olczyk said. "And that's all that matters."

The road trip got off to a good start. The Penguins won 4-3 in New Jersey before an announced crowd of 10,134 that looked to be half that size, a far cry from the rowdy sellout of opening night. I heard laughter in the dressing room after the game for only the second time all season. The Penguins had a night off before they were to meet the Islanders at Nassau Coliseum on Long Island. At practice on the off-day, the players, especially Sidney, were relaxed and happy. Again, another mass of reporters descended, this time many from New York preparing stories on the young player who was now widely being referred to as Sid the Kid.

Crosby played a game of basketball, trying to sink his balled-up ankle tape into a waste basket set halfway across the room. It kept falling short or wide. He kept grabbing the tape back and trying again, a half-dozen times until it fell in. Whenever a ball of tape or an empty water bottle didn't land in the waste basket, Crosby would throw it again and again until he sunk it. He never gave up until he succeeded, even when it came to tossing out the garbage.

"I'm too competitive," he said. "I mean, I'm not a freak. I can play ping-pong and not break a paddle. But I can't quit, and if I'm competing against someone else, I'm going to match it. That's why I can't train with anyone."

The New York media wanted to know how he felt about visiting the bright lights of the big city five nights hence. "I'm happy to go everywhere," he said. "Every place is fun to go right now. It's all new. But my focus doesn't change when I go to a bigger venue than normal or a place where

I might be more.excited. I've never looked at it as a burden, and I don't think I ever will. It's exciting. It means that people are interested in hockey, and that's important. That's the best part about it."

The next night, Crosby had his first multi-goal game in the NHL. He had two goals – as many as he had in his first twelve games – and added an assist. The Penguins trampled the Islanders 5-1. Crosby, Lemieux, and Recchi combined for three goals, and Crosby scored a beauty from in close off a mid-air pass from Lemieux. With Lemieux playing centre, Crosby also didn't have to worry about taking so many faceoffs, the one area where he still needed work.

"I think the three of us really found it," Recchi said afterwards. "This was our third game together, and I think we're really starting to figure things out."

They lost in Boston 6-3, the victims of bad penalties and too many five-on-three chances for the Bruins. It didn't seem so terrible coming off two consecutive victories, their first of the season. Crosby's grandmothers, Linda Crosby and Catherine Forbes, made the twenty-hour trip by charter bus from Halifax to watch the game. He was held pointless, but they cheered their lungs out anyway, sitting in the stands wearing yellow sou'wester hats and waving Nova Scotia flags every time he took a shift. His grandmothers said they could barely watch him play, and had to cover their eyes with their sweaters because they were always afraid he would get hurt.

Crosby loved his first trip to the Big Apple. When the Penguins arrived on Sunday from Boston, he wandered around Times Square with some of his teammates. He couldn't get over the lights and noise that never ceased. "It's a lot bigger than Cole Harbour," he said. He couldn't believe the traffic. He had never seen anything quite like it. Some of the older, more adventurous guys, Talbot and Malone, went out for the evening. Crosby, as he always did, ate dinner out with some of the team and then returned to his room to watch movies and get some sleep.

In New York, the Penguins rediscovered their winning ways. Crosby's Manhattan debut saw the Penguins play a tight and tidy game to win 3-2. Lemieux, Crosby, and Palffy scored. When he was introduced before the game, the hockey purists at the Garden paid their respects to him with some hearty applause; there were also a good deal of boos from the hardscrabble members of the crowd.

Mark Messier was sitting in a box. The crowd gave him a standing ovation when they realized he was there, and he waved back at them. Crosby, on the bench, saw Messier too. He scored on his next shift.

Crosby was the game's first star. He was pumped in the dressing room afterwards. "It's so special to come here," he told a crowd of more than two dozen reporters. "There's so much tradition here. The atmosphere was awesome. It was an incredible night."

The next morning, the *New York Daily News* proclaimed across two pages: Sidney a Star on Broadway.

MELLON ARENA, PITTSBURGH, PENNSYLVANIA, NOVEMBER 10, 2005: At the morning skate on the day of his first game against the Montreal Canadiens, Crosby was as relaxed as he had been all season. He liked seeing old friends, and there were some in the travelling media contingent of more than a dozen reporters who had covered him in junior. He did interviews in French and English.

Crosby scored the Penguins' first goal, and the team battled to a 2-2 draw in regulation time and through the extra period. Suddenly the kid who grew up idolizing the Canadiens found himself in a dream situation against his dream team.

With the puck sitting at centre ice and the referee having given him the green light to go, Sidney Crosby dug his skate blades into the Mellon Arena ice for his solo rush towards José Théodore in the opposing net. Everyone in the crowd of 16,254 was standing. Five shooters had already tried and failed in this shootout.

Michael Ryder, Alex Kovalev, and Alexander Perezhogin were stopped by Jocelyn Thibault. Théodore turned aside Mark Recchi and Mario Lemieux. Now he was staring down the rookie, who needed only two strides to get up to speed and gather the puck on the almost straight blade of his stick.

This game was out of the ordinary for Crosby, who had grown up watching the Canadiens play on television, had Habs wallpaper in his bedroom, and had his parents take him to his first NHL game in the Bell Centre in Montreal.

Earlier in the day, at the morning skate, he was happy and excited. "It's going to be special. It's the team I grew up watching. It's pretty cool." He smiled, shaking hands with all the familiar Montreal reporters who were in town for the game. Crosby's dad and a cousin would also be here tonight. He wanted to perform well.

During the game, Crosby had staked the Penguins to an early lead. He was passing to a wide-open Ziggy Palffy, parked at the corner of the net, when the puck hit the skates of defenceman Francis Bouillon and caromed into the goal. Lemieux then chipped in a Palffy pass for a 2-0 lead. Rookie Penguins defenceman Ryan Whitney inadvertently tipped in a Craig Rivet slapshot for a Montreal goal in the second period, and Chris Higgins scored at 16:29 of the third to force a tie. Overtime yielded no scoring, bringing on a shootout.

On the bench awaiting his turn in the shootout, Crosby studied Recchi's shot. They were both left-handed. Théodore went for Recchi's deke but managed to stop him.

"Did he commit to you after you faked the shot?" Crosby asked Rex when he got back to the bench. "Yeah," Recchi answered.

Crosby decided to take the same path and use the same fake. But he decided instead that he would draw the puck back onto his backhand and look for an opening.

Just before he went onto the ice, when Perezhogin was taking his turn, Palffy uttered some words of encouragement. "If he misses this, you have a chance to win it," Palffy said. Sure enough, Perezhogin missed. Crosby took his spot above centre ice, the puck waiting for him.

The entire arena fell into a hush, church quiet. He set off. He sold his fake to the extent of picking up his right foot as if going for a shot. Théodore committed. Just as he had visualized it, Crosby gathered the puck back onto his stick, cruised across the goalmouth, and then lifted a sweet backhander over a helpless Théodore. The water bottle on Théodore's net popped up before the red light came on, and Crosby raced to the jubilant arms of his teammates. The crowd erupted. In their seats, Troy Crosby and Dee

Rizzo jumped into each other's arms and jumped up and down like prizewinners on a game show.

Olczyk hadn't even watched. He had looked on during the shootout against Carolina in the season's second game, and the Penguins failed to score. So he decided not to look, casting his eyes downward as Crosby skated in. The eruption of cheers told him his youngest player had come through.

"To do it in this type of game, with all the emotion and against the Canadiens, it's awesome. It was my favourite team growing up," Crosby recounted later. "Just to do it at home, it's a pretty amazing feeling. The fans stayed with us. They gave us that energy we needed."

Losing two-goal leads had become a disturbing pattern for the Penguins, who had played the night before and were coming off a five-game road trip while the Canadiens watched them get beat by Atlanta on television in the comfort of their Pittsburgh hotel rooms. But they were able to gather themselves against the NHL's most storied franchise and Crosby's childhood favourites. It felt storybook, the sweetest of their few victories so far.

"It's kind of hard to believe," Crosby said. "It's always fun to win. One of the funnest things in hockey is when you pull together as a team. It would have been easy to get frustrated. We didn't lose our focus like we might have in the past."

It was his first shootout goal; his first shootout win. He had been stopped in Carolina and hadn't made any of his attempts in the pre-season. He was coming along.

In the dressing room, Maxime Talbot, who took a hard hit from Montreal centre Steve Begin, was nursing a broken nose.

Nearby, Lemieux was ebullient over Crosby. "He's quite amazing. I've said it time and time again, for him to be able to do the things he's doing and he's only eighteen . . . Some of the things he does on the ice are quite amazing. He's a true professional. He's only eighteen."

Back home in Canada, the goal was replayed on the sports networks all the next morning. A few days later, Crosby was asked if the night had felt like a coming out party because so many people at home had been able to see it. He nodded enthusiastically. "I like to be in that situation. If we need a goal late in the game, that's the funnest part in hockey. To be in that situation, to give my team an extra point is fun. I was pretty excited. The first career goal was exciting too, but that was more of an important one. Joce kept us in the game. That kind of gets lost."

On the morning of the game against the Habs, a report was published in the *Kansas City Star* that said that the Penguins would be the city's first choice for a hockey franchise to occupy their new Sprint Center, an 18,500-seat arena managed by Anschultz Entertainment Group (AEG).

"If Pittsburgh doesn't have an arena deal done a year from now, they're gone," said Tim Leiweke, president of AEG and the Los Angeles Kings. "The Pittsburgh Penguins can be the Kansas City Penguins, no question about it. That team . . . will sell out every ticket in advance, end of story. That team will be a huge instant home run in Kansas City. And that kid, Sidney Crosby, is unbelievable."

Kansas City was courting the Penguins, and they weren't doing it quietly. They thought Crosby had the potential to be a huge hockey star who could sell the game in a mid-west market that loved football and barbecue.

None of that ever noticeably mattered to any of the Penguins players, other than Lemieux. The team's future didn't distract Crosby, who had thirteen points in his last eight games.

But as great as the Penguins were against the Canadiens, they were awful two nights later against the Rangers. In front of a standing-room-only sellout of 17,132 fans, the Penguins were clobbered 6-1. Recchi scored the only goal. Crosby looked short on energy for the first time all season. Almost everyone in the crowd walked out before the final buzzer. It was one of those nights where everything went wrong.

The Penguins had to shake off the loss. They had a big home-and-home series coming up against their archrivals, the Philadelphia Flyers. Those games weren't going to be easy. No one expected they would be pretty either.

7

THE FLYERS

He's grown into a man tonight.

AT THE BEGINNING of the season, Mario Lemieux promised to make a long-shot attempt at playing all eighty-two
games for the first time in his seventeen-year NHL career. It
seemed an attainable enough goal. He had arrived at training camp lean and fit, arguably the best shape he had ever
been in. But just before the twentieth game of the year, the
Penguins' second trip to Philadelphia, Lemieux's dream died.

The forty-year-old captain and owner had been playing
pretty well. He had nineteen points in as many games, but
he reluctantly begged off making the trip across state,
saying he had been battling a low-grade flu for several
days. Coach Eddie Olczyk urged his boss to stay home in
Pittsburgh and get well. The lineup was also missing
defenceman Sergei Gonchar, who was sidelined with a
sore groin.

History had not been kind to the Penguins when they
played the Philadelphia Flyers. They typically struggled

against their cross-state rivals, especially on the road. Pittsburgh had won just one of nine previous games there and tied another, losing the other seven. At the moment, the Flyers were in possession of a 9-1 home record, the best in the league so far. Canadian-born winger Simon Gagné was on a roll, too, with eight goals in his past nine games.

By contrast, the Penguins were in terrible shape, having won just five games in total. Now they were heading into their twentieth of the season against these formidable Flyers, who had beaten them 6-5 in overtime a month earlier in Philly.

Crosby had seven goals and twenty-one points so far, the highest total on the team, but he wasn't happy after the Islanders game a few nights earlier. The Penguins lost 3-2 in an overtime shootout. In regulation, Crosby scored a beautiful goal on Rick DiPietro, beating him in the five-hole. He also netted one in the shootout, but Jason Blake won the game when Ryan Whitney failed to answer the Islanders' final shot with one for the Penguins. It was a bittersweet loss, because they had worked hard and it was a game they could have won.

At practice the next day, Sidney, who was still playing on the wing under Olczyk's direction, said he was discovering that he had to be "more aware" as a winger. He had played the position a bit in junior, and as versatile as he was – and he may well have been more aware than any young hockey player on the ice anywhere in the world – the wing was not his natural position.

"Your mistakes are more exposed in this league," he said. "You can play well even if you lose, but you can't often have a bad game and win."

I asked him how he was feeling about only having won five games so far this season. He thought for a few seconds and wrinkled his nose, as he often did when he wasn't entirely happy.

"I don't feel embarrassed," he said quietly and defiantly. "You just don't want to cheat your teammates."

That should have been his last worry. Crosby was easily the hardest working among his teammates. But it was apparent by the way he spoke when things weren't going well that he was struggling emotionally, more than some of the others, with losing and what to do about it. Though he never shirked his media duties, lately he had been more tense and serious during his daily question-and-answer sessions. Usually conducted in his long athletic underwear and bare feet, he often curled his toes up as if making a fist and held the position tensely the whole time he was talking to us. To be fair, sometimes the questions, especially by the media members who only showed up when the Steelers had their day off, got so repetitive it was painful to listen to them, never mind what it must have been like to answer them. When you've only won five of nineteen games, what is there to say? Everyone dealt with it in their own way. Lemieux didn't talk to the media every day. Crosby never missed a session. LeClair and Recchi were frustrated. But everyone still thought it was fixable.

"I think we have the personnel here to make it work," Lemieux said. "At some point if it doesn't work, that's when you make changes. But it's still early in the season. It's frustrating for us all."

Olczyk could not fathom why his team, so talented on paper, couldn't get it together.

"When we skate, we can play with any team in the league," the coach said after the loss to the Islanders. "But where's that consistency? We got that goal from Sid and I thought, 'Yeah, we have a chance.' And then. . . ." His normally soft voice trailed off so quietly as to become inaudible. Olczyk had no answers either.

Before he showered, Sidney met his dad in the players' parking lot outside the Igloo. It had rained relentlessly the night before, but it was unseasonably humid for November, and in some ways, while putting off winter should have felt good, the warm temperatures served more to make everyone feel slow and lethargic. Sidney, hands shoved deep in the pockets of his warm-up jacket, smiled as he and his dad chatted. It would be the last time Troy would see his son's perfect, wholly original front teeth.

WACHOVIA CENTER, PHILADELPHIA, PENNSYLVANIA, NOVEMBER 16, 2005: The start to the night was not promising. In the warm-ups, goaltender Jocelyn Thibault was accidentally struck in the throat by a puck shot from teammate Konstantin Koltsov. He struggled to breathe and was rushed to the hospital, where he spent most of the night.

Young Marc-Andre Fleury, who had been the number one draft pick a few years earlier and was expected to be a franchise goalie for the Penguins in the coming years, had been recalled as the backup a few days earlier when Sebastien Caron strained his leg. Fleury was pressed into service.

The Flyers were looking for their tenth straight win at home; the Penguins, now playing the game without a backup goalie on the bench, were just looking to survive. Lemieux had the flu, the team said, and hadn't made the trip.

The scoreless first period was chippy, but nothing like what was to come. It started with about six minutes left in the second period, as Crosby fought for the puck along the right wing boards with big Flyers defenceman Derian Hatcher looming right alongside and, sometimes, on top of him.

Near the Penguins bench, the ornery blueliner pivoted and suddenly attacked Crosby in the face with his stick, pushing the teenager's head back until he tipped over onto the ice. Hatcher was huge compared to his prey – a half-foot taller and forty pounds heavier. As a physical battle, it was no contest. Crosby crashed atop Hatcher's stick, and the defenceman dragged him along for a few feet, face-down, blood dripping from his gashed upper lip and the bottoms of his two front teeth jaggedly broken off. Hatcher smirked and tried to skate away nonchalantly as Crosby clung to the blade of his attacker's stick like a riled rag doll.

The officials either did not see Hatcher's handiwork, or did not see fit to call a penalty. At the time, either scenario was difficult to believe. Two months later, Stephen Walkom, the NHL's director of officiating, told me that referees Kevin Pollock and Dean Warren, after watching a recording of the game, realized they had erred in judgment and should have penalized Hatcher for high-sticking. He likely would have received a double-minor – four minutes for drawing blood and causing injury.

Hindsight was worthless to Crosby that night. He left the ice and went to the dressing room, where one of the Flyers' doctors closed the wound with four stitches. And less than five minutes later, just in time for a Penguins power play, he was back.

Hatcher was waiting for him. This time he used his stick on Crosby's throat just before the faceoff near the Philadelphia net. Sidney shoved him back and turned to the referee, complaining. It was this act of defence and defiance the officials chose to recognize. They slapped Sidney with a two-minute unsportsmanlike conduct penalty.

Enraged and in disbelief, his mouth swollen and teeth broken, Crosby skated to the penalty box and slammed his helmet against the boards as the crowd cheered wildly.

The game remained scoreless into the third period, but there were still scores to settle. The Penguins struck first, on the power play, as Mark Recchi lugged the puck up the ice, passed it over to the left to John LeClair, who pushed it through traffic to Crosby, who fed it back across the ice to Ryan Malone, who finally scored.

"Nice!" Crosby shouted of the tidy tic-tac-toe play as the four men, each of whom had ties to this place – two former Flyers, one native Pennsylvanian, and an emerging enemy to Philadelphia – skated into a celebratory embrace. It was 1-0, with 17:57 left to play. Less than a minute later, Crosby kicked his revenge into high gear, slapping the puck past goaltender Antero Niittymaki through a tangle of legs and skates and sticks in the crease.

Crosby was exuberant in his celebration. He pumped his gloved fist in the air and waved his stick, hollering, "Yeah, fucking right!" to no one and everyone. It was his eighth goal, and at 2:59 of the third period gave the Penguins a fast and rare two-goal lead in a most hostile building.

The crowd of 19,687 at Wachovia Center instantly deflated. An anemic "Let's go, Flyers" chant rose softly but quickly receded.

But Finnish defenceman Joni Pitkanen scored two quick power play goals for the Flyers to tie the game. The hard-scrabble crowd – and none of us had seen anything yet in that regard, as it later turned out – booed and cursed the Penguins rookie, and alternately cheered Hatcher's every bullying move. Thanks to Pitkanen, everyone, the players and the fans, were back in it.

What the Flyers didn't realize, however, but what had been emerging for some time, was that Crosby was the kind of player who became better the angrier he got. Bullying, churlish opponents didn't throw him off his game, they focussed him intently. He had worn a microphone for the OLN broadcast, as he often did throughout the season, but that night, during the third period, he ripped it off on the bench and tossed it to the floor. He said it was dangling and in the way, but it seemed more likely he was worked up enough that he didn't want the network to hear his emotional and often profane utterances.

The Flyers' comeback lifted their own emotions and energy, and they dominated in overtime, peppering Fleury with five shots compared to none for the Penguins. But the young francophone was brilliant in turning back every puck.

With less than a minute left to play, and the game appearing to be headed to a shootout, Crosby vaulted over the bench for his final shift. At the same time, across the rink in the corner near the Penguins' net, Ryan Malone corralled the puck onto his stick. The rangy sophomore forward looked around for an open man and the near pass, but then he spied Crosby off near centre ice, just starting to head across the zone. The rookie was wide open and all alone. Flyers defenceman Kim Johnsson was far out of

position, off to the side, when he should have been protecting the open ice. So Malone fired a long lead pass to his
teammate straight up the middle of the rink.

Just over the centre line, Crosby pulled the puck in and
charged into the Flyers zone, all the anger from earlier con-
tained entirely on the blade of his stick. The only thing
between him and Niittymaki was less than ninety feet of
well-worn ice. The Finnish goaltender shimmied out of his
crease in an attempt to cut down the view of the net, but
Crosby was churning so hard and so fast he quickly backed
up. Sidney spotted an opening on Niittymaki's stick side,
and in an instant he shot and scored.

He raised his arms and shouted. He circled back towards
centre ice, all broken teeth and fat lip and unbridled rage
and joy and sweet revenge at once. The crowd roared its
displeasure. It was a sound he would get used to hearing in
Philadelphia.

After, in the dressing room, a crowd of reporters pressed
around Crosby. Nearby, Malone was still in awe.

"I just turned and looked, and Sid was wide open at
centre ice," he said. "I was wondering where the defenceman was, but I didn't see anybody, so I just tried to fire it
up the ice as fast as I could. Then, I just sat there and
enjoyed the moment."

Crosby, whose mouth was aching, answered questions
patiently, but it was clear he was emotionally spent and still
upset about the beating he took.

"Hatcher got away with one, then the next shift I come
out and get another one," he said. "I was surprised he got
away with two. Obviously [the official] didn't like what I
said, so I got two minutes.

"To get away with one and then to be gone for five minutes and get another one on the next shift, it's frustrating.
It wasn't good on my part to take those two minutes and
give them a power play, but my emotions got the best of
me. It's not something I'm going to make a habit of."

Why didn't he stick up for himself, and maybe take his
own stick to Hatcher or give him a beating? He smiled
wanly. He was not the kind of player who responded with
fisticuffs when finesse served him so nicely.

"When that kind of stuff goes on, it's nice to answer
back. But I'm not going to answer back with my stick or
drop my gloves."

Two thrilling goals, two perfect teeth lost. Crosby's big
night came at the price of his smile. What would his mother
think?

"Yep," said the player who never liked to wear a mouth
guard as he finally, almost a half-hour after leaving the ice,
bent to unlace his skates. "She's going to be pissed."

The following afternoon, back in Pittsburgh, Crosby had
his million-dollar grin restored during a two-hour visit to
the dentist.

In addition to his overtime and moral victory over the
Flyers, he now had nine goals and fifteen assists in
twenty games, best in the league among rookies and
three points ahead of his closest rookie rival, Alexander
Ovechkin, the Russian sniper who went number one in
the 2004 draft.

After practice at the Igloo, a little less than twelve hours
after the emotional, game-winning goal, his normally full,
bee-stung lips were sore, stitched, and swollen. He looked
more TKO than *GQ*.

That morning, the Philadelphia papers were filled with snide and vitriolic words about Crosby. The *Philadelphia Inquirer* accused him of diving three times in the game and questioned whether he behaved "like the ambassador of the new league." Flyers coach Ken Hitchcock was quoted as saying, "Other than the breakaway, I didn't notice him."

The Philly coverage had an overtly spiteful tone, even while Crosby maintained a measured view the morning after.

"I don't mind a guy hitting me clean," he said. "But to get away with two high sticks in a row, one that cut me. I was off for three minutes and came out for the next shift and the same guy hits me again."

He shook his head and continued. "You have to respect referees. You have to be careful about what you say. But it's an emotional game. It's easy to say that now, but when stuff's going on out there, it's one of those things where sometimes your emotions get the best of you and you say something."

The outcome of the Flyers game was terrific for Crosby, but it was also the most complete game he had played in his young NHL career. He melded toughness with pure goal scoring and crafty playmaking in the right measures, and mixed in zealous and timely backchecking. He showed that he would not be pushed around, and that if poked and prodded, he would make his opponents pay where it really hurt, on the scoreboard.

Throughout the Flyers-Penguins game, OLN analysts Neil Smith, the former New York Rangers general manager, and Keith Jones, once an NHL all-star winger, were ebullient over his play and posture.

"Crosby has grown into a man tonight," Smith enthused. "He's the complete package."

But the game also launched the start of Crosby's problem with referees, and the Flyers' comments in the papers frantically fuelled the problem. Suddenly, people were talking about whether or not Sidney Crosby was a diver. The wire game reports that ran that night and the next day on both sides of the border said the Penguins rookie was penalized for diving, rather than unsportsmanlike conduct. Just like that, the undeserved reputation was cast. Corrections appeared the following day, but the damage was done.

Meanwhile, Eddie Olczyk, reacting to the Flyers' obvious and public lack of respect, took a sarcastic tone, going out of his way to praise the Flyers' coaching and even saying they were favourites to win the Stanley Cup, which wasn't remotely true.

The situation was made even more potent because the two teams were scheduled to meet again in about forty-eight hours, on Saturday night at the Igloo. Suddenly, there was more fodder than the beat writers could fit into an off-day story.

MELLON ARENA, PITTSBURGH, PENNSYLVANIA, NOVEMBER 19, 2005: With Thibault back and no worse for taking a puck in the neck, Fleury had been dispatched to Norfolk, Virginia, to catch up with the Baby Penguins and his AHL job. He had made forty-five saves, many of them acrobatic and eye-popping, in holding off the Flyers long enough to give Crosby a chance to win the game, but it was a financial decision to keep him in the minors. He earned $942,000 in the

NHL but only $92,500 in Wilkes-Barre, and had incentive clauses in his contract that could earn him $3 million if he played twenty-five or more games in the NHL. Besides that, the Penguins expected Thibault to soon find his legs and start playing to his veteran potential.

Tonight's game was a standing-room-only sellout – 17,132 had come to hurl insults at Derian Hatcher. One group of fans had hung a banner announcing: These Broad Streeters Can't Bully Sid the Kid. Another said: Get Well Alexandra, for Olczyk's ten-year-old daughter, who was suffering with a mysterious stomach ailment that left her in almost constant pain, preoccupying the already beaten-down coach with serious, personal problems.

At practice the previous day, even as the Philly papers continued to accuse Crosby of being a diver, the kid said he was trying not to think about this quick rematch as a revenge game. He had already gotten his revenge with the overtime game winner, but he was also being careful not to fan the flames.

"It's not something I think about," he said. "You can't think about getting guys back too much.

"It's always tough after emotional games like that. You have to make sure you close the book and move on."

To a man in the dressing room, the Penguins players were either outraged or bemused by the veiled comments in the papers made by Coach Hitchcock and the blatant, clumsy editorializing done by the Flyers beat writers. The coach himself issued a terse "no comment" when asked about Crosby by the Philly writers because he said he did not want to be fined by the league for accusing the player, who had never been penalized for diving, for doing just that. But the Philadelphia writers interpreted Hitch's comments for him, making it quite clear that the feeling among the entire organization was that the rookie star was being disrespectful of the game itself, perhaps the most insulting thing that could be said of him.

In the NHL, where most players believe they should always fight to stay on their skates, diving is regarded as a scourge. Players who go down easily and in exaggerated fashion in hopes of drawing interference, hooking, or tripping penalties are considered weak and the act nearly sacrilegious. Some players have garnered reputations as divers through their careers; ironically, one of the best-known was Forsberg when he played with the Colorado Avalanche, so much so he was nicknamed Floppa, a play on his real Swedish nickname of Foppa.

Olczyk was dead serious over those few days when asked repeatedly if he thought his young star a diver. "Absolutely not, absolutely not," Olczyk repeated firmly. "Absolutely not." But he, too, was stunned by the reaction from across the state.

"It's always been an accepted part of the game where players make comments about other players," he said. "I can accept that. But I can't accept when Hitch mentions about Sid, not noticing him except on a couple, certain shifts. That shows a lack of respect, not only to Crosby, but to me and our team. I expect more from Hitch when it comes to that kind of stuff, because to me it's a lack of respect. Take the high road, or you worry about your team and let me worry about my guys."

Truth be told, Crosby had been dealing with being unfairly roughed up with slashes and smacks to wrists and ankles and cross-checks to the back since he was about twelve years old.

"I'm used to it," he sighed.

Like the Penguins, the Flyers had won two Stanley Cup championships, and like the Penguins, they were hoisted back to back, making for a sort of mini-dynasty at the time. But Philly's dated back considerably further to the Broad Street Bullies teams of 1974 and 1975, compared with the Penguins' relatively recent Cup wins in 1991 and 1992, won on the finesse play of Lemieux and Jaromir Jagr.

Still, the Penguins had never fared well against the Flyers. Over the years, their longest winning streak against the Flyers was just four games, while Philadelphia had beaten Pittsburgh eleven straight times. Prior to the other night, Pittsburgh had not won in Philadelphia since January 12, 2004.

The intra-state rivalry was many layers deep and went back years. Both teams were founded at the same time, June 5, 1967, the day the NHL added six additional teams to the Original Six, in the league's first expansion in forty years.

The rivalry extended to Major League Baseball's Pirates and Phillies, though it didn't seep into the National Football League, where the cities' teams play in different conferences and the Steelers enjoyed a rust belt rivalry with the Cleveland Browns. In size and culture and as part of the northeast urban corridor, Philadelphia shared more in common with Boston, New York, and Washington than with down-to-earth, blue-collar Pittsburgh.

When the lockout ended, part of the NHL's plan to sell the game was to remake the schedule and put more of an emphasis on rivalries by expanding divisional and conference play. The downside was that Eastern teams played far fewer Western opponents and vice versa. Teams would play inter-conference opponents only once every several years, robbing Western Conference fans of the opportunity to see stars such as Sidney Crosby and Eastern Conference fans of seeing up-and-comers such as talented defenceman Dion Phaneuf of the Calgary Flames.

The significant upside was that frothing, rabid rivalries would be encouraged to develop and simmer and even boil over between geographically near clubs such as Toronto and Ottawa, Florida and Tampa, Calgary and Edmonton, and Los Angeles and Anaheim.

The new collective bargaining agreement ensured that each team would play eight games against each of its four division rivals, thirty-two in total. Each team would also play four games against each of the other ten teams in the conference, creating a sort of secondary set of rivalries, with only ten inter-conference games.

Previously, division rivals met only six times. This season, for the first time, the Penguins and Flyers would play each other eight times.

Taking just hockey into account, the Flyers have had more heated rivalries over the years with the New York Rangers – they have met ten times in the Stanley Cup playoffs, with Philadelphia capturing six of those series.

And the Penguins had more of an antagonism with the Washington Capitals, who have been beaten by the Penguins six of the eighteen times they have appeared in the playoffs, more than any other team. But any Penguins-Flyers game was always a hot ticket in both arenas, and now, in a single game, Sidney Crosby had guaranteed entertaining contests on several fronts for years to come.

"The Philadelphia-Pittsburgh rivalry has always been there," said Mark Recchi, who had played for both sides. "It kind of dropped off a little the last few years, mainly because we hadn't beaten them all that often."

Everyone expected an emotional, fight-filled rematch. Even Pittsburgh Pirates outfielder Jason Bay, a British Columbia kid who had been voted the National League rookie of the year, was in the stands.

The fans hoped tough defenceman Brooks Orpik might take a run at Hatcher, or that Lyle Odelein would go after one of the Flyers' stars. But the Penguins didn't want to lose the game in the penalty box and seemed determined to play with cool heads.

Hatcher was booed during the player introductions and every time he touched the puck.

The Flyers opened the scoring in the first period, when Simon Gagné beat Thibault from just inside the left circle, but it didn't take long for Crosby to retaliate. He slapped the puck past Niittymaki after scooping up a beautiful blind, backhand pass from John LeClair. It was his tenth goal of the season, and it tied the game at 1-1. Mike Richard and Ziggy Palffy traded goals in the second period to tie the game at 2-2.

Emotions, which had been mostly bottled until then, spilled over. Late in the period, Flyers defenceman Mike Rathje smacked Sidney in the skates with his stick, causing him to lose his balance. As Rathje was sent to the box for tripping, Forsberg started yapping at Crosby and made a diving gesture at him. Then he yelled at Sidney, "Look at the replay."

Crosby, taken aback by Forsberg's action, cursed at him from across the ice.

The teams traded goals again to force another tie, but Thibault gave up two soft scores in just more than a minute and the Penguins squandered two extra-man opportunities when they were trailing. Philadelphia coasted to a 6-3 win.

Afterwards, Crosby seemed stung by Forsberg's act. The Flyers superstar, a thirty-two-year-old franchise player who won two Cups with Colorado and an MVP honour before arriving in Philadelphia in the off-season as a free agent, had always been a sort of reluctant superstar, a demeanour that demanded respect from fans and players alike.

As much as Crosby had been compared to Gretzky and Lemieux, Forsberg often as not was the one many people talked about in the same breath as Crosby – a finesse player who could score goals but also physically overpower opponents. Both were slick and precise passers who preferred playmaking to scoring their own goals. To say that Crosby looked up to and admired Forsberg was an understatement. His comments and gestures cut to the quick.

"I was surprised from him, yeah," Crosby said with a disbelief that gave away his hurt. "I didn't think he'd say anything like that. It was pretty obvious that I didn't dive."

Far on the other side of Mellon Arena's concrete bowels, in the visitors' dressing room, Forsberg flatly told reporters, "I thought it was a dive. It looked suspicious."

Crosby knew that the Flyers were just trying to get inside his head, get him off his game. But he did not understand how two high sticks in a row could have gone unnoticed, or how Forsberg could have accused him of one of the most disrespectful acts in the game.

"It's pretty obvious why they're doing it," he said. "It's just better not to talk about it, because this is exactly what they want, for you guys to ask me questions about it. It's a lot nicer when they don't talk about it, but obviously, [Hitchcock] wants to try to get me off my game. That's what he's doing. You don't need to do that. But if that's the way it is, that's the way it is. I'm not going to change my game. I wish that wasn't the way it is, but if that's how they're going to try to get the edge, let them do it."

And they did. The next day, in reporting the Flyers' 6-3 victory, the Philadelphia media again suggested Crosby had been diving. The contrived controversy continued. It would not end any time soon.

Sidney Crosby, who as part of an elementary school project wrote letters to the Philadelphia Flyers asking for autographed hockey cards and photographs and delightedly received them, was now an enemy across the state.

"As a kid, it was amazing to get them and really nice of them," he said, recalling the school assignment and how thrilled he was to hear back from the Philly players. I suggested it was probably the last good experience he would ever have with the Flyers. He laughed heartily. "I think you might be right about that."

THE **OTHER** ROOKIE

*They're in the same solar system
and so we get to enjoy both.*

A FEW DAYS after the controversy with the Philadelphia Flyers began to quiet down, the next wave of drama around Sidney Crosby started unfolding: his first meeting with Alexander Ovechkin, the Russian sniper who was a co-favourite to win the rookie of the year honours along with Crosby.

Ovechkin was the number one pick in the 2004 entry draft, but the lockout delayed his NHL debut. The talented left winger was part of the double cohort draft class that had been so impressive already this season.

He was twenty years old – twenty-three months older than Crosby – and had spent the cancelled season at home playing with Dynamo Moscow in the Russian Super League, where he had a respectable but relatively underwhelming thirteen goals and thirteen assists in thirty-seven games.

But here in the NHL, he already anchored the Washington Capitals lineup. Like Crosby, he quickly became his awful team's best player. He was a franchise guy that the team would be built around. Like Crosby, he was his team's future and that of the league. Like Crosby, he was thrilling to watch but for entirely different reasons.

Alexander Ovechkin had a face that was impossible to forget, big and square with a smile so broad it almost devoured his own face. On a freezing cold night, shortly before midnight on January 5, 2003, I was walking in downtown Halifax with colleagues Roy MacGregor of the *Globe and Mail*, and Cam Cole, then with the *National Post*. We had watched the Russian world junior hockey team beat Canada 3-2 to win the gold medal. The Canadian players did not wear their silver medals to the media session following the game, depressed they had fallen short. Outside, the Russian players wandered the streets, celebrating with their gold medals around their necks.

One young forward, then seventeen-year-old Ovechkin, his arms draped around two teammates, laughed and shouted, showing off his medal to everyone who passed, with that grin stretched from ear to ear. At the time, he was the most promising player eligible for the 2004 NHL entry draft. I'll never forget his smile that night, his laughter hanging in the cold night air.

If Sidney Crosby was all polite polish, Alexander Ovechkin was brash and bold and wore his confidence on his sleeve. They both knew everyone was intrigued by their first NHL confrontation, but Ovechkin was a little more colourful in expressing his thoughts. "He is a very good player. But there are some other good rookies in the league, such as Jeff Carter, Mike Richards, and Dion Phaneuf. We will see at the end of the season which rookie will win the Calder Trophy. Everybody talks about Crosby when I turn on the TV. I don't mind. It is not unfair for me. He is a great player, a special player. We have different styles of play. We cannot all play like Gretzky and Lemieux."

Both of them said they would approach the game at the Igloo like any other, but given that it was their first head-to-head matchup in the NHL, it was hard to see it as just any game. It was a showcase for the league's two best young players. "I admit it will be special to play against Mario Lemieux," Ovechkin said. "He was my favourite player when I grew up."

They had plenty in common, but it wasn't their first meeting. They played opposite each other in the gold medal game of the World Juniors in December, where Ovechkin sat out the third period with an injured shoulder after Crosby delivered a big hit.

It was a sign of new times that the NHL realized just what they had in their two best young players and arranged a conference call for reporters with both Crosby and Ovechkin on the eve of their first big league meeting. The game was being compared to the first between two promising players who turned out to be legends, Mario Lemieux and Wayne Gretzky. That night ended in a 3-3 tie. Gretzky had a goal and Lemieux an assist.

The NHL, banking on Crosby and Ovechkin as two of the game's next superstars, smartly hyped the game, even though both players were doing so well on the ice that neither needed additional advertising.

League officials and hockey fans from Russia to Rimouski were waiting, not just for what one game might bring, but for what these players, who both led their respective teams in scoring, might offer over long careers to come.

Crosby tried to maintain perspective about the upcoming game. "This is the first time we'll meet, and we're twenty games into our rookie seasons in the NHL," he said. "We're both enjoying the experience and trying to get better, but we have a long way to go before we can start comparing ourselves to Lemieux versus Gretzky. We both realize that, but being two first overall picks, there's probably going to be some buildup."

Heading into the game, Crosby had ten goals and fifteen assists in twenty-one games. Ovechkin had fifteen goals and six assists in twenty games. There had not been a rookie-of-the-year race shaping up so early and with so much intrigue in many years.

"You've got two dynamic players that people are talking about outside of their cities," Olczyk said. "It's going to be very exciting."

Even though everyone wanted to debate who was the better player, it was difficult to compare them, because they were so different. Crosby, at five foot eleven and 193 pounds, was compactly built, but his lower body was so strong he was nearly impossible to knock off his skates. He could split defencemen thirty pounds heavier and a half-foot taller with ease with his speed and slick skating. He was primarily a playmaker – he was ranked among the NHL top ten in assists, but his goal tally was mounting rapidly with each game. He liked to battle along the boards and would sneak the puck away from opponents that way.

Ovechkin was two years older and bigger, at six foot two and 212 pounds. He bullied his way into the crease without much effort and delivered devastating hits. Last year, while playing in the Russian Elite League, he put Sergei Gonchar in the hospital with a concussion. He possessed a wicked slapshot and pure goal-scoring abilities already among the best in the league. He was tied for fourth in the NHL in goals and was the only player to go three for three in shootouts.

It really did seem impossible to answer the question everyone was asking: Who is better, Sid the Kid or Alexander the Great?

Mike Emrick, the veteran play-by-play man and voice of the NHL on OLN, said their differences made it impossible to say. "I don't put any qualitative differences on either player," he said. "Because Ovechkin's a goal scorer; he's got the blade that's tilted at a nine-iron angle and he's going to score goals. That's what his talent is. But the other side of that is Ovechkin may be all that Washington really has in terms of star power. But I see Crosby as a potential leader of the team as well as a point leader. He's a great passer, and he contributes that way.

"It's the same thing they used to say about Mario and Wayne. Who cares who the better player is or who someone thinks is the better player? They're in the same solar system and so we get to enjoy both."

Ovechkin wasn't so cheeky he couldn't praise Crosby's game. "He is a great passer like Gretzky."

He admitted he desired the Calder Trophy as the league's top rookie; Crosby insisted he wasn't thinking about it, because it was simply too distracting.

"As a hockey player, with this being my first year, consistency is big, and I can't get caught thinking about anything other than being my best every night," he said. "Other people decide [the Calder]. If I put my focus on helping the team win hockey games, then after eighty-two games I can be satisfied with the way I've played. But if I'm preoccupied with other things, I can't accept that. I can't worry about other guys.

"Every night you play in this league, you're against good players; you're always aware who you're playing against. He's a fast player, he's strong and a powerful skater. He's a good all-round player, from what I've seen. I think he's got everything. He's dangerous when he's out there. He's a player you have to respect when you play against him. He's had a great start to the season."

Lemieux said the rivalry was great for the game and that the buildup reminded him of the comparisons made between him and a young Gretzky, even though he joked he was too old to remember what happened that night.

Recchi took the more skeptical view of an old warhorse. "Let's not get ahead of ourselves. They're both terrific young players, and they've earned all the praise they get. Mario and Gretzky were great players for a long time, and in three or four years, when they're at the top of the league, we'll be able to say that."

MELLON ARENA, PITTSBURGH, PENNSYLVANIA, NOVEMBER 22, 2005: Not forgotten in the frenzy over Crosby and Ovechkin was the sore fact that the Penguins had still won just six games and were four points behind Buffalo for the last playoff spot in the Eastern Conference with a quarter of the season already over.

Olczyk, who was getting increasingly desperate to find a formula that would work, dramatically juggled the lineup.

Forwards Rico Fata and Konstantin Koltsov and affable defenceman Rob Scuderi, who had been scratched the past seven games, were put on waivers. Centre Matt Hussey and right winger Michel Ouellet, a quiet francophone from Rimouski with an intense stare and magic marker eyebrows, were called up. Gonchar, who had missed three games with a strained groin, was expected back in the lineup.

Eight minutes and seven seconds into the much heralded matchup between two top draft picks, the kid with the reputation as the wily playmaker showed the sure-shot sniper a lesson in dramatic goal scoring.

Skating up the middle, Crosby caught a pass from Palffy on his left skate, scooped it onto his stick blade, and chugged towards Capitals goaltender Olaf Kolzig. He shoved through two defenders on the way and flipped a backhand shot almost vertically into the net, knocking Kolzig's blue water bottle into the air and onto the ice. The goal gave the Penguins a 3-0 lead and Crosby first bragging rights over Ovechkin.

The Penguins handled the Capitals easily. Like barn cats playing with church mice, they had a 4-0 lead at the end of the first period on goals from Palffy, Jackman, Crosby, and Lasse Pirjeta. For the first time all year, the crowd gave the home side a standing ovation at the end of the first period.

"He's an impressive player," Crosby said of Ovechkin afterwards. "He's a strong skater, he's fast. He made some incredible moves out there. He can do it all, I think. He's really dangerous."

Down the hall in the dumpy visitors' dressing room, Ovechkin praised his rival. "He's a great passer, and he sees the ice real well. He's a passer like Wayne Gretzky and the way he sees the ice."

The Penguins won the game 5-4 in front of a standing-room-only sellout crowd of 16,978, who saw the young stars overlap for just seconds here and there when Crosby skated off and Ovechkin on, until the second-to-last shift of the game when Washington pulled Kolzig for an extra skater to try and tie the game.

The paying customers got their money's worth, nonetheless, and the NHL got a glimpse of the future. It was an eye-popping clinic in hockey moves. In the second period, Crosby displayed his sixth sense. He was working along the boards with the puck in the Capitals zone but was held up by centre Brooks Laich. Crosby simply dropped to one knee, spun around, and without looking threw a backhand pass across the ice to pass to Palffy, who caught it on the tape and scored.

Ovechkin started out slowly but was most impressive in the game's second half. He set up the third goal by weaving the puck through his own legs while charging at full speed into the Penguins zone, then passing to Matt Pettinger.

Even Olczyk was delighted, though the Penguins win might have had more to do with it.

"It's exciting to go from where we've been, with eighteen months without hockey, to have two young players who've performed to the expectations everyone had for them," Olczyk said. "It's a great boost for the league, the teams, and these two guys."

At the end of the night, Crosby remained leader of the rookie scoring race with eleven goals and sixteen assists for twenty-seven points in twenty-two games. Ovechkin had fifteen goals and seven assists for twenty-two points in twenty-one games. And Crosby had the prize of being the game's best performer. He seemed to rise to the challenge that playing Ovechkin offered, as though it was a chance to answer any critics.

Ted Leonsis, the Washington owner, enthused that Crosby and Ovechkin had all the makings of the passionate basketball rivalry between Larry Bird and Magic Johnson, but at least one of the young players said neither had been around long enough to deserve the lofty comparison.

"I try not to think that far ahead," Crosby said. "It was really exciting to be out there, and it's exciting for the crowd, but you play against great players every night in this league, so I try not to think too much about that or change my game. But you want to be up for the challenge when it's built up like that."

At practice the next day, Ryan VandenBussche spent some time trying to teach Sidney how to fight. He showed Crosby how to land a punch. He kept grabbing Crosby's sweater, trying to pull it up over his head as Sidney squirmed. It looked like they were dancing.

9

GREY DECEMBER

The guy has a lot on his mind.

THE U.S. THANKSGIVING weekend did not go well for Crosby. In Sunrise, Florida, he took a puck off the instep of his skate in a 6-3 blowout to the Panthers that wasn't half as close as the score suggested. Before he was injured, he scored his twelfth goal of the season, a one-timer past Roberto Luongo on a behind-the-net pass from Ziggy Palffy forty-eight seconds into the third period, to spark a rally and cut Florida's lead to 4-2.

But with eleven minutes left to play, Crosby stuck his left foot into the path of a slapshot from six feet out by big Panthers defenceman Mike Van Ryn, and when the puck made contact, Crosby collapsed to the ice in a heap. He hobbled to the dressing room and returned several minutes later to take a shift. But he could not continue. The puck was travelling about 150 kilometres an hour and hit with a thundering thwack heard by everyone on the bench.

"It sounded like someone taking a baseball bat to a piece

of leather nailed to a tree," Phil Bourque said. "For him to be able to walk and put most of his weight on it is a good sign. If there's no break, it's all about your pain threshold."

Afterwards, the reporters were waiting in the hallway outside the Penguins' dressing room to find out how Crosby was. He limped around the corner with Penguins trainer Scott Johnson at his side talking softly about the X-ray Crosby had a few minutes earlier on his foot.

A few minutes later, we filed into the secondary visitors' dressing room – teams often use one to put on and shed their equipment and another to shower and put their street clothes back on. Some of his teammates, such as LeClair, had already showered and dressed and were on the bus. Others were still in the shower or knotting their ties. Everyone was quiet, but that was hardly unusual after a loss.

Crosby limped out of the shower and gingerly began to get dressed. "It's just a bruise, we'll see tomorrow, it's usually the next day you can tell the severity," he said. "I was trying to block the shot and I turned a little bit and it got me in the side of the foot."

He was in a lot of pain. As he pulled his slacks onto his right leg, he winced and had to support his weight on a nearby chair. "I was in a lot of pain, and they said just forget about it and stay off it. No point getting hit there again. I wasn't sure if it was broken. But it's just a bruise. Tomorrow I'll see how it feels."

Somehow, despite the ache in his foot and the curious crowd around him, he managed to keep his sense of humour. When I asked him to confirm it was his left foot, just to make certain, he chuckled wryly, "You can just say 'foot.'" He didn't want opponents taking advantage of his injury.

The Penguins flew to Tampa after the game and practised there the next morning. They didn't play the Lightning until the following afternoon. I went to see how Crosby was doing. He didn't practise; instead he got a precautionary CAT scan at a hospital in the morning and then watched his teammates work out from the stands at the St. Pete Times Forum. Even though it wasn't a game day, he wore a black suit and an open-necked white shirt. His ankle peeked from the gap between his left shoe and hem of black slacks. It was his first NHL road trip to Florida, but he was already sporting the bare-feet-in-dress-shoes look that was preferred by locals.

A rectangular bandage was affixed below the bump of his bony ankle, covering a cut from the puck that left a deep bruise and threatened to slow the snappy scoring pace he had established with twelve goals and twenty-eight points in twenty-three games. He was still ahead of Ovechkin. He had scored ten goals in his past eleven games, his best pace of the season.

Out in the hallway on a workbench, long-time Penguins equipment manager Steve Latin was working on fashioning a pad for his skate to cushion the bruise so that he could play the following afternoon if the swelling had receded enough. If Crosby couldn't play, it would be because his foot was too swollen to put on his skate.

Crosby had stayed awake until four o'clock Saturday morning layering bags of ice on his hoof, keeping roommate Matt Murley awake. "I was up most of the night making sure I kept the swelling down as much as I could," he said. "It's never fun waking up in the morning. You don't know how it's going to be. But it was better than I feared. Usually you expect the worst, but I was able to move it a little bit. It's just one of those things that happens. I've had a few in the foot before, but that's the hardest I've ever gotten hit. I was the most nervous about this one."

Blocking shots was a risky but necessary move, one he didn't regret making but for the injury. Everyone in the dressing room could empathize. Almost all hockey players have been hit with a frozen piece of rocketing rubber in that tender area with little meat and many small bones.

"You feel like throwing up," Eddie Olczyk said. "It's a feeling that takes your breath away, and then you realize how much pain there is. Van Ryn has quite a shot. It's a frozen piece of rubber getting up to 100 miles an hour. That play happens a lot. When it does, you realize it's probably lucky more guys don't get taken out that way."

Lemieux, who said he'd taken many pucks that way over his career, felt bad for his young star and worried a bit about where it left the team. "Any time you lose a top guy, it's a big loss," he said. "The kid's a phenom. He's shown he's one of the best in the league."

The next day, Sidney managed to pull his padded skate on and play against the Lightning. He would have been better off resting it. His scoring streak was broken in the 4-1 loss. The Penguins had dropped the third game of their last four.

In addition, Lemieux sat out the game with a sudden bout of stomach flu. He didn't even leave the team's waterfront hotel, just steps from the arena, to watch the game in person from the press box.

Afterwards, outside the dressing room in the chilly hallway of the St. Pete Times Forum, Olczyk held his usual post-game question-and-answer session.

The coach was routinely soft-spoken and thoughtful. He never raised his voice and never spoke without carefully choosing his words. After a handful of questions about the game, he was casually asked about Lemieux's health, and Olczyk's answer was startling.

"Let's be perfectly clear. When people look at him, they look at him only as a player. But he's got the arena situation, the ownership stuff, he's leading a team and being counted on for a lot of things. The guy has a lot on his mind. He's a unique individual; there's no other guy in sports [who is an owner-player]. A lot is going on. He's a dad with four kids. Being run down is one thing, but he's got a lot of things on his plate besides playing. We have to make sure we get him right."

The remarks were spontaneous and heartfelt and rife with subtext. He had raised more questions than he had answered.

In the same manner as October went, so did a horrible November finally end. The Penguins' record was now a disappointing 7-12-6, woefully short of where they thought they would be at this point in the season when training camp began. Even worse, they were thirteen points out of the final playoff spot in the East.

The players and Olczyk agreed that if the Penguins were going to start picking their way through the standings and have a hope of sneaking into the playoffs, December was the month they would have to do it.

By way of an accidental Christmas gift, the NHL schedule makers had given the Penguins a friendly schedule for the month. There were only four road games, to New York, Detroit, St. Louis, and Buffalo. The other eight were at the Igloo, and they were sprinkled throughout the month with a stretch of four days off in early December and a stretch of five days off the week right before Christmas. There would be a lot of time to rest, and practise.

On December 1, the Penguins found themselves in New York to face the Rangers. They had played what was arguably their best game of the season at Madison Square Garden on November 7. That night, which ended with a 3-2 victory for the Penguins and Crosby being named the game's first star after he scored a brilliant goal and played an all-round terrific game, had the Penguins feeling as though their luck was about to change.

Lemieux scored that night, and Sebastien Caron had played well in goal. But Olczyk knew even back in training camp that Lemieux sometimes wasn't going to look like Super Mario.

"The way Mario carries himself and competes and communicates the professionalism to the other guys . . . You see the points and the goals, but the example he sets is the highest in the league," Olczyk said. "It's not always going to be there every night, and he knows that. That's why the supporting cast he has is important." They were about to become even more so.

The defeats, some of them embarrassing, continued to mount in December. Crosby hadn't missed a game with his sore foot, which was slowly healing, but it had clearly affected his game. He didn't register even an assist in losses to Tampa, Buffalo, and the Rangers, the three games his longest scoreless streak of the season. When the holiday month opened, he started to regain his scoring touch. Wins, however, continued to elude the Penguins, most of whom now often seemed visibly shaken after games.

A return to New York yielded a 2-1 loss to the Rangers, and back at home they fell 3-2 to the Calgary Flames. After games, Crosby kept repeating the same old lines: They weren't far from winning these games; they had to play smarter hockey. On some nights lately, the eighteen-year-old rookie was the only member of the team aside from the goaltender waiting in the dressing room when it was opened to the media shortly after the end of the game. Sometimes he would ride the exercise bike for fifteen minutes before he came out to talk to us. Sometimes he rode it afterwards for a half-hour. After the Calgary game, he stayed at the arena until well after midnight, sprinting up and down the stairs.

HEART BREAK

I'm not the future anymore.

FOR THE PAST several weeks, there had been quiet chatter around the woefully underachieving Penguins about the effectiveness of Lemieux, who had turned forty on the first day of the season and was aging, as all professional athletes do, in the spotlight before fans and television cameras.

Fans and some people close to the club were asking rhetorically if Lemieux could still help the team, if he was too old to exploit the rule changes that would have helped his offensive talents soar even higher as a younger player, if the years had turned Le Magnifique into L'Ordinaire.

Lemieux was playing in his seventeenth NHL season, and he had moved far beyond having anything to prove. He had 690 goals and 1,031 assists, seventh among the all-time leaders.

Though he had accomplished feats too numerous to list, and was on pace to play seventy-six games and score sixty-one points this season, he had never played a complete season. If he managed to accomplish it, and it was a big "if," given his history with chronic back problems, it would be his most productive and consistent campaign in a decade.

Olczyk was keeping Lemieux's shifts shorter to keep his legs fresh; he was saving him mostly for the power play. But Lemieux himself was the first to admit he found it difficult to adjust to the new rules aimed at helping skilled offensive players like him do what they did best.

"It's been a tough adjustment for the older guys," he said. "It's been a lot different game for so many years, and now it's a lot faster and you have to react a lot quicker, be in a certain spot at just the right time. The game expects a lot of guys used to playing differently."

Lemieux was at the front of the pack of players who lobbied loud and long for just these rule changes, but here he was, unable to take advantage of them. He was already in the Hockey Hall of Fame, but he often looked his age on the ice, especially next to Crosby. Lemieux wasn't bitter. But he was bittersweet.

"It's frustrating, but it's good for the game, and that's the main thing," he said. "We want the game to get better, for it and the fans. And we're finally going in that direction. I wish it would have happened fifteen years ago, but that's just the way life is."

After a 3-2 loss to Buffalo, the first game after the Tampa game that saw Lemieux sit out with "the flu," I went across the street from the Igloo to the Steelhead Brasserie Wine Bar, a popular after-hockey gathering spot for fans and the occasional site of the ESPN post-game show hosted by Mark Madden, an irascible but hockey-loving Pittsburgh radio personality. The crowd at the bar was a mix of Penguins fans and Sabres supporters who had made the four-hour drive.

On the wall behind the ESPN set hung an enormous colour photograph of the Penguins celebrating their 1991 Stanley Cup victory. At the centre of the picture is Mario Lemieux, hoisting the treasured trophy and grinning ear to ear.

Madden had Olczyk on for a few minutes, and then took calls from listeners. One suggested the Penguins captain be sent to the club's minor league team across the state to "get into shape." Madden, a staunch defender of Lemieux, exploded in rage and sarcasm. "Sure, jerk," he barked into his headset. "You're going to send the owner of the team to Wilkes-Barre. Thanks for the call, jackass!"

I talked to him a little later. He said he received a handful of calls each day bearing the same sentiment about Lemieux. "My feeling is that it's a small but vocal minority who feel that way. These are people who like to bring him down. It's my theory that they are disgruntled Steelers fans, angry because he has been the biggest sports hero in Pittsburgh for two decades. This city is tough on its athletes. But if people were really down on him, you'd hear boos at Mellon Arena." And that you never heard. When Lemieux hit the ice, there were only cheers. When he strolled through the Igloo Club for a press conference, the only discernible reaction was reverence.

Before the season began, Lemieux was openly excited about three things: passing the torch to Crosby, who he saw as a young phenom in his own mould; finishing a proposal to land the club a new arena and keep the team in Pittsburgh; and making a playoff run with this team assembled under the new salary cap with a blend of young talent and high-priced veterans.

But not everything was going according to plan. The Penguins' horrible start to the season – they were 7-14-6 and thirteen points out of a playoff spot through early December – put them out of contention almost before Christmas, even though no one on the team would admit defeat just yet. And while it was unfair to measure the forty-year-old Lemieux against the eighteen-year-old Crosby, there was no doubt that Crosby's youth and sudden impact amplified Mario's age.

"Is Mario the player he was ten years ago?" Madden said. "Of course not. Who would be? But he's still a damn good player who brings a lot of class to this organization."

When I raised the notion to Crosby after practice the next day, he said he didn't know how Lemieux juggled it all. "It's amazing; you forget he's been through so much. It's important for us he stays healthy. He has to feel his own body, but he's one of the greatest who has ever played because he's been able to adjust his game and adapt. There's a lot there. As a pro hockey player, there's enough pressure to perform. Couple that with owning a hockey team. He's obviously had to learn to balance it. It's pretty amazing. It's something I could never do."

The first indication that anything was wrong with Lemieux to those outside of Pittsburgh was his reluctance to commit wholeheartedly to participating in the upcoming Olympic Games in Turin. A few weeks earlier, he had slyly dropped the notion to reporters after practice that he might not be ready to take on another Olympics. In December 2000, Lemieux had stunned the hockey world when he returned from an early retirement forced on by his battle with Hodgkin's disease and chronic back ailments. At that point in his career, still young at thirty-six, Lemieux was named captain almost a year before the Salt Lake City Olympics took place.

Early in the 2001-2002 NHL season, he suffered a hip injury and limited his playing time in an effort to save himself for the Games. He had two goals and four assists in the tournament, which saw Canada win its first hockey gold medal in fifty years. He was the team's leader and spokesman.

But his participation effectively ended his season with the Penguins, and he was harshly criticized by fans as the team crashed in the standings and missed the playoffs, winning just six of thirty-one games from the end of January until the end of the season. "I couldn't skate. That's why I was taking games off," Lemieux said. "It was important for me to play in the Olympics and represent my country. That way, I was giving myself the chance to go to Salt Lake and be a part of it. Salt Lake City, I knew that was probably the last time I was going to play. I came back in Pittsburgh and played, I think, one or two games. I knew that I was going to have surgery on the way back. Now, physically, I'm feeling a lot better."

Lemieux played a bit of a cat and mouse game when it came to talking about the Olympics. He wasn't being deceitful. In retrospect, it seemed as though he was having trouble with the idea that he might not be able to play. He said he was still committed to playing a full season in Pittsburgh, but that easing off wasn't out of the question.

"I don't know," he sighed one day after practice. "A lot depends on the schedule. We've played a lot every second day. We have a little break coming up in December, and that helps a lot. You can take a day or two to recharge the battery."

Olczyk was inclined to let Lemieux set his own pace. Still, he managed three multi-point games in his first ten of the season. "Mario's no different than anyone else with the inactivity of last year. Unfortunately, he got run down and sick. But he's a pro's pro. He's frustrated, but he knows he's part of the solution and continues to believe in getting the job done."

In the meantime, Lemieux was beginning to lay the groundwork for sitting out the Olympics. "When you look at the young Canadians, there are so many playing well right now," he said. "You shouldn't be on the team just because you're a name or on what you've done in the past. It should be about the present."

It seemed he wanted to get the message out to the people back home that he might not be all right to represent Team Canada one last time. But he was careful with his words. He wasn't ready to be definitive. He seemed to want to break the news gently, maybe as much to himself as anyone else.

No one in the hockey world – not even Wayne Gretzky – had more going on in that last season than Mario Lemieux. He marked the start of his seventeenth season in the league by turning forty and looking forward to the end of a four-year fight to build a new arena.

"It's been a long process," Lemieux said. "We've been working on it for the last four years. It's frustrating at times, but I think we're getting close to finding an answer and knowing what this franchise is going to do in the future."

People around the Penguins were worried about him. You could see it daily in Olczyk's kind face. Eddie Johnston had been impressed by Lemieux at training camp and the shape he had arrived in but was troubled by his nagging "virus."

"Hopefully, he's on his way back," Johnston said. "He got off to a pretty good start, but illness has taken a lot out of him. He's under a lot of pressure, and it takes a lot out of him. He's trying to keep our team in Pittsburgh. He's been working so hard on the rink. It's an every day thing. He plays, and then he goes across the street and talks to politicians and tries to negotiate. It takes its toll. It's tough to play with both hats on.

"He's feeling the losing as an owner and a player. He's frustrated because our expectations were higher than what is happening. I think he's committed right now to playing the whole season. But he's got to pace himself, take a day off here and there. He'll be fine. You'll see him rebound. He'll be stronger in the second half. Crosby has brought energy to Mario."

That, and a sense of loyalty. Lemieux may have had another motive for wanting to stay home from the Olympics. If he wasn't well enough to play, he wanted Gretzky and his assistants to consider taking Sidney Crosby in Lemieux's place. His words were a way of letting Team Canada bosses know what his wishes were if he couldn't make it. It was good timing.

Gretzky planned to be in Pittsburgh in a few days, for a Saturday night game against the Avalanche. His visit was partly to see Crosby play, and also to have a talk with Lemieux.

"It's important to bring him on Team Canada," he said
that day in front of the Toronto reporters. "Even if he
doesn't play a lot, let him see how it works. He's going to be
the future of a lot of world cups and Olympics in the future.
It would be wise."

Passing the torch to Crosby was also an important part
of Lemieux's season. Although he had seven goals and fourteen assists in twenty-five games this season, a respectable
number, to be sure, Lemieux knew he wasn't in it for the
long haul much longer.

"It's important. He's the future of this franchise. I'm not
the future anymore. And that's something that I'm going to
have to prepare myself and everybody else for."

No one was prepared for what occurred on December 7.
Lemieux checked himself into the hospital for observation
because he had a racing and irregular heartbeat after practice earlier in the day. He had been on the ice for the team's
energetic workout that lasted more than an hour. Lemieux
seemed fine, albeit flushed, when he left the ice. It wasn't
the first time it had happened. Suddenly, it was obvious that
Lemieux's ailment was something more than stomach flu.

The following day, the Penguins were scheduled to play
the Minnesota Wild. News of Lemieux's condition hit the
wires around dinner time the night before, and several
dozen reporters, including a couple of sports television
crews from Canada, showed up at practice.

Afterwards, Craig Patrick spoke in the lounge adjacent
to the dressing room and explained the events surrounding Lemieux's hospitalization. His tone was even and calm
and made the whole thing sound rather routine. Lemieux

had been diagnosed overnight with atrial fibrillation and was being discharged that afternoon. The condition was considered relatively common, affecting about 2.2 million Americans each year and occurring when the heart's two small upper chambers quivered rather than beating in proper time. As a result, blood couldn't drain and could pool and clot. Medication was used to help restore a natural heartbeat. Lemieux would start taking it immediately and probably resume working out in about a week. Patrick predicted the aging legend would not be out of the lineup for long.

It sounded terrifically optimistic – too good to be true. Patrick said the condition wouldn't affect Lemieux's career.

"We expect that he will be able to begin exercising in a matter of days and return to the lineup in a brief period of time," he said, finally admitting that the rapid heartbeat that sent Lemieux to the hospital the previous night had flared up a handful of times since the summer.

It had flared up during the road trip to Florida over the U.S. Thanksgiving weekend. It had flared up earlier in the season in Buffalo. In Tampa, a doctor advised him not to play. "The doctors said that the next time it happens we should get him into a hospital and hooked up to a monitor so they could figure out what it is," Patrick said. "We weren't really worried [Wednesday] when it happened, because he went right in. He's actually really happy to know what it is now."

Doctors didn't know what triggered Lemieux's condition other than the fact that a number of factors, including stress, could have been the culprit.

The previous night, Crosby had visited his teammate in the hospital. The health crisis left him a bit shaken. "It was pretty shocking. Being around the family, you feel it a bit more," he said. "But everyone was pretty positive. Everyone was pretty high-spirited. He didn't really want to talk about it.

"Obviously, I'm sure it's never easy to go through that, but if anyone can handle it, he can."

Lemieux had suffered with a lengthy history of medical problems since he was chosen number one overall by the Penguins in 1984. He battled Hodgkin's disease in 1993, which forced him to miss the 1994-1995 season. He missed more than half of the Penguins' 1990-1991 Stanley Cup championship season with chronic back pain. He retired for three and a half years but returned in December 2000, though hip problems forced him to miss parts of subsequent seasons.

Despite Craig Patrick's optimism, Lemieux's dream of playing in all eighty-two games, or even in most of them, was now completely unattainable. It also meant that it was highly unlikely he would be selected to Team Canada for the trip to Turin in February. The timing was eerie, with Gretzky on his way to Pittsburgh in a few days to watch a game.

Lemieux was now preoccupied with his health and the arena situation. He had decided it was time to let the newspapers know just how dire he thought the situation really was.

"I think we're running out of time," he said, his voice heavy with frustration. "We probably ran out of time already. It's been unfortunate that the city and the county hasn't been willing to work with us over the last two or three years.

"We're going to sit down with everybody to understand what's at stake with our investment and what's best for the future. By the time we'd get the arena built, it's going to be another four or five years. Can we afford to stay here for another four or five years and assume the losses? I'm not sure."

There was no way that the Penguins could be expected to remain in Pittsburgh without a new arena. Even if they sold out every game on the way to the Stanley Cup, it was a money-losing proposition and it couldn't go on forever.

At this point, the most likely candidate to buy the two-time Stanley Cup champions was the Kansas City group headed by Los Angeles Kings owner Tim Leiweke, owners of a new downtown arena that needed a tenant.

The previous June, Lemieux had agreed to sell his interest in the Penguins to San José, California venture capitalist William Del Biaggio III. But that was just before the lockout ended and the Penguins won Crosby. He took the team off the market after the draft, but now, facing a health crisis, he wasn't sure how long he could hang in. The city said there was no public money to fund a new arena, even though millions in tax dollars helped build a new baseball park for the Pirates and a new football stadium for the Steelers a few years earlier.

No one knew that the Penguins were working to secure a partnership with the Isle of Capri, a Biloxi-based gaming company that had committed to financing the entire cost of a $290-million arena should the group win the slots licence, and would announce the plan in a matter of days.

Lemieux had more going on than he could handle, and while it pained him to think of the Penguins leaving and his own career coming to an end, now his heart really was broken. And fixing it wasn't as simple as building a new rink or winning a string of hockey games.

11

A FRESH START

It's going to be his team.

IT WAS A COINCIDENCE that the fan promotion for that night's game was a DVD featuring Lemieux's NHL comeback game from five years earlier. The legend wasn't there watching from his box as he often did when he was out of the lineup, usually with his son, Austin, and sometimes Nathalie. He had been discharged from the hospital the previous morning, but decided to watch the game from home.

That night was bitterly cold. If the Penguins could beat the lowly Minnesota Wild, they might be able to dream about salvaging their season. The Wild weren't faring much better in the standings at 10-12-4. If the Penguins could manage to score some goals, they might be easy enough to beat.

It was the worst game of the year. Most of the Penguins just floated through the game. They were trampled 5-0. It was the worst game Crosby played all year. He almost seemed to be playing down to everyone else's level. His body language spoke volumes: if you're not going to give it everything you have, well then neither am I. Recchi called it the low point of his career.

Crosby seemed furious after the game. He rode the bike so long that hardly anyone waited around to talk to him. When he finally emerged from the exercise room, he hadn't cooled down much. "We are not working hard as a team," he said. "We're not trying."

In the hall outside the entrance to the weight room, Troy, Dee Rizzo, and Pat Brisson stood in their usual spot, waiting for Sidney to come out and visit after the game. They looked grim. I waved, just barely, as I went by. It was not a night for small talk.

Across the street from the Igloo, where I waited for the bus, snow continued to fall steadily. Several inches had accumulated during the game, and the arena was covered in snow. For the first time all season it resembled its namesake. A glow from the streetlights bounced off the snow and reflected off the slate grey sky. Cars slowly inched along and spectators slipped towards the nearby parking lots and garages.

The snow had stopped falling by the next morning; it had piled up, muddy and wet and dark, much like the Penguins' hopes of saving their season. I was actually surprised to find Olczyk running the practice, but I was also relieved. He was a nice man – soft-spoken, smart, and thoughtful. He carefully considered every question, was never dismissive, and possessed a deep understanding of real life outside of hockey that he wore on his sleeve in a way some coaches did not.

It was easy to imagine him as your dad, your brother, your husband, your friend. He was human. It was tough to imagine him getting fired. He wasn't necessarily the problem, though he probably wasn't the solution either. He had much on his mind of real-life consequence. His daughter continued to suffer with a stomach illness that left her hurting for more than twenty hours a day. A sick child could make winning hockey games seem a trivial pursuit.

Under Olczyk, the Penguins had never held particularly gruelling practices. But they stayed out for a long time that day, an hour and forty-five minutes, so long Troy left before it was over.

In the dressing room, some of the players were surprised. "Holy shit, it's almost one o'clock," Andre Roy said.

"Yep, an hour and forty-five," quipped Ryan Malone.

Crosby was in a better mood than the previous night, and answered questions easily and without any emotion.

Olczyk still had Crosby playing on the wing. The rookie had scored just one goal since injuring his foot in Florida. He had put on a valiant effort of appearing chipper in the daily scrums, but in private, when he thought he wasn't being watched or he was just hanging around the dressing room engaged in his routine, sometimes he looked depressed.

On December 10, the Penguins welcomed a rare Western opponent; the new schedule designed to build rivalries with conference opponents meant that Western teams were rarely on display. The Colorado Avalanche was in town. And Wayne Gretzky came to the morning skate.

The morning skate was a game-day ritual dating back to the seventies, introduced in North America by the Russians, and used as an attendance taking to make sure players who may have been out carousing the night before finished sweating the alcohol out of their system before the game. In the modern age of stricter conditioning and fewer opportunities to carouse – teams used to stay in cities overnight after a game, but now they charter out immediately afterwards for home or the hotel at the next destination – the morning skate is a routine some believe has passed its time. It has the added benefit of offering reporters a chance to do some prep work for that night's game, prepare early edition notebooks, and for broadcasters to collect nuggets for commentary during the game. Players use it to practise drills, plays, and get a little skate in.

It was sort of startling to see Gretzky, the executive director of Team Canada, sitting in the stands. The reason for his visit was two-fold. He was there to talk to Lemieux about Team Canada and the Olympics. He was also interested in scouting Crosby.

He was clear that the evening's game was "not an audition" for the young player. "Oh, no. We know what he can do as a player."

Gretzky was peppered with questions about the young man whom he had picked a few years ago to break his prodigious points records. "He's a breath of fresh air for the NHL. He's tremendous for our game."

Gretzky planned to make his roster decisions in about ten days. It was unlikely Lemieux would play, and Steve Yzerman, the venerable Detroit Red Wings forward who was now forty years old with a bad knee, also wouldn't be going. It was likely younger players such as Crosby, Jason Spezza, or Eric Staal would get a chance. "All three have a legitimate chance. What Sidney brings to the table is something special to the league," Gretzky said. "He's one of the players we've been watching. He's been under the microscope. He understands what everything is about. He's handled himself pretty nicely."

Gretzky praised Crosby's vision and work ethic and passing skills. "And he loves coming to the rink every day. He's mature beyond his years. He's way more mature than any eighteen-year-old I've ever been around. How can you get a better combination than that?" he said.

Crosby was aware that Gretzky was in the house and would be watching the game against the Avalanche, but he said it wouldn't be a distraction.

"It's an honour to be considered. But my approach will be the same as it's been – to prepare myself for tonight's game and to do everything I can to help my team win. I can't be thinking about other things."

Gretzky and Lemieux shook hands and had a brief exchange in the dressing room. Gretzky was disappointed when Lemieux called on Wednesday to say he wouldn't be participating in the Olympics, but said he understood. "His personal health is more important."

The Penguins managed to beat a pretty good Avalanche team that night by a score of 4-3. Sidney was decent if not spectacular and had an assist. Some nights it looked as though they were playing the same bad game as the night before. On other nights they could look like world beaters. Everyone seemed surprised, albeit pleasantly so, by the effort, and it was almost difficult to explain. The victory bought Olczyk another day, and the Penguins prepared to leave for back-to-back Western Conference road games.

SAVVIS CENTER, ST. LOUIS, MISSOURI, DECEMBER 14, 2005:

The Penguins played one of their worst games of the season the previous night in Detroit at Joe Louis Arena, losing 3-1. The score flattered them. They had barely shown up. After playing one of their best games of the year against Colorado, they suffered an immense letdown, looking listless and failing to capitalize on two five-on-three chances. They blew a terrific effort by Marc-Andre Fleury in net and were outshot 19-3 in the first period. Crosby set up Recchi for the late third period goal. Olczyk was as close as I'd seen him to speechless afterwards.

Here in St. Louis, things surely couldn't get worse. The Blues were an awful team, below the Penguins in the standings, and they played most nights to a half-empty arena.

The only team in the league with a worse record than the Penguins shut them out 3-0. Nobody seemed to know what they were doing. Crosby was trying to do too much, sometimes playing out of position to try and compensate for others' shortcomings. It was a painful game to watch. I felt bad for Fleury, who was the only reason the Penguins weren't completely blown out on the scoreboard.

After the game, almost all of the players were in a room across the hall where the showers were. The main dressing room was empty except for Fleury, who was struggling to remove his pads off in one corner, and Crosby, who was still in his skates, pants, and pads, his head in his hands and dark curls sprouting through his tightly clenched fingers.

Karen Price of the *Pittsburgh Tribune Review* and I approached him slowly. As much as it was my job to talk to these guys every night, it did become difficult because there wasn't much to say. This seemed like the worst night yet. He just looked at us, his face blank. "I don't know what to say anymore. I don't care what happens, but I'm not going to give up."

When Olczyk came out, he didn't say much about the game itself or his future with the team, which was now obviously and painfully very likely over. He spoke about how special a goaltender Fleury was, and as he did, it hit me that Olczyk also realized he had coached his last game for the Penguins. He was giving Fleury a parting tribute because he knew it would be his last opportunity.

It felt funereal in the visitors' dressing room in St. Louis that night.

The next morning, after a two-hour flight back to Pittsburgh that had him home around 3 a.m., Crosby got up at his usual time of 6:30 and went to the gym to work out. The next day, the Penguins announced that Eddie Olczyk had been fired.

Michel Therrien became the head coach of the Pittsburgh Penguins on December 16, 2005. He had been coaching the Baby Penguins in Wilkes-Barre, the best team in the American Hockey League. Therrien, who had been working towards a second head coaching job in the NHL since he was fired in 2003 by the Montreal Canadiens, jumped at the chance to take over behind the bench of the worst team in the NHL.

At a hastily called press conference at the Penguins' secondary practice facility outside of the city on Neville Island, Craig Patrick looked worse for the wear. The bags under his eyes and his sallow complexion suggested he had been up all night and agonizing over having to fire his friend. He had no choice, however. The players, many of them anyway, had quit on Olczyk, and even Patrick had to admit as much. "The Minnesota loss was very disturbing," he said. "The team had shown its face, and for whatever reason, they weren't listening."

Therrien brought with him his staff from the minors, assistant coach Mike Yeo, goaltending consultant Gilles Lefebvre, and strength and conditioning coach Stephane Dube.

Therrien arrived with a vastly different attitude than Olczyk, who had been more of a friend to the players and at thirty-nine was about the same age as some of his veteran players. Olczyk, who was a former team broadcaster and had no coaching experience at all when he was hired in 2003 near the end of the season, left with eight wins in thirty-one games. His team had lost eight of its last nine games.

Therrien was forty-two, had coached the Montreal Canadiens for the better part of three seasons with a 77-91-22 record before being fired, and had a reputation as a disciplinarian. He was expected to bring a more structured approach to the Penguins, who had long been criticized in hockey circles for having lazy work habits. It was a common joke among the visiting teams' beat writers that Pittsburgh ran the shortest practices in the NHL. Therrien preached puck control and creating turnovers in the transition game.

The young guys who had played in Wilkes-Barre – Talbot and Whitney and Murley among them – said more than anything Therrien hated to lose.

"He's a no-nonsense guy," Patrick said. "It's either his way or the highway. We look pretty on paper, but what are we? Now we'll find out what we're made of."

His first practice ran over two hours and included push-ups and suicide sprints, a punitive drill from blue line to blue line usually given to punish poor effort. In Therrien's first week, the Penguins did more push-ups and sprints than they had done all season. One practice resembled the famous scene out of the film *Miracle*, where Kurt Russell as Herb Brooks made the players sprint until they fell down and Mike Eruzione declared, "I play for the United States of America!" "I keep expecting Ziggy Palffy to stagger to his feet and shout, 'I play for the Pittsburgh Penguins,'" Karen Price said dryly.

The Penguins were a league worst 23-47-8-4 during Olczyk's first season and had an eighteen-game losing streak that would be an NHL record but for one loss that came in overtime. He did lead them to a strong finish, with twelve wins in their last twenty games, giving the front office hope that he had grown into the role.

Crosby was distressed by the firing of his first professional coach. "Eddie never once gave up on us. I've had coaches in the past who weren't like that when you went through tough times. They left us to handle it. Eddie didn't. It would have been easy to quit on us, and he didn't. When we were hurting as a team, he was hurting too.

"We're a family. When you lose a guy like that, it's like losing people in your family. He was always there. He was the first one to take the blame and held himself responsible. As a player, it's not something you like to see. The coach doesn't put on his skates and go out and play. There's only so much he can do. He cared about us as a coach, especially me. I'm eighteen and he gave me an opportunity to play here, and I feel fortunate for that."

But he also wanted to win. And he was about to find out what getting an opportunity really meant.

Therrien was excited about getting his hands on Crosby. "He's got so much skill and speed, for a coach it's fun to have an opportunity to work with that. I want to give him a chance to expose his talents. He's going to be able to do a lot of good things out there. I'm going to give him a lot of opportunity. He does such amazing things on the ice. I was impressed when I saw him in training camp, but I never thought he'd be this good."

The first thing he did was anoint Crosby an alternate captain, saying, "He is going to be the leader of this team. It's going to be his team in the future." Therrien wanted to see how the team's best player would react to the additional responsibility, and he wanted to reward him. Crosby was thrilled and honoured and took it very seriously. Even though he was eighteen years old, it made sense. It would have been dishonest to pretend that it wasn't already becoming Crosby's team. Predictably, criticism began to emerge from some powerful voices, most notably Don Cherry, the host of the CBC *Hockey Night in Canada* staple, *Coach's Corner*.

"The only opinions I care about are the ones from the guys in this room," Crosby said. "I'm young. I have a lot of guys I can learn from in here," he said. "It's a little more responsibility. I think it's something that can make me a better player."

It was around this time that I began hearing idle chatter that some of the veterans, namely Recchi and LeClair, were unhappy with their young teammate being made an alternate captain at such a young age. When asked, both denied it and said they were happy for him. It wasn't the first time there had been something in the wind about supposed bad feelings between Recchi and Crosby, but this was the first time it seemed there might be legitimately hurt feelings. But Recchi vehemently denied any problems between the two. So did Crosby.

"To take that step is fine," Recchi said. "It's not a big issue in our locker room. He's eventually going to carry the torch for this team, and Michel wants to put the responsibility on him. It's a big step, but it's a process he's been going through."

On December 16, the Penguins lost Therrien's first game behind the bench, 4-3 in overtime to Buffalo at the Igloo. But already they looked like a more cohesive team, lending credence to the theory that much of Olczyk's failings had come about because he didn't have a solid system implemented. Therrien brought the system he had used in Wilkes-Barre, and a lot of the younger Penguins who had played for Therrien on the farm already knew it inside and out. They skated much better, especially five-on-five, played tighter defence, and equalled the Sabres' twenty-seven shots on goal. Their penalty killing and power play still needed work. Everyone, especially Crosby, seemed encouraged after that first game under the new coach.

"We're going to get better at that, but for the most part we played pretty decent," he said, pulling off his sweater with the A stitched on. He registered his nineteenth assist, had a career-high six shots, and played a career-high twenty minutes and nineteen seconds. Therrien was giving Crosby extra ice time and more opportunities. He also moved him from the wing back to his natural and preferred position at centre. He was happier all around.

"Any time you get a new coach, there's more energy in that first game, and it's important we keep that and apply the things we're taught. We have to get things organized, and for a day and a half, I thought we looked pretty strong."

Ziggy Palffy scored at 17:43 from Crosby and Mario Lemieux, his new linemates, to tie the game and force overtime. The goal was awarded after a video review. Michel Ouellet, the young right-winger Therrien recalled a few days earlier, scored his first NHL goal at 3:28 of the second period on the power play. Ryan Malone also scored.

Therrien was a demanding coach who preached hard work and wouldn't tolerate a losing attitude. He said he thought things were "going in the right direction." Then he dropped a bombshell, saying he didn't think most of the players "were in shape," an incredible notion at this point in the season.

"Cutting down scoring chances and shots against is one thing we accomplished," he said. "It is going to be positive, but I know they can play better eventually. Conditioning-wise I don't think we're right there. When you're in good shape, you make better decisions."

Therrien had already brought more discipline to the club, as demonstrated by longer, harder practices and a better overall effort last night. The Penguins would travel to Buffalo for another game the next night against the Sabres, who were on a 10-1 run.

Crosby was just thrilled to be back at centre. He would get more chances and more time quarterbacking the power play. He actually looked noticeably happier. "It felt pretty good. There was more room to skate, and I think it's good to get you into the game," he said. "You battle a little more in your own end, for me to be able to move my feet and jump on loose pucks and create turnovers. I enjoy it."

HSBC ARENA, BUFFALO, NEW YORK, DECEMBER 17, 2005:

Lemieux had been scratched, and Jocelyn Thibault had been given one more chance to show Therrien what he could do in goal. On the Sabres radio broadcast, commentators Rick Jeanneret and Jim Lorentz had criticized Crosby for talking too much to the referees. "He has to stop doing that, he's eighteen years old. He should just shut up and play." People were starting to notice that Crosby, more and more the target of dirty play, had become more vocal with the officials. Don Cherry commented on air the previous week that Crosby complained too much, but Cherry and others didn't see the high sticks and slashes to Crosby each night that so often went uncalled.

The Penguins had five days without a game after a second 4-3 loss to the Sabres in as many nights. Therrien began holding ninety-minute practices. He had the players doing more push-ups and suicide sprints, so many Ziggy Palffy almost vomited on the ice. They studied Therrien's system, which relied on a team concept and emphasized puck control, creating turnovers in the transition game. Under Olczyk, the Penguins were allowed to play a more wide-open free-flowing game that more often than not collapsed around them. Therrien's system was more rigid. If everyone did their jobs, there was less chance for error. There was a new competitiveness among the guys I hadn't seen before, not even in training camp. During a one-on-one drill,

Brooks Orpik and John LeClair fought for control of the puck all the way down the ice until Orpik pulled the veteran down and pushed his helmet off, then skated away without a word.

The team Christmas party was being held at Mark Recchi's house later that night, and there was a family skate the following night at the Igloo, followed by the front office's party across the street at the Marriott hotel.

The Olympic announcement was coming out late the next afternoon. Everyone expected Crosby to be named to Team Canada, but I made arrangements to find him at the skating party no matter what the outcome, even though I was certain he'd be on it and I wouldn't have to look too hard to find him.

THE OLYMPICS

*There's a good chance Sidney
could be leader of the team in 2010.*

THE ANNOUNCEMENT of the Canadian men's Olympic hockey team had been greatly anticipated for weeks, even months. Hockey columnists had been speculating on the roster, making their predictions, and reasoning why one player should be on it while another wasn't as deserving. In the early days, Crosby was not necessarily considered a lock, but over the past few weeks his inclusion had gathered favour with columnists and broadcasters.

The NHL's participation in the Olympics was part of the new collective bargaining agreement; the league would shut down during the Games to allow full participation. Twenty-three NHL players would be selected to the Canadian squad with three more named to a taxi squad. In the beginning of the debate, most figured that Crosby was a little too young, a little too inexperienced. But as the date of the announcement drew closer, most everyone was putting him on their roster. Not even the taxi squad, but on the main roster.

Crosby had always been the youngest player on his team. In Timbits hockey, he was five competing against seven-year-olds. In midget, he was fourteen going up against sixteen-year-olds. He was the only player younger than eighteen invited to be on the World Junior team in 2003-2004, and was the youngest player to ever score for Canada at the tournament at sixteen years, four months, and twenty-four days.

Craig Patrick, who was an assistant coach of the gold medal–winning U.S. Miracle on Ice team in 1980, said Crosby had the skating ability for the big ice surface. "His game is made for the international ice."

A few hours before the announcement, he arrived back from practice, held on this day at a rink on Neville Island, on the team bus. I was waiting to chat with him because I wanted to make sure he was going to be around later in the day. He schlepped in wearing his hockey pants, sweaty stocking feet in shower sandals, hair wet, and hockey bag over his shoulder, three sticks in hand. He stopped to sign a fire hydrant–sized bobblehead of himself. "Ah! A life-sized Sid!" crowed Andre Roy. Sidney chuckled when he saw it, and signed the little chest with a gold Sharpie.

I asked him if he was nervous about the pending announcement. "Actually, I totally forgot about it until we were on the bus after practice," he said. "Some of the guys were talking about the U.S. team [named the previous day], and it wasn't until then that it crossed my mind. It'll be good to know. If it happens, great, but if not, that's okay too, maybe next time."

He was upbeat and cheerful, and we made plans to talk after the team had been named, for better or worse.

Crosby would have been the youngest player named to the team in its history, but he was playing exceptionally well and showing he could handle the pressure of adjusting to the NHL.

He had thirty-three points in thirty-three games and was the third leading Canadian scorer in the league. Having been named alternate captain of the Penguins hadn't hurt his reputation as a leader; he had earned the confidence of a tough coach. It all bode well for his chances of making the team.

At 3 p.m. I was up in the Igloo press box starting to write what would form the skeleton of a story on Crosby being named to the Olympic hockey team in anticipation of word coming from Vancouver, a few hours from now.

On the ice below, many of the Penguins players and their wives and children glided around the ice. Craig Patrick skated in swift, broad circles, in slacks and a sweater, looking like an aging member of the Ice Capades.

When Crosby came out, he played with Jocelyn Thibault's small daughters, softly passing the puck to the pink- and blue-toqued tots as though he did not have a care in the world. He didn't skate so much with them as play hockey with them. He posed for photographs with Ryan Malone's fiancée.

When it got close to 5 p.m., Crosby was still out on the ice, playing around. I was watching the Internet, waiting for the roster to be revealed. I was down at ice level, standing off near the runway where everyone was coming on and off.

Nathalie Lemieux was there, with the kids. For a few minutes she was talking intensely with a young woman I didn't recognize. Nathalie was crying. I wondered if she had been talking about Mario's health. Was she having an adoptive mother's reaction to Crosby not being named to the Olympic team? The roster was just now being revealed.

Crosby pulled his cellphone out of his jeans and poked at the keypad. He was phoning his agent, Pat Brisson. He asked him if he would have received a call by now had he been selected. Brisson solemnly told Crosby that Team Canada officials had already begun announcing the roster. And then Crosby disappeared.

I hung around outside the dressing room to wait. About forty-five minutes later, he emerged with Keith Wehner, Tom McMillan, and Todd Lepovsky, the full Penguins media relations staff. They had been waiting for him to walk over from the Christmas party. At least near the arena, it was difficult for Crosby to walk down the sidewalk without being asked for dozens of autographs.

He carried a suit bag over his shoulder but wore jeans and a plaid shirt.

He came over by himself wearing a sheepish smile on his face, but his disappointment was obvious. He was crestfallen. I told him I was sorry to hear the news.

"Yeah, it was tough," he said softly. "But there are so many good players. I knew the opportunity was there, I knew I was in the mix. But hopefully down the road I'll have an opportunity to represent Canada. I really hope so."

After Gretzky's visit a few weeks ago and so much speculation that his terrific rookie season would land him a roster spot, Crosby didn't make the twenty-three-man roster or even the three-player taxi squad. He had fallen to second in the rookie scoring race, behind Ovechkin, and was top thirty in the NHL with fourteen goals and nineteen assists. But it was not his time. He was disappointed, but also upbeat and introspective.

"It would have been nice, definitely. But there are so many good players in Canada, and being so young, I don't think I expected to be picked. I prepared myself. I tried to have the best first half possible and give myself an opportunity, and I was right in the mix. I'm not there, but at least I can say I gave it a good shot. Like with World Juniors, when you play so much hockey you always know there's other teams to play for. But if you focus on playing for your own team, everything else takes care of itself. For me, that's the way it was. I just tried to worry about helping the team here. If I can contribute and make things happen here, then that's the best way I can make a difference."

Kevin Lowe, Team Canada's assistant executive director, who made the announcement because Gretzky went home to Brantford to be with his ailing mother, Phyllis, who was dying of cancer, dealt with reporters' questions about why Crosby was snubbed. "There's a good chance Sidney could be the leader of the team in 2010," but the team wanted to go with veteran players.

Crosby, who was fifteen when he volunteered to be a stick boy with the 2003 World Junior team for the experience, would have benefited enormously even from being selected to the taxi squad.

"It's a competitive nature to say you want to be there," Crosby said. "But it's not up to me, and it's just one of those things. There are so many guys that are so close, and it depends on so many things. It just wasn't one of those things that worked out."

The Canadians would be trying to defend the gold medal won in Salt Lake City in 2002, their first in fifty years. Mario Lemieux was captain of that team, and when he stepped aside, Crosby, his young protegé, was supposed to step in – at least that's the way Hollywood would have written it.

It was easy to believe that Crosby had a legitimate shot, especially since Lemieux, who removed himself from consideration because he had been suffering with an irregular heartbeat and was out of the Penguins lineup indefinitely, said last month he should be on the team.

"They can only take so many guys," Crosby said. "It's easy to say 'I'm young' but when you're that close, you want to do it. But those guys definitely deserve it, and I wish them the best. I'll be watching."

The next morning after practice, three times as many the usual number of reporters showed up. They all pressed around Crosby, who had barely removed his helmet, in the Penguins dressing room, hoping to hear how upset he was over being snubbed for a spot on the Olympic team.

Naturally, the kid hurt. Who in their right heart and mind would not? Crosby may well believe he had what was required to be on Team Canada – he is as competitive as they come – but it was unlikely he would ever say he should have been included.

"It's not one of those things I try to think about like that," he said the next day, his mood more detached and less revealing. "I try to go out and give myself an opportunity to play. I'm not second-guessing any guy there. They all deserve to be there. It's tough because I thought I had a chance, but it's not tough because I think I should replace someone else. It's not like that at all."

In three months of chronicling Crosby's rookie NHL season, of seeing and talking to him nearly every day, of watching up close most every game and practice, there is no doubt he deserved a spot on the twenty-three-man roster.

He had been consistently good while handling more scrutiny and attention than any athlete his age, with the exception of basketball player LeBron James. Productive on the ice and graceful off it, he would have been a fan favourite in Turin. Hockey Canada executives had called him the future of Canadian hockey. The action was inconsistent with the message.

It was similar to the enormous public debate held over whether or not English soccer player Michael Owen should go to the 1998 World Cup in France. He was a teenaged sensation for Liverpool, but many felt he was too young and therefore too big a risk. He went, and played, and ended up scoring one of the greatest goals in World Cup history against Argentina. England lost the game because David Beckham got sent off for a stupid reaction to a foul. In a single tournament, Owen established himself as someone ready for the world stage.

"We would have liked to have seen him get on it," Recchi, who was on the 1998 team, said. "But it's right the guys who played on it before and won gold be on it. There are so many good players. That's the problem."

Team Canada would be long on experienced veterans but short on youthful magic, the kind Crosby, even playing a limited role as a newcomer, could provide. He won gold at the World Junior Championships last year. He made the adjustment to the NHL from junior without missing a beat. He could take over a game, as he did last month when the Penguins posted a rare victory in Philadelphia and Crosby had a goal, an assist, and the game winner on a breakaway in overtime, all after having his mouth bashed in with some dirty stick work.

Michel Therrien said the Olympics would have been "a great experience" for his star rookie, but that he shouldn't take his exclusion too hard. "For an eighteen-year-old, just to be mentioned in conversation that he has a good chance to make the Canadian team, it's just phenomenal," Therrien said. "He's going to have plenty of time to participate in the Olympics. As far as I'm concerned, I would have liked for Sid to go there. Just for his name to be mentioned, you don't see that often for an eighteen-year-old."

Lemieux also was disappointed, but he refrained from criticizing Hockey Canada brass. "He's young, and he's going to have many opportunities. I know he was disappointed, but there are so many good young players now with a little bit more experience. It's unfortunate, but he'll be there for the next one."

Twenty-four hours later, Crosby had a more distanced view of it and didn't give away as much emotion as he had the night before when we talked. "When you're that close, it's tough, because you don't know what's going to happen when you're twenty-two or twenty-six; you don't know if the opportunity's still going to be there," he said. "It definitely gives you something to think about and something to work toward for the next one. It's up to me to earn that opportunity and to play for that opportunity in four years."

It was easy to dismiss Crosby as too young, but I had a sinking feeling the moment the roster was announced that it was a team loaded with bad karma. With controversial power forward Todd Bertuzzi on the roster, there was an instant old-boys loyalty quality to Team Canada and a distinct lack of youthful energy. Why wasn't Staal or Spezza on the main squad? The second-guessing hadn't even really started yet. Meantime, Alexander Ovechkin had been named to the Russian Olympic team, as had nineteen-year-old Evgeni Malkin, the Penguins prospect who was playing in Russia and who would likely join the NHL club the following season.

The next night at home against the Philadelphia Flyers, Crosby scored a pair of highlight-reel goals forty-five seconds apart and registered an assist, sparking a rally that fell just short in a 5-4 loss.

Mike Lange, the Penguins' venerable play-by-play man with the smoky voice – the one who exclaimed "Slap me silly, Sidney!" whenever the kid scored – asked sarcastically of no one in particular on the air, "So, Sidney Crosby isn't ready for the Olympic team?"

After the game, Crosby, who had chartered a plane to get him home to Halifax for Christmas, was philosophical about the loss and happy with his own efforts. He was off for two days to see his parents, sister, aunts and uncles, and grandparents, and eat his mother's baking and turkey dinner. He was really looking forward to it. The next morning, I went to the airport to catch my own flight, a commercial one to Toronto to visit my own family for a few days over Christmas.

It was his first Christmas in Cole Harbour in four years, and he brought his parents and ten-year-old sister, Taylor, back to Pittsburgh with him to see some home games and celebrate New Year's Eve. Taylor bunked in at the Lemieux manse. "It was a nice family atmosphere. It's been four years. I enjoyed it. It was a short stay, but it was worth it." Was the gift exchange more extravagant now that he was a millionaire? Not in his household. "No matter how much money you have, it's still family. My grandmother still gives me twenty bucks. That never changes. I still get Subway gift cards. That's the way I like it. I enjoy it just as much." He did buy his mom and dad expensive watches, but "nothing too crazy. I can't show up with just me," he said, laughing.

I asked him how his life had changed now that he could buy anything he wanted. He grew up in a middle-class household. His parents were young when they had him; they lived with his paternal grandmother, Linda Crosby, when Sidney was a baby. There wasn't a lot of money for extras. The often-told stories about the family delivering newspaper flyers for extra cash to pay for Sidney's hockey equipment and tournament fees were true. It was something that helped shape the values he now holds dear. "For me, a lot of stuff wasn't easy. It wasn't like I had to work five hours a day to get things, but nothing was really given to me. I was treated well as a kid. I got a new pair of skates for Christmas, but I got what I needed and not a lot more. When it came to hockey, I'd get new skates and a stick. But I learned that you get what you need and not so much what you want. My parents instilled in me that you don't need everything you see. You work hard for what you get, and a lot of things in life don't come easy. That was a lesson I got from my parents.

"When you're younger, you don't even know the difference. Then in junior high you start seeing kids wearing nicer clothes and you maybe feel you want a certain shirt or something. But now you can look back and think, 'Why did I ever care about that?' I was always more than happy with who I was growing up, but I always felt I had to fight a little hard to keep up."

It made it difficult for him to blow his new-found wealth, but he was glad for it. Money hadn't really changed his life, unlike the teenaged millionaires in the NBA who rush out to buy Hummers and gaudy jewellery.

"It's hard for me to spend it, to be honest. I can't reason with myself to spend a lot. I got my car [a silver Range Rover]. I got my parents a car [a silver Mercedes SUV] and big television so they could watch some games. I got some clothes, because playing in the NHL, you're a professional, and part of it is about wanting to look good and set a good example when you're on the road and going to games. When everyone's looking at you, you want to feel confident. But outside of that, I don't spend money on anything I don't need. A lot of guys get into hobbies, but that's not me. Having money hasn't made me more inclined to get stuff."

Troy did quit his job as an office manager at a Halifax law firm a few months before the draft so he could help his son with some of his hockey-related business. Crosby felt proud that he was able to support his family in the way they supported him growing up. He loved having his father around all season, he said, travelling to more than half his games. "It's a pretty unique situation, and it's nice I can do it. How many parents get to watch their children start their careers? It's been good for all of us."

When he returned to Pittsburgh for the last three games of the year, against the Toronto Maple Leafs, New Jersey Devils, and the New York Rangers, he brought his parents and sister back on the chartered flight so they could continue their holidays. The previous two years from Christmas until after New Year's had been spent attending the World Junior tournaments, and before Sidney was a part of the team, the holiday weeks were spent with the family watching the games on television.

The Rangers game was an afternoon affair on December 31. The Penguins won 4-3 in overtime. Crosby scored the winning goal. The Penguins didn't win their tenth game of the season until New Year's Eve.

And in another important development that week, a string-bean right-winger from Saskatoon named Colby Armstrong was called up from Wilkes-Barre after three seasons in the minors to bolster the Penguins' penalty kill. Maxime Talbot also rejoined the team.

BACKLASH

Look, I've got nothing against the kid.

NOT EVERYONE loved Sidney Crosby.

As the season resumed after Christmas, word of Sidney Crosby's growing troubles with the referees began to spread outside of Pittsburgh and the biting criticism began.

Much of it seemed to spring from one source: Don Cherry, the controversial hockey commentator and Canadian hockey celebrity. Cherry's sentiments started to be repeated time and again by others, as if hard fact.

Cherry's show was consistently the highest rated portion of the *Hockey Night in Canada* broadcast, and his influence extended to the hockey media as well; at Toronto Maple Leafs games on Saturday nights between the first and second periods, the press row emptied out almost entirely as reporters gathered around the television in back to hear what hockey gospel Cherry was offering from his pulpit that week. At the very least, they found it highly entertaining, but in truth Cherry shot from the lip so carelessly at times that he often became the story. And that is how it was with his feelings about Sidney Crosby.

The seventy-two-year-old former coach of the Boston Bruins held impossibly strong opinions, never hesitated to share them, and rarely reneged once his views were formed. He had often called Mario Lemieux "a floater" and criticized European players as "soft." Cherry had criticized Crosby in November 2003 when, then just sixteen years old, Sidney scored a flashy goal against the Quebec Remparts in a junior game. With the Oceanic leading 4-0, he scooped up the puck on the blade of his stick, brought it up about waist high, and then reached around to the front of the net and dropped it in behind the goaltender, as if in a lacrosse match. It was a move he had been practising for weeks, a move made famous in 1997 by London, Ontario–born winger Mike Legg at the University of Michigan; it won Legg an ESPY award for most outrageous play of the year.

The following night, Cherry called Crosby a hot dog on *Hockey Night in Canada* and accused him of showing up an already overmatched goaltender and exhibiting poor sportsmanship by celebrating the goal, Rimouski's fifth in a game they won 7-1.

"I like the kid," Cherry said that night. "But I've seen him now after goals. He slides on the ice on his knees. You talk about a hot dog."

A few days later, Crosby dodged controversy by evenly telling reporters, "I'm not shaken by his words. It's his style to make controversial remarks. I can't please everyone."

But many of his fellow Nova Scotians were enraged by Cherry's national put-down, voicing their displeasure on letters-to-the-editor pages and flooding the CBC switchboard with complaints. Cherry was seen to be picking on a young boy for being exuberant. Amazingly, even with Crosby in the NHL, it was still on his mind two and a half years later.

Early on the morning of December 27, I flew back to Pittsburgh after spending two days at my parents' home for Christmas. Shortly after 6 a.m., I settled into a seat near the departure gate and began planning my next piece for the newspaper series. It was time to address the backlash that had been bubbling around Crosby. I needed to talk to Don Cherry.

With his flamboyant attire and polarizing position on everything from visors to francophone players, Cherry was outspoken on television. But he was regarded as intensely private in his personal life and a notoriously difficult interview to land. I once enlisted mutual acquaintance Brian Williams, now the face of the Olympic Games for CTV and quite possibly the nicest man in broadcasting, to broker an interview with Cherry when I was researching a piece on his business interests nearly a decade earlier.

Then a serendipitous thing occurred, a sort of late Christmas gift. Don Cherry strolled past me and sat down nearby.

The Leafs were playing the Penguins later that night, and the entire *Hockey Night in Canada* crew was on my flight to Pittsburgh.

To understand the heft of Cherry's sometimes inexplicable influence you need only to consider these two things: that he was voted among the top ten greatest Canadians in a 2004 CBC poll, a list that also included Tommy Douglas, Pierre Trudeau, Alexander Graham Bell, and Wayne Gretzky; and you had to bear witness to the commotion Cherry caused at the airport over the next hour.

In a giddy, steady stream that did not cease until Cherry boarded the plane, dozens of delighted fans came to him, seeking signatures and snapshots and handshakes. Dressed in his trademark high-collared shirt, a black fedora, and a long black trench coat that made him look like a villain from a film noir, Cherry mugged for fans. His *Coach's Corner* sidekick, the demure Ron MacLean, was with him, but it was Cherry that stole the spotlight.

He signed a young woman's arm, a man's newspaper, one teenager's copy of the book he was reading, *God's Devotional Journal*, and several people's notebooks and boarding passes. One girl couldn't decide between offering her breast or her shoulder blade, but MacLean made that decision for the two of them; the pair signed the back of her shoulder.

Then, as Cherry made his way along the hallway for the stairs that led to our gate, I asked if he had a few minutes to talk about Crosby. He obliged while continuing to scrawl his autograph and pose for photos with MacLean and their admirers.

"Look, I've always said he was a good hockey player," he said. "In fact, he's going to be a great hockey player. But my problem is that he showed up that goalie. You get a reputation like that."

But there was much more to it. Over the past month on *Coach's Corner*, Cherry accused Sidney of diving, echoing the sentiments of Flyers coach Ken Hitchcock and several of his players. He also criticized him for yapping to the officials, and said Crosby supported the firing of Eddie Olczyk, something that was blatantly not true. But what really stuck in Cherry's craw was the fact that Crosby had been made an alternate captain by the Penguins' new coach, Michel Therrien.

"An eighteen-year-old kid?" he said. "Give me a break. What do you think Lyle Odelein thinks? What do you think Johnny LeClair and Recchi think?"

If LeClair and Recchi felt that way, it might have made some sense, but they certainly weren't telling anyone they felt that way. Cherry's emotions hadn't softened from ten days earlier on *Hockey Night in Canada*, when he had launched his most passionate rant yet about the teenager.

"Therrien makes the kid an assistant, please, an eighteen-year-old kid? He's going to give them ideas? Come on, that's ridiculous. I almost gagged when I heard about it. No kid should have as much to say as he's got to say. . . . Yapping at the referees, doing the whole thing, golden boy. This kid is really taking over the whole thing."

On the air, Ron MacLean suggested Cherry may have had a vendetta against Crosby.

"I don't have a vendetta," Cherry snapped.

Cherry, who took the Bruins to the Stanley Cup finals twice only to lose both times to the Montreal Canadiens in 1977 and 1978, the latter lost on a call for too many men on the ice that also cost him his job, was well-known for his dislike of European-style hockey. He made a comment on air in 2004 that visors are most popular among "Europeans and French guys," who were "turning into sucks" for protecting their eyes. It prompted an outcry in Quebec and an investigation by the federal Official Languages Commission. The CBC imposed a seven-second delay on *Coach's Corner*, but it was abandoned for the 2005-2006 season.

The Quebec media have often accused Cherry of being racist and a xenophobe. Yet his audience and his celebrity, as evidenced that morning in the airport, had only grown.

Cherry figured Hitchcock, who called Crosby a diver after his infamous near-single-handed win over the Flyers on November 16, knew what he was talking about. And because Hitch's sentiments were echoed by Peter Forsberg and the Philadelphia media, and then picked up and repeated enthusiastically without any first-hand knowledge by Sabres announcers Rick Jeanneret and Jim Lorentz, Cherry felt the knocks on Crosby were widespread enough to be valid.

"Now, Ken Hitchcock said the same thing I did. Buffalo said the same thing I did. Forsberg said the same thing I said. So that's not too bad company," he said. "Look, I've got nothing against the kid. He just can't act the way he acts. He can't be yapping at the referees. You just don't do that when you're eighteen years old."

Therrien didn't have much time for anyone second-guessing the faith he showed in his young star, and dismissed Cherry's views. "He's a mature kid. Obviously, he's one of our best players. We want him to learn. He's surrounded by guys who won the Stanley Cup. It's important that he's learning from Stanley Cup winners," Therrien said. "There's a lot of controversy in Toronto over anything you're doing. There was no controversy in Pittsburgh. Eventually, this is going to be Sidney's team. I'm not afraid

ABOVE: The rookies Crosby and Erik Christensen break the ice at training camp.

Billy Wareham/Pittsburgh Penguins

BELOW: Crosby and Colby Armstrong made a terrific pair on and off the ice.

Billy Wareham/Pittsburgh Penguins

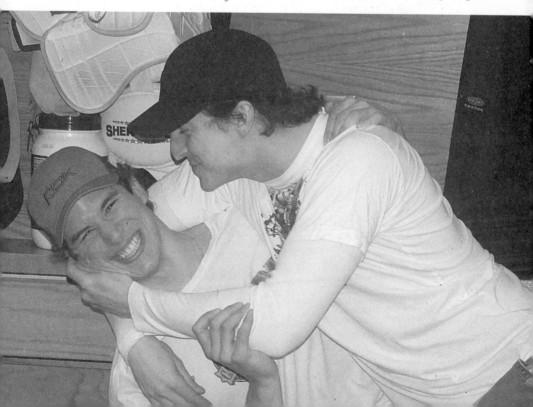

ABOVE: Sidney and Marc-Andre Fleury share a joke after the power goes out at the Igloo during a game against the Leafs, March 19, 2006. *Matt Polk/Pittsburgh Penguins*
BELOW: A rink rat at heart, Crosby talks with assistant coach Mike Yeo long after practice is over. *Billy Wareham/Pittsburgh Penguins*

The legend Lemieux watches the prodigal son warm up before taking on the Montreal Canadiens, November 10, 2005. *Matt Polk/Pittsburgh Penguins*

ABOVE: Crosby looks to the officials for a call after taking a stick in the mouth against the Devils, October 20, 2005. *Matt Polk/Pittsburgh Penguins*

BELOW: Sidney and linesman Tony Sericolo exchange pleasantries during a game against the Flyers after a call goes in Crosby's favour. *Matt Polk/Pittsburgh Penguins*

Sidney looked relaxed and rested in his first game after the Olympic break.
Matt Polk/Pittsburgh Penguins

INSET: Lemieux congratulates Crosby after he beat the Habs with a shootout goal, November 10, 2005. *Matt Polk/Pittsburgh Penguins*

ABOVE: Games against the Flyers brought out all of Crosby's grit and determination. *Matt Polk/Pittsburgh Penguins*

BELOW: Sidney celebrates his game-winning goal that beat the Rangers in overtime on New Year's Eve. *Matt Polk/Pittsburgh Penguins*

These bee-stung lips made the girls crazy from Halifax to Hershey.

Matt Polk/Pittsburgh Penguins

Sidney basks in the glory after scoring his 100th point in the last home game of the season. *Matt Polk/Pittsburgh Penguins*

to say it. He's so mature. The most important thing for me is I want him to learn."

In response to Cherry's rant, everyone descended on Crosby, who refused to be drawn further into what was so far a one-sided controversy.

"It's fine. He's there every Saturday night. He's always been opinionated. I always watch Saturday night to see what he's going to say. In my case, he's mentioned my name [in] probably not the best of ways. Everyone's entitled to their opinion.

"He's a hockey analyst. When guys watch hockey, everyone sees things different ways. He has his viewpoints. They're his opinions. That's fine. If he thinks those things, then he's entitled to that. I think that everyone can form their own opinions from watching.

"I'm sure he's not the only guy who's criticized me, but that stuff happens," he said. "Everyone's not going to have a great opinion or a nice opinion of you, no matter what you do. So, it's the same way whether it's something good or something bad. You take it in stride.

"People are allowed to have their opinions. We have to respect that. The only opinions I care about are the ones from the guys in this room."

Some reporters and broadcasters in Canada kept vaguely mentioning that some of the veteran players were bothered by Sidney's accession to prominence. Mark Recchi, who had been charged by Olczyk as a mentor of sorts for the teenager at the start of the season, was the player most often mentioned when it came up. In some ways, it was difficult to imagine. They sat next to each other in the dressing room at home and on the road, and they were roommates on road trips. After the first month of the season, some of the roommate assignments changed because of injuries and player movement between Pittsburgh and Wilkes-Barre, and Crosby began rooming with Matt Murley on the road, who was twenty-six. Recchi, who was thirty-eight and just a year younger than Sidney's father, decided to exercise his veteran's right to a single room.

"It's good for him to room with some of the younger guys," Recchi said, adding that Crosby already had the ultimate father figure with Lemieux in his life.

At the time, it made sense, but the rumours of a rift between Crosby and Recchi continued to circulate. No matter how many times either one was asked about it, and the questions occurred on a daily basis through much of December, both denied there was anything wrong between them. The questions began anew when Crosby was named alternate captain. But Recchi only ever publicly voiced support. And Crosby visibly got tired of people asking about it.

Privately, it seemed more likely that something had happened between them. A number of people familiar with the matter spoke of an incident earlier in the season, back in November during the game in Philadelphia. After Crosby was called for unsportsmanlike conduct for complaining to the officials, Recchi allegedly bawled him out between periods and lectured him about taking unnecessary penalties and keeping his emotions under control. Olczyk had already spoken to Crosby about it, and the rookie accepted that – Eddie was the coach. But after Recchi and even Lyle Odelein allegedly chimed in, telling the kid he shouldn't be taking penalties, a frustrated Crosby told them that he'd gotten the message. Then, angry and stung, he went out and essentially won the game by himself.

But if Rex (Recchi) was bothered by any of this – the penalties, the A, the attention the rookie was getting – he wasn't about to admit it, and neither was Crosby.

Later that night, with the Leafs at the Igloo and the national anthems being sung, Cherry and MacLean did their pre-game routine near the ice. Boos rained down on the man in the bright plaid sports coat.

The game was the Penguins' first national appearance on *Hockey Night in Canada*; fans from Coquitlam to Cole Harbour would see Crosby play on television for the first time.

Hockey Night in Canada had asked the Penguins if Sidney could do a live interview between periods. Initially there were mixed opinions about making him available for it, but team officials decided it was the best way for their star player to rise above the criticisms. Sidney was keen to co-operate and came off as polite and even-tempered, even when he was asked about the conflict with Cherry. He had a jaw-dropping assist in the game when he fought off two Leafs players to drag himself on one knee into position near the corner of the net to stickhandle the puck to Michel Ouellet in the crease, who scored in the 3-2 loss. Don Cherry didn't even come up in the post-game question-and-answer session and seemed to be forgotten.

The Maple Leafs' Eric Lindros, who came into the league as an eighteen-year-old saddled with exceptionally high expectations and suffered a number of public relations setbacks, had an insightful perspective on Crosby's situation.

He told Rosie DiManno of the *Toronto Star*, "You think he went in there and asked for that A? When you're eighteen, nineteen years old, things that happen can really crush you. Crosby's still a boy, but I don't see that happening to him. He just loves to play so much, takes such joy in it. You can just see that. This other stuff doesn't matter."

The cheap shots continued as the Penguins set off on a road trip that took them into America's heartland and struggling hockey markets Columbus, Chicago, and Nashville. At the United Center against the Blackhawks, Crosby got a fat, tender lip, not likely his last, when a defender elbowed him hard in the chops on a surge to the net. No penalty was called. He was not surprised. And in a new approach to things, he did not argue for one. He had been talking to the officials less and taking his lumps, chalking them up to growing pains. It was the latest challenge in navigating his first professional season, and it was a perplexing problem more suited to philosopher than hockey player: how at once does a man change yet find a way to stay the same?

Crosby had realized that the aggressive and uber-competitive style that made him the consensus number one draft choice had not earned him any breaks from referees, on calls and non-calls both for and against him. He had learned his reflex to object could hurt his team, which was struggling horribly with just eleven wins, second fewest in the league.

Crosby led the Penguins in penalty minutes with sixty-four, but he knew he had to reconcile his refusal to mute the feisty manner of play that made him successful with knowing when to shut his mouth.

"You go through tough times sometimes," he said. "It's never a smooth ride. I'm learning as I go, and I still have a lot to learn. It doesn't happen overnight. But I've always played an aggressive game, and I'm not going to change that. It's what's made me successful, to be emotional and passionate and driving. I'm not going to change."

I had been exchanging e-mails with Bruce Hood, who was widely considered the game's top referee when he retired in 1984 after twenty-one seasons. Hood had been watching the treatment of Crosby and had an interesting point of view for a former referee, so I called him up one day. He said the officials were largely ignoring many of the flagrant cross-checks, high sticks, and the interference dished out against Sidney almost nightly.

"I get incensed at a player of Sidney's talent being put through so much abuse," Hood said. "The referees are sup-posed to be there to protect him. But they see so much physical activity against him, and he continues to sparkle. They lose sight of the fact there are serious infractions on him. It's sickening. Maybe there is a tendency for some officials to not call something obvious to show they are not intimidated by a tremendous young hockey player."

Stephen Walkom, NHL director of officiating, who over-sees the league's seventy-seven referees and linesmen, called Hood's view of things "ridiculous" when I phoned him for comment.

"No official would allow things to happen intention-ally to any player," he said. "It's blown out of proportion because Crosby is such a great player. Any time anything happens to him, it's noticeable. All players in the game have emotion and at one time or another interact with officials.

Some of the best players are the most emotional. I think our guys as a whole really respect Sidney Crosby and the talent he is.

"Over time he's going to build up an excellent rapport with officials, because he's a great guy."

But Walkom did say the high-sticking should have been called in the infamous November 16 game in Philadelphia during which Crosby was cut in the mouth.

"When a high stick happens, no official on the planet wants to miss that," he said. "It's certainly not intentional. When they do miss a call, no one feels worse, especially when it involves a player being injured or a goal being scored."

Hood, who blew the whistle on all the greats, from Orr to Gretzky and Gordie Howe, said he saw Crosby's rookie experiences mirroring a young Gretzky's.

"Gretzky was deemed a whiner because he was always talking to officials," he said. "But if you have any kind of courage in your body at all, you speak up."

Crosby said the comments about him being a whiner didn't bother him, but his scoring pace had slowed considerably. In his first ten games under Therrien, he went on his best pace of the season, scoring eight goals and registering nine assists. But on the heels of his well-publicized troubles with the officials, he had just one assist in three games. Therrien didn't want him to change a thing.

"Sidney plays with a lot of pride. He plays with a lot of emotion. This is what makes Sidney Crosby. We're proud of him because he's one of the best players in the NHL, because he plays with emotion. We want him to be aggressive. Why would we want him to change?"

John Davidson thought it was just part of the growing process for a kid in the NHL.

"Gretzky did it a lot. Look, he's a competitive kid. He'll learn. He's real good. He's a generous kid with his time off the ice, and he's so competitive on it. If the opposition finds a weakness there, well maybe that's getting him too emotional. He's going to find himself in the penalty box. And if you're playing the Pittsburgh Penguins, where do you want Sidney Crosby? In the penalty box.

"Like John McEnroe used to tell me, he had to get really emotional to play. Crosby's the same way."

Davidson said he thought if there was one place that Crosby actually showed his age it was in his dealings with referees. "Don't you think that's where the real eighteen-year-old shows? He'll learn. He's already such an important part of the league that he'll learn to use the calls to his advantage. But you've got to earn it."

Lucien DeBlois, the Canucks scout who sat next to me at a Devils game and first saw Crosby play in junior when he faced off against DeBlois's son Dominic, had seen Crosby play five times in the NHL and thought he weathered a lot of dirty play.

"Some people say he's a whiner, well, he takes a lot of abuse out there," DeBlois said. "They all do it. Mario did it. Gretzky did it better than anyone. He's only eighteen. He's a kid. Leave him alone and let him play. He can't be perfect all the time. But he's come pretty darn close. And I don't even know him. It's just what I've heard and what I've seen. He's been amazing on the ice and for the game."

In assessing the officiating near the end of the season, John Davidson thought it was inconsistent – that veteran guys had done a good job, but the younger officials were too preoccupied with the restraining fouls from the waist down.

"They are missing a lot of the stuff to the head. The high sticks, and the elbows, and the things that can really cause devastating injuries. Older officials have learned how to watch the whole package. That's a tough process to go through. But the league is going to have to look at that if they want to get to where they are hoping."

The officiating troubles dogged Sidney throughout the season. Near the end of the year, the *Toronto Sun* ran a lengthy piece on his image as a diver, a whiner, and player who was not yet ready to be alternate captain. It surprised me, because in Pittsburgh he didn't have that reputation.

Crosby had been known as a vocal player everywhere he had played, with the Subways in midget, at Shattuck, in Rimouski, and with the World Junior team. Emotional and vocal, he was a passionate player who believed in sticking up for his teammates and himself. I saw him curse at referees – it was Gordie Howe who said all hockey players are bilingual; they speak English and profanity – but I never saw him be disrespectful, and I never saw him disrespect the traditions of the game, which he held in high regard.

I saw it as a learning curve in his leadership abilities. He spoke up, but he always tried to set the first example on the ice and he had. He wasn't talking and not contributing. Maybe he was simply struggling with growing into his role.

Was it a strange jealousy? If Crosby had been playing for the Leafs or the Canadiens or the Oilers, would so much have been made of how vocal he was on the ice? Were some Canadians turning on him because they were envious he wasn't completely one of ours any longer?

Gzowski wrote about the backlash that hit Gretzky as soon as he got really popular – that Canadians were generally uncomfortable with attention. It was true. In the United States, if something receives much attention, it becomes further validated and even more popular. In Canada, it is considered instantly overexposed and, soon, unworthy. Is this what was beginning to happen with Sidney Crosby? Watching him play with such joy and passion every night, it was hard to imagine anyone saw that in him.

He handled the criticism better than most his age might have, probably because he had weathered it for years. Growing up, his abilities made him a target for cheap shots and barbs from hockey parents and other players. It was largely behind the family's difficult decision to send Crosby to play and finish high school in Minnesota. Crosby said it had always been harder on his parents than it had been on him.

"They heard a lot more of it. For me, I was always able to reason that it's hockey. As personal as it gets, it's still hockey. If I realize that, it doesn't bother me so much. If someone says the same thing in a school or real-life atmosphere, you take it a different way. But in a hockey rink, the emotion catches people, even adults. So you have to reason it out and be the better person. Maybe they don't realize what they're doing. As you go along, you develop a thicker skin. That's how I've always thought of it."

OH CANADA

Even with Mario it was nothing like this.

THE PENGUINS arrived in Canada on New Year's Day with every member of their three-man media relations staff in tow.

It was the club's first road trip of the season north of the border, and the excitement had been building for over a week. The Leafs game a few days after Christmas meant the Toronto media were in Pittsburgh writing big advance stories of Crosby's first NHL game on home soil. The upside of a road trip to Toronto – widely considered the epicentre among National Hockey League cities – is it guarantees enormous exposure for a rising star such as Crosby.

The less desirable side is that a Toronto stop often raised controversies, often exaggerated, and fuelled by Don Cherry.

The Penguins played the Leafs on January 2 and the Montreal Canadiens the following night. The back-to-back games meant a frenzied schedule at the best of times;

that they coincided with the Crosby's first visit to Canada intensified matters.

And it wouldn't be hectic for Crosby just from a media standpoint. He would have dozens of friends and relatives making the trip to both games, which meant terrific support, but also commitments to visit people, and personal obligations were always difficult to fit in on road trips.

Crosby arrived in Toronto with forty-two points and on the heels of a one-sided feud with Don Cherry. Alexander Ovechkin had forty-six points. But Crosby was gaining. Since Therrien moved the natural centre from the wing back to centre, he had exploded for six goals and four assists in his past five games, including the overtime winner against the New York Rangers on New Year's Eve.

The Penguins held their morning skate at the Ricoh Coliseum on the grounds of the Canadian National Exhibition, a few miles from the Air Canada Centre. Crosby was scheduled to speak with reporters before the practice and came over early in a town car with Tom McMillan from the Westin Harbour Castle hotel, where the team was staying. Before they left the hotel, he invited twenty or so children who had been huddled out on the sidewalk in the damp winter cold into the lobby, where he signed autographs for them.

When he eventually left, with McMillan by his side, another dozen autograph seekers, these ones considerably older, and in a scene right out of *Hard Day's Night*, jumped into taxi cabs and trailed the pair over to the arena. When their driver couldn't immediately find the entrance, McMillan started to get a little nervous, but after a few minutes they pulled under a garage door, avoiding a crush of fans.

Nearly two dozen reporters, including ten television cameras, were waiting for him. The Pittsburgh reporters stood off to the side. They didn't need to ask him anything. The scene was the story.

Predictably, Crosby was asked about how he felt playing in Canada for the first time as an NHLer, how he felt about Don Cherry's unflattering comments, how he would feel the next night playing against the Canadiens, the team he worshipped as a young boy. He was asked about living with Mario Lemieux, how he liked Pittsburgh, how he felt about the officials targeting him.

He gave uncontroversial, politically correct answers to every question. "I'm just trying to approach it like a regular game," he said. But of course, that was impossible. After more than twenty minutes, McMillan signalled to Crosby that his obligations were done, and he padded off to the dressing room to get ready for practice.

After the skate, the same crush of reporters pushed into the cramped visitors' room to interview Crosby's teammates. He was sequestered in a back room, with none of his teammates near him and McMillan standing watch to make sure no one tried to sneak another question in.

There was such a commotion around Crosby every time he went to any new city that his teammates didn't always relish sitting beside him in the dressing room, because it invariably meant they were also squeezed by the intruding cameras.

On occasion, in cities such as Toronto and Montreal, when the pack outnumbered the team, guys like Ryan

Whitney would wisecrack, baa-ing like a sheep as the TV cameras stormed in, mocking the media herd.

While Crosby didn't enjoy doing podium interviews because he didn't want to be singled out and treated differently from his teammates, he would occasionally agree with the media relations staff, as he did on the trip to Canada, that getting in front of a podium outside the room made everything easier on both him and his teammates.

The Air Canada Centre was buzzing before the puck was dropped. Dozens of Crosby sweaters dotted the crowd, and kids pressed up against the glass during the pre-game warm-ups. But Crosby's first game in Canada was a relatively anti-climactic affair. The Penguins lost 3-2 in overtime when Toronto defenceman Bryan McCabe scored a fluky goal by having the puck deflect off of him and past Jocelyn Thibault. Crosby was held to a single assist, on the Penguins' first goal. But it was a beautiful one. Off a rush deep in the Leafs zone, Crosby carried the puck down the left side. Just as he seemed to be running short of space, he dropped the puck around behind his back to put it on the tape of Ziggy Palffy's stick, without so much as a glance. Palffy's shot was turned away by Ed Belfour, but Sergei Gonchar, who was bringing up the rear on the play, fired the rebound into an open net.

It was Crosby's tenth point in the five games since he was left off the Olympic team. He may not have put on a show for the Toronto fans, but he may have subconsciously been putting one on for Wayne Gretzky.

BELL CENTRE, MONTREAL, QUEBEC, JANUARY 3, 2006:

Sidney Crosby had been here once before, in 1999. He was eleven years old and his parents brought him to see a playoff game between the Habs and the Buffalo Sabres. It was the first time he had seen an NHL game in person. They sat high up in the nosebleed section. Montreal lost, he remembered, but every moment of the night was still a dream come true for him. He had grown up worshipping the Canadiens.

Though his father never made it to the big leagues, father and son both loved the Habs. There is a photograph of the two of them in Habs jerseys hanging on the family room wall, among Sidney's hockey mementos. He cheered his lungs out for them from his living room. About forty relatives and friends, including a huge contingent from Rimouski led by Yannick Dumais, were in attendance.

Shortly before noon, he padded to another podium, in his long black underwear and sneakers, and answered questions in English and French for nearly a half-hour.

"It's special, not only for my dad, but for my whole family," he said. "We pretty much all grew up Montreal fans, but with him being drafted by them, seeing me playing in this building against a team that drafted him, I'm sure it's a little more special.

"It was definitely one that I paid attention to and that a lot of friends and family seemed to be talking about since the start of the season."

Normally when the Penguins visit Montreal, it is home-town hero Mario Lemieux sending the fans into frenzy. But with the team's owner-captain out of the lineup indefinitely with an irregular heartbeat, the hoopla fell on the new rising star.

Sidney made jaws drop in his first game against the Habs with a shootout-winning goal against Théodore, for a 3-2 win in Pittsburgh on November 10. The backhand shot sent Théodore's water bottle flying and made the highlight reels for a week.

When Crosby was announced as the Penguins' starting centre, the crowd of 21,273 at the cavernous Bell Centre offered a long and lusty cheer rarely heard for visiting players.

"It was a nice reception," he said. "You never know what to expect in other team's buildings, but that was an added bonus. I can't thank them enough."

The game in Toronto the previous night might have been his first in Canada as a professional, but that proved to be just the appetizer.

When he beat José Théodore with a slick wrist shot from the red circle for the game's first goal and his twentieth of the season, at 4:33 of the first period, the crowd roared.

The Penguins dominated the first period. After Crosby's goal, forward Shane Endicott scored his first NHL goal in a short-handed breakaway that left even his teammates shocked and awed, and Montreal-born Maxime Talbot scored to give the Penguins a 3-0 lead. But Fleury surrendered one to forward Jan Bulis with twenty seconds left, and the Canadiens surged in the second period with forwards Steve Begin, Jonathan Ferland, and defenceman Sheldon Souray scoring three unanswered goals to take a 4-3 lead at 6:43 of the middle period.

Late in the period, Souray was called for high-sticking Crosby in the face, and the power play allowed Michel Ouellet to tie the game before the intermission.

Crosby scored the game winner in the third period to give him twenty-one goals for the season and forty-five points, and to extend his torrid scoring spree; he had eight goals and five assists in his last seven games. It was the fifth loss in six games for the Habs. Ouellet added an insurance goal later in the period to cap the 6-4 victory.

Crosby also hit the post once and might have had the hat trick but for his shot on an empty net that sailed wide as time ticked down.

The win was special for a number of the Penguins, starting with Therrien, who was from Montreal and had spent three seasons as the Habs' head coach. Fleury grew up in Sorel, Ouellet was from Rimouski, and Talbot the Montreal suburb of Lemoyne. Jocelyn Thibault was also from Montreal and had played three and a half seasons with the club in the late nineties. Mark Recchi spent four seasons with the Habs, and John LeClair and Lyle Odelein won a Stanley Cup with them in 1992-1993.

"It was a special day for a lot of our players," Therrien said. "And for Sidney to play his first game here, I felt before the game the guys were excited. There were a lot of people rooting for Sid."

Crosby was named the game's first star. He skated out when his name was called, looked up into the crowd, and found his family in the stands. "It seemed like yesterday I was up in the crowd watching my first NHL game, and now I am skating here," he said after leading the Penguins to a 6-4 win over the Canadiens. "It's something I'll remember forever."

After the game, most of the players went out to celebrate the victory. A lot of the French players had family and friends in town, and they went out for late dinners or drinks. Some, like LeClair and Recchi, had played for the Habs, and Montreal was always a favourite road city. Usually, the team would hop on their charter flight home or to their next destination, but they had scheduled practice here the next morning and so were spending the night in the city.

Crosby went back to the Ritz-Carlton and climbed into bed, where he watched a taped game of the World Junior tournament. "I was exhausted."

The next day, the French papers carried twenty pages about Crosby and Therrien and the Penguins' visit.

The Penguins were scheduled to practise at a junior rink in Verdun. Their next game, against the Thrashers, wasn't for three nights. They were flying to Georgia later that afternoon.

Word spread quickly that the Penguins were practising at the junior rink that was home to the Verdun Junior Canadiens in the eighties, Troy Crosby's old team. The stands began filling up with kids and fathers in tow. Some of them were old friends of Therrien's whom he had invited to watch practice and meet Sidney. Crosby was delighted to be practising in his dad's old rink – it brought back fond memories of watching his dad's old game tapes.

By the time the players began coming off the ice, shortly after noon, the crowd had grown deeper and many had moved down to ice level near the hallway to the dumpy dressing rooms.

Some older gentlemen, in badly mismatched equipment, waited for the Penguins to finish practice so they could get in their lunch-hour rec league game. They craned their necks to try and catch a glimpse of the players as they came off the ice.

Crosby clomped off and was ushered by Tom McMillan into one of the small dressing rooms. He talked to reporters for a while, and then some kids and their dads, friends of Therrien's, piled in with sweaters and photographs to be autographed. He gamely signed and shook hands and posed for snapshots for over a half-hour. All of his teammates except for Marc-Andre Fleury were already on the team bus, and as usual, they were waiting for Crosby. McMillan and Keith Wehner were anxiously eyeing the exits and the swelling crowd, trying to figure out the best way to the bus. The side door to the arena was the closest exit. The bus sat idling thirty feet beyond.

Crosby tried to leave. As they inched along the wall, scores of people pressed forward. When he had the elbow room, Crosby signed whatever was thrust at him as best he could, but it was almost impossible to move, let alone sign autographs. Children and teenaged girls shrieked "Sidney! Sidney!" as he and McMillan moved closer to the door. After about ten minutes, they had travelled the ten feet and emerged into the cold air and bright sunlight, where nearly a hundred more fans waited outside.

Crosby kept shuffling and signing. McMillan, who was as slim as Crosby was sturdy, was swept up in the wave and flattened against the side of the bus as some of the Penguins looked on from inside with bemused impatience.

"Come on, kid, get on the bus," McMillan urged as they both slipped safely on board.

I desperately wished I had brought my camera, because in more than a decade of writing about sports, I had never seen anything quite like that.

"Even with Mario, it was never like this," McMillan said the next day at practice in Atlanta, where Crosby could have strolled down the street carrying a sign announcing his name and no one would have bugged him. "We got to that point eventually, but he was from there. The whole French thing with him made that a scene. But with Sidney they actually treat him like he's from there too. For a non-French player to cause such a reaction in Montreal is really unbelievable."

Crosby, who played his junior hockey in Rimouski, Quebec, had been embraced by francophone hockey fans as if he were their own. In many ways, he was.

While living in the remote and almost wholly French town of 40,000 on the south shore of the St. Lawrence River 300 kilometres east of Quebec City, Crosby, who knew no French when he arrived, learned to speak the language.

The Montreal stop foreshadowed how he could one day capture the hearts of anglophone and francophone hockey fans in equal measure, something Wayne Gretzky and Mario Lemieux never quite accomplished.

"Ultimately, if you are French, if you want to move on to the National Hockey League, you're going to need English," Crosby reasoned.

He spoke solid, albeit uncomplicated French but practised constantly to keep improving. "If you are English, having French is a good thing. It gives you something extra to have both."

Unlike Eric Lindros, who enraged Quebeckers when he refused to report to the Nordiques after being drafted number one overall by the club in 1991, Crosby and a handful of other anglophone Oceanic players from the Maritimes, including Tampa Bay Lightning star Brad Richards, immersed themselves in Rimouski's francophone culture, delighting locals.

"I thought it was the right thing to do in a place where everyone else was French," Crosby said. "I kind of spoke a little, a word here and there my first year. But by my second year, one night instead of doing my post-game interview in English, when he asked me the question in English, I answered in French. Everyone was kind of surprised, but after that I would always do my interviews in French."

When Lemieux was drafted by the Penguins in 1984, he was a shy francophone kid who arrived in the Steel City with hardly a word of English in his vocabulary.

"It was tougher for me when I first got here," Lemieux said. "I didn't speak the language. I was a little bit shy. He's very mature. He makes a few phone calls in French on the way home. He's very good at French."

Renaud Lavoie, a reporter with RDS, the French-language sports network, said he was amazed by how quickly Crosby learned French and that he continued to practise it.

"He knows it's important for his hockey career," Lavoie said. "He is going to be captain of Team Canada one day, and for him to be able to speak both official languages of his country is incredible.

"In Canada, there are a lot of people in French Canada who love Mario Lemieux, and a lot of people in English Canada who love Wayne Gretzky. There's some crossover, but Gretzky was never totally embraced in Quebec because he didn't speak French. Sidney is going to be the next Jean Beliveau."

Crosby only knew how to say hello when he arrived in Rimouski in 2003. His billet host, Christian Bouchard, helped him with French, and Crosby and his roommate, Eric Neilson of New Brunswick, practised on each other.

"We would have a rule where at the dinner table you could only speak French," Crosby said. "At first it could be interesting, a little frustrating. But eventually I got to where I could carry on a conversation and say most of what I needed to say. I used it around the town, and people were really good about helping me along. It's a big deal there to do it, and it means a lot to people."

He had plenty of teammates to practise with this season. The Penguins had eight francophone players on their roster.

"The fact that he's an English guy who made the effort to learn French is huge," said goaltender Marc-Andre Fleury, one of Crosby's closest friends on the team. Crosby counted on Fleury to keep him sharp.

"Salut, mon chum" was their usual greeting, though they often resorted to the humorous, salty language of typical young adults and locker rooms.

"You always learn the bad words first," Crosby laughed. "I could tell you, but you can't print them."

"He's not bad. He knows a lot of words, a lot of slang," Fleury said. "It's great for him and will help him, because he played, too, in Quebec. He has become such a big star for the English people but is also a big star for the French people."

As a francophone and former coach of the Canadiens, Therrien had a unique perspective on his people's take on Sidney. "He's had a huge impact, especially in Canada. I heard there were a lot of things like this with Mario, but this seems so unique. I had never seen something quite like this. It's really very special."

There was little doubt something special had happened, and that it would happen again and again, each time Crosby visited Montreal.

GROANING PAINS

He plays with emotion.
Why would we want him to change?

AFTER BEING CHASED in Toronto and mobbed in Montreal, that Crosby and his teammates could make the ten-minute walk from the Ritz-Carlton Hotel through downtown Atlanta, right past the CNN building to the Philips Arena and back afterwards, stopping for lunch in various restaurants, all without being noticed by a single passerby was a nice reprieve.

On Thursday morning, with no game until the next night, the Penguins had scheduled a late-morning practice. Crosby had to show up a few hours early because *ESPN Magazine* was sending a crew to photograph him for an upcoming issue that would put him on the cover, a rare showcase for a hockey star in a magazine that usually looked out from the newsstands with baseball, basketball, and football stars on the front.

Crosby posed for a portrait and had some shots taken on the ice in full gear. Towering light stands had been set up all around Crosby so the lights would appear as stars shining on him in the photo. Everything went smoothly with the shoot until the photographer asked one of the crew to fix the angle of one of the lights. The crew member raced down the ice in his street shoes and wiped out, as if hitting an imaginary banana peel. He crashed and slid into a big heap, knocking over the equipment, shattering light bulbs all over the ice. The shoot ended soon after. Crosby and McMillan barely made it into the dressing room, they were laughing so hard, Crosby's breathless giggle a hysterical gale.

PHILIPS ARENA, ATLANTA, JANUARY 6, 2006:
This was the first game of a home-and-home series with the Thrashers, with round two taking place back at the Igloo the following night. The Thrashers had been on a roll lately, winning eight of their last thirteen games. But the Penguins were feeling pretty good about themselves, something that hadn't happened too often. They had beaten the Devils and Rangers at home, lost a close game to Toronto, and had a big night in Montreal, the best stretch of results so far this year.

But things quickly went wrong, not the least of which was that the Penguins were exhausted from their back-to-back games in Canada and were overpowered by the Thrashers almost immediately. Atlanta scored three goals in the first ten minutes of the game on just nine shots against Jocelyn Thibault. Therrien pulled Thibault from the game and sent Marc-Andre Fleury in to replace him.

A little before the halfway mark of the first period, the brash Russian forward Ilya Kovalchuk crushed Crosby into the boards from behind, leaving Crosby dazed and more than a little shaken up. He was also angry. He cursed at Kovalchuk and moments later gave him a chop on the shin. The referee blew his whistle. Crosby had been caught slashing.

As the game went on, the Thrashers scored at will against the exhausted Penguins. Crosby and Kovalchuk kept finding each other on the ice. They exchanged dirty looks and insults. Kovalchuk whacked Crosby on the arm with his stick. On the next shift, Crosby shoved Kovalchuk hard.

With just more than two minutes left in the second period, and Crosby sitting in the penalty box serving another slashing minor, Kovalchuk fired a slapshot from the top of the left faceoff circle past Fleury. The goal made it 5-0, further embarrassing the Penguins. Kovalchuk turned towards Crosby, who was just getting up to leave the box, and pointed his gloved finger at him, holding the pose for several seconds to make sure Crosby didn't miss it.

Up in the press box, Karen Price and I stared at each other, expecting referee Bob Langdon to call unsportsman-like conduct on Kovalchuk. The call never came.

Crosby didn't say a word. Head down, he skated to the Penguins bench.

In the third period, the Penguins rallied to score four goals in thirteen minutes. The veteran John LeClair started the comeback, and the Penguins converted their next three power plays. Colby Armstrong got his first NHL goal. But they fell short and lost 6-4. Crosby had one assist, his twenty-fifth of the season, and extended his scoring streak to nine games. Kovalchuk ended the game with an empty net goal that gave him a hat trick.

Afterwards, in the Thrashers' dressing room, Kovalchuk was arrogant and unapologetic. I asked him why he taunted Crosby after the goal.

"Which goal?" he said with a smirk. "Crosby takes those stupid penalties all the time, and he's an eighteen-year-old kid, and he can't play like this. If he wants to play tough, we can play tough. He can finish his checks. He's not Mario Lemieux yet."

Bob Hartley, the Thrashers' coach, had a close friendship with Therrien and reprimanded Kovalchuk after the game. He didn't think much of what his star player had done.

"I didn't like it and I told him," Hartley said. "They are two great young players. They're two young roosters in one barn trying to prove who is best."

Down the hall in the visitors' dressing room, Crosby wouldn't say too much.

"If he wants to do that, he can do that," he said quietly. He would never retaliate by fighting. "There's no point. I'm not a fighter. I'm not going to go out there and drop the gloves with him. He's a skilled guy and he's a great player. I respect him as a player, but that's as far as I'll go."

LeClair, who had seen a lot over fifteen NHL seasons, was stunned. "I couldn't believe what I was seeing. I was really surprised. A player who is that good doesn't need to do that kind of stuff."

The next day in the *Pittsburgh Tribune Review*, Karen Price called Kovalchuk's move "a gross display of disrespect."

Therrien alluded to, if not revenge exactly, some kind of counterplay. "What Kovalchuk did, well, it's a long season."

MELLON ARENA, PITTSBURGH, PENNSYLVANIA, JANUARY 7, 2006:
Emotions were still running high when the teams met again twenty-four hours later. The fans hoped to see Penguins tough guy Andre Roy stand up for Crosby and put a beating on Kovalchuk.

The Russian star was booed every time he touched the puck or jumped over the boards, but it only seemed to motivate him as he continued to toy with the Penguins. He scored twice to elevate his total to thirty-two goals, tops in the league, on the way to a 4-3 Thrashers win.

Crosby, who had two assists, got four penalties, a season high. Late in the second period, he was flying down the slot at top speed when Niclas Havelid hooked him from behind, causing Sidney to go down. It didn't look like a dive. He fell when Havelid's stick came up and smacked him in the face. When Crosby gestured to Stephane Auger from the penalty box, the second referee came over to the scorekeeper's box and Crosby tried to insist he didn't dive but was hauled down by a high stick.

Crosby got an unsportsmanlike conduct penalty for his protests. "I don't know if he knew what I said," he said later. "He just saw me talking to him from inside the box."

It wasn't a good night for Crosby, as far as the officials were concerned. On his first penalty of the game, a hooking call early in the second period, Kovalchuk scored.

But Crosby's playmaking kept the Penguins in the game. Michel Ouellet tied it up 1-1 late in the first period when Sidney made a backhand pass to Ouellet across the slot, while falling forward onto his face. He found Ouellet again late in the second period to tie the game again at 3-3.

After the game, Crosby felt stung. He had taken six penalties in the last two games against Atlanta, two for slashing, once in retaliation, and for hooking, diving, unsportsmanlike conduct, and interference.

During the second game of the series, Thrashers winger Jean-Pierre Vigier was whistled down for hooking Crosby, who was so used to being called he thought the infraction was on him and reflexively started to head to the box before realizing it was on Vigier. He was the second most penalized player on the team, with sixty minutes. Only feisty defenceman Brooks Orpik had more penalty minutes, and just a single minute more at that. Kovalchuk had gotten under Crosby's skin, which may have bothered him as much as anything else.

He sat in his stall after that Saturday night, head down and arms folded across his chest, answering questions quietly.

"It's tough to do anything when you're sitting in the box the whole game," he said. "I've got to improve on that."

"I've just got to keep my head down and play. Try to play hard, and if I get called for penalties, suck it up and go. I have to make sure I'm paying attention to what I'm doing out there, that I'm not committing any infractions. Because if I do right now, it seems like I'm getting nailed for it."

He was most irked about the diving call. "I don't usually go down from a hook that easy. I can't control if a stick hits me in the face and I go down. I have to get tougher, I guess."

His sarcasm was barely veiled.

Crosby's strong, fast skating style meant that when he fell he fell hard, but not on purpose. Diving, exaggerating a fall after a hook, is the most demeaning call a player can get because it suggests disrespect for the game.

But even Hartley, who was asked if he thought Crosby dived, said, "I can't say that."

As an alternate captain, Crosby had the right to talk to the officials during a game on behalf of himself or his teammates. But he had been trying to do so less often. He realized that using the A "as an excuse to talk to them all the time" wasn't a good idea.

In Toronto that night on *Coach's Corner*, Don Cherry stuck up for Sidney Crosby. He showed footage of the rookie being targeted for extra-tough physical play by the Thrashers and condemned the Penguins for not sticking up for their star. "They have to get someone to ride shotgun with him. He's an eighteen-year-old kid. It's ridiculous." Of Kovalchuk's gesture while Crosby was in the penalty box, Cherry said, "Someone should have broken his arm."

Even the cynical Don Cherry would no longer deny that Crosby was getting a rough ride in his first year in the NHL.

For all Crosby's physical play – his ability to battle along the boards and keep others from the puck, his obsession for sticking with the play, and his willingness to burst through defenders far bigger than he – he was not the kind of guy who was going to get in a fight.

"Trust me, there have probably been a number of times I would have loved to do that. But, in the best interest of the team and best interest of me, I don't think it's the right thing to do. If I hurt a hand or a shoulder, to be off the ice is not worth doing that. You can still play tough and not fight. I like to think I play a pretty tough game."

Therrien told reporters after the game that he was proud of the way his young star handled himself. "Sidney Crosby plays with pride. He works hard. He battles. He plays with a lot of emotion. This is what makes Sidney Crosby. He's one of the best players in the NHL because he plays with emotion. Why would we want him to change that?"

Thrashers coach Bob Hartley said it was Crosby's emotion that made him so dangerous. "He can beat you so many ways."

Crosby said he had no plans to change his style. "It's what has made me successful, to be emotional and passionate and driven."

But he also felt he had let his teammates down by spending so much time in the penalty box during those two games.

When he arrived home later that night, Sidney and Mario talked about the rookie's struggles with the referees, and Lemieux gave him some advice.

"He has the passion to be successful," Lemieux said. "That's a great thing to have. But you have to control your emotions. I know it's not easy. Every time he has the puck, he's getting hooked and grabbed. But it's always better to make the officials your friends. And that's what I told him."

The following day, Crosby was more reflective. "I'm emotional when I play, but I can control whether I argue something," he said. "Sitting in the penalty box is tough. You're putting your team down. Being alternate captain, I want to lead by example, and sitting in the penalty box is in no way leading.

"I'm not going to change who I am because of that, but maybe there's a little more responsibility because I'm looked on as a role model, and I take that very seriously. But I'm not going to change."

Lemieux, who watched the first Atlanta game at home on

television, said he was bothered by Kovalchuk's taunting. "It was a stupid thing to do. I don't think he'll do it again."

Monday morning dawned unseasonably warm for January in Pittsburgh. By the time the Penguins began arriving at the Igloo for practice, it was almost forty-five degrees Fahrenheit. Crosby was a winter kid – not surprisingly, it was his favourite season – and he felt most at home in Pittsburgh when there was some snow on the ground and a chill in the air.

Even though they lost both weekend games to the same team, they had an easy workout and found time to play a game with the puck that resembled baseball or cricket. One at a time, players on one team flipped the puck out from the corner and skated furiously to the blue line, across the ice and back to the goal, as if running the bases, before the other team scored. There in the middle of it all was an unexpected sight: Mario Lemieux.

It was the first time he had practised in nearly a month. He was worried about getting back into skating shape because he intended to rejoin the lineup as soon as he could. Doctors had adjusted his medication the previous week. Other than not being able to taste anything he ate or drank, he was feeling pretty good.

"It was a good day to come back," Lemieux said. "I got a good feel for being with the guys. It was a good first day."

He was going to make the Penguins' upcoming road trip to Columbus, Chicago, and Nashville, though he had no plans to play. "It was a breath of fresh air to see him out," said Therrien, who added that he wouldn't rush Lemieux into the lineup. "We want to make sure that when he comes back, he's at 100 per cent."

The next night, the Edmonton Oilers beat the Penguins 3-1. Centre Shawn Horcoff scored his first career hat trick: on a power play, short-handed, and even strength. Crosby was held off the score sheet for the first time in ten games and had just two shots in the first period. He also didn't get a penalty.

The whole team was flat, but the defence was terrible. Therrien was livid afterwards.

"It's a pathetic performance," he said. "Half of the team doesn't care. That defensive squad, I am really starting to believe their goal is to be the worst defensive squad in the league. They turn the puck over, they have no vision, they are soft. I have never seen a bunch of defencemen as soft as this. The guys don't care. They pretend to care, but I know they don't care. We should take 50 per cent of their salaries, because they only play 50 per cent of the time.

"What's the solution?" Therrien asked, shaking his head in disgust. "I'm going to find the solution."

The players may not have realized it, but Therrien was issuing them a challenge to play better and prove him wrong.

It didn't quite work out that way. The Penguins were embarrassed in Columbus. The Blue Jackets' Rick Nash scored on the game's opening faceoff, the fastest goal in franchise history, starting the roll to a 6-1 win.

Crosby failed again to get a point. He was whistled for roughing in the second period, a penalty of frustration with the game already out of control, and again for holding in the third period. The game degenerated into a fight-filled mess, with 152 minutes in penalties being handed out to both teams. "If we're down five goals, we're going to be a little more edgy," Crosby said.

Therrien didn't insult his team this time. Even though

the lowly Jackets got more goals on two shots than the Penguins managed all game, the Pittsburgh players, out of frustration or embarrassment, stuck up for each other and fought often. That pleased Therrien, who was happy just to see some passion from most of his players. "For the first time this year, that team seemed to stick together," Therrien said. "That's a good start. Even though we're in January, I like the way they responded. It's a positive thing to stick up for each other, and we're going to build on that." Crosby failed to score a point in his second consecutive game. Goalie Dany Sabourin had been called up earlier in the day, but was thoroughly overmatched. Marc-Andre Fleury came in early in the second period.

When Crosby was in the box in the third period, a couple of fans sitting nearby stood up and leaned over towards the box, calling him a crybaby and more vulgar things he later wouldn't elaborate on. Crosby hollered back. The score-board camera put him up with the caption "Baby Cam." The fans jeered.

"I'm not going to start something with a fan, by any means," he said. "But it gets to a point where some of the things they say cross a line. You feel the need to say something back. I wasn't hanging over the glass screaming at them or anything."

Even though he hadn't scored in two games – Crosby's longest pointless streak to date was just three games, after he hurt his foot in Florida – he said he wasn't playing more tentatively in order to avoid being called for penalties.

"I don't think so," he said hesitantly. "I'm trying not to change my game."

The Penguins arrived in Chicago with an off day before their Friday night game. Therrien, who wasn't happy with the way the team had been playing, imposed a 12:30 a.m. curfew even though the next day was only a practice day. Crosby had dinner with some of the team at Gibson's Steakhouse and relaxed in his room.

It had been a good week for Chicago hockey fans. Earlier, they got to see Alexander Ovechkin and the Capitals play at the United Center, and now it was Crosby and the Penguins, the only visit they would make in three seasons.

The Blackhawks' owner, Bill Wirtz, lifted the long-standing ban on televising home games to permit Comcast SportsNet to carry the Penguins game. It was the only home game they would show all season. Crosby was almost sheepish when he heard about it. "I don't know what to say. It's good if there is a little bit of excitement. I've been in situations where there is probably a little more buildup than usual."

The game was sold out with 20,541 fans for only the second time in twenty games. Only the Detroit Red Wings ever packed them in at the United Center. The Blackhawks had some of the league's worst attendance and had had for seasons, and were among the league's worst teams.

In a city that basketball's Michael Jordan had ruled for years in the eighties and nineties, and where the Cubs and White Sox do battle on both sides of the city, hockey had faded considerably. It was a franchise clinging to history. Greg Couch, sports columnist for the *Chicago Sun Times*, called the Blackhawks "hockey's Neanderthals" in his column that week about the new NHL and the arrival of Sidney Crosby.

Before the game, Denis Savard, the former Blackhawks star from the eighties, was flashed on the scoreboard to tell fans, "We have a great player here today."

It was a far cry from Columbus, where Crosby was mocked on the big screen. Even if the Blackhawks were stuck in the Stone Age, Chicago was a once-great hockey city that could appreciate a player like Crosby.

On Friday the thirteenth, the Penguins lost again, 4-1. Crosby had several decent scoring chances and assisted on Colby Armstrong's only goal for Pittsburgh. Andy Hilbert, the Blackhawks' rookie winger, scored two pretty goals. Even though the Penguins would not see the Blackhawks again for several years, it was not the last they would see of Hilbert.

In the third period, Crosby was elbowed along the boards by a Hawks blueliner. His lip was split but no penalty was called.

The team looked sloppy and run off their feet. Therrien's system hadn't yet started to sink in, but it was difficult for the players to explain why.

"We need to trust each other," Crosby said. "This is not easy. We have to pull together."

In a room off the dressing room, Lemieux sat stone-faced, his chin in his hands. He looked miserable.

In a bit of good news, Colby Armstrong was coming on and starting to show he was plenty good enough to play in the NHL. In the way of bad news, the team got to spend the night in the Windy City but had to practise at ten o'clock the next morning.

GAYLORD ENTERTAINMENT CENTER, NASHVILLE, TENNESSEE, JANUARY 15, 2006:

The arena was across the street from the city's famous honky-tonk scene – Tootsie's, The Stage, the Orchid Lounge, Legend's Corner, the Lipstick Lounge, and B.B. King's Blues Club. The Ryman Auditorium, made famous by the Grand Ole Opry, was just around the corner. It wasn't typical hockey country.

Even though Nashville was a relative newcomer to the NHL – 1998-1999 was their inaugural season – the arena announcer told the crowd they were getting a chance to see one of the best young players in the NHL and urged them to enjoy it. Crosby was the reason for only the fourth Predators sellout of the season.

In the press room, where teams keep the game notes and popcorn and soft drinks for reporters, the Dixo-American attendant asked us if we were from Pittsburgh.

"Ah, I shoulda brought my gun tonight," she drawled. "That's what you do with birds, ain't that right? You shoot 'em."

Again the Penguins fell behind early, 5-1 through two periods. Again they made a spirited comeback, scoring three unanswered goals in twenty-three minutes in the third. Again, it wasn't enough. It was their sixth loss in a row.

Things had really collapsed. After winning three games in four and getting eight of a possible ten points in five games, the Penguins were in free fall. The players had no confidence. Since their plucky win in Montreal, they had been outscored 28-14.

"They get one goal on us and it's like we put our heads

down and feel sorry for ourselves," Colby Armstrong said. "We can't bounce back."

Outside the press box and coaches' boxes, Mario Lemieux and Craig Patrick paced in short lengths, looking frustrated and not speaking much.

Therrien's approach at this point was simply to keep practising and working on the most basic fundamentals of the game – puck possession and keeping turnovers to a minimum.

Crosby was frustrated, but he tried to keep a good face on. "We're having a really tough go right now," he'd say, then instantly follow it with a hopeful remark about how he felt they weren't that far from being a competitive team. It made me think he was trying to convince himself, as much as anyone else, that success could be just around the corner if only a few more things started going right on the ice night in and night out.

And there would be no rest. After they lost in Nashville, they flew home to face the Vancouver Canucks the very next evening.

A high-flying Canucks team handed the Penguins consecutive loss number seven. Crosby scored his twenty-second goal of the year on the power play in the first period of the 4-2 defeat. Despite coming off back-to-back games, he looked energized and played desperately. He generated a lot of scoring chances and had a season-high six shots on net, despite taking what looked like a season-high amount of abuse at the hands of a big Canucks team.

He fought back, receiving roughing and slashing penalties. He drew one too, when Sedin upended him when he didn't even have the puck. In the second period, when he was cross-checked into the boards, Therrien shouted at the officials from the bench and Recchi talked to referee Paul Devorski. Crosby just picked himself up and didn't say a word. He was going to let Recchi do the talking.

Colby Armstrong continued to improve, chipping in an assist. He hit Canucks centre Ryan Kesler in the open ice so hard, Kesler went flying and the partisan Igloo crowd roared. Then Armstrong blew Kesler a kiss.

Armstrong had been recalled from the minors on December 29, and was one of the best young players in the Penguins lineup. The right-winger could kill penalties and score goals, and he was one of the few players who could skate with Crosby and set him up, his skating prowess perhaps the result of long-time childhood figure skating lessons.

At six foot two and 190 pounds, Armstrong seemed scrawny out of his hockey equipment but was the team's most physical player. He threw his body into opponents as if he were a much larger man. He didn't back down from roughing or a fight, and he had started to jump to Crosby's defence, rushing in to take on Jarkko Ruutu when the Canucks winger started shoving the rookie.

He and Crosby started rooming together on the road and were becoming close friends.

"He's not the biggest guy, but he plays big and has a big heart," Crosby said.

But in the players' lounge, where Therrien had hung the league standings board, the Penguins were back at the bottom of the list after their loss to the Canucks, which in that room put them just above the garbage can.

16

NEW YEAR'S LEAVE

There are things in life you can't always prepare for.

JANUARY HAD STARTED eventfully, with Crosby's first Canadian appearances as a Penguin, the difficult games with the Thrashers, his battles with Kovalchuk, and his struggle to adapt to the NHL officiating.

But after the Penguins returned from a disheartening three-game Western road swing, they hadn't won a game since that glorious night in Montreal, and everyone's mood was as low as it had been all season. They had only won three games since Therrien took over from Olczyk on December 15. Even though sometimes the Penguins looked to be playing more cohesively, other times it didn't look as though much had changed at all.

Their next game was at home against the New York Rangers, and they prepared and practised hard in hopes of ending what was now a seven-game losing streak.

Ziggy Palffy, the mercurial Slovakian right-winger, had been one of the league's most consistent scorers over the past decade. He had been Sidney's most dependable linemate all season, with eleven goals and thirty-one assists, second only to Crosby on the team. He was also the only player on the team with a positive plus-minus rating at plus five.

The Penguins landed the free agent over the summer, but he didn't come cheap. Palffy had signed a three-year deal that paid him $13.5 million. It was seen by some as a risky move; Palffy had already undergone shoulder surgery twice, but Craig Patrick thought he was worth taking a chance on. In nine seasons with the Los Angeles Kings and New York Islanders, Palffy had scored sixty-five or more points six times. But the quiet thirty-three-year-old was struggling. He hadn't scored a goal in his last fourteen games and looked like a man who had lost his passion for the game.

On the morning of January 18, shortly after nine-thirty, Palffy strode into Craig Patrick's office.

"Can we talk?" he asked the general manager. Patrick said it didn't take him long to figure what was coming next.

Patrick announced Palffy's retirement during the morning practice and said Palffy was leaving for personal reasons. At the same time, a Slovak newspaper reported the player was quitting because of his lingering shoulder problems, and they even quoted Palffy as saying so.

He had missed the final forty-two games of the 2003-2004 season to recover from surgery to repair a dislocated shoulder, but rebounded as a point-per-game player during the lockout with Praha Slavia in the Czech League.

"We didn't sense there were any problems with his shoulder," Patrick said. Palffy had passed a physical shortly after he signed his contract.

The moody winger walked away from roughly $11.5 million. It seemed there was more to it than a painful shoulder. But Palffy was gone, his agent wasn't talking, and Patrick had said all he wanted to on the matter.

"We talked about a lot of things," Patrick said. "At the end, he just said he wanted to retire for personal reasons. After the discussion, I understand all his issues, and I also respect his decision. He's ready to move on from hockey."

Crosby was shocked but said he knew his linemate had been ailing. Palffy weathered a monstrous hit from Darcy Hordichuk, a squarely built, six-foot-one, 215-pound winger, in the Predators game three nights earlier.

"I knew he was hurting," Crosby said. "His shoulder, his back, his back hurt him for a long time. And with that hit, I think his shoulder was pretty sore."

To a man, the Penguins were stunned by Palffy's departure. Therrien's comments were most revealing. "He was not playing the way he wished to play, and he's not getting any younger. He's got some personal reasons, and we have to respect that. But for sure, he wanted to contribute a lot more to the team, and for him, I think, he's ready to move on."

The next day Palffy told Karen Price of the *Pittsburgh Tribune Review* that he thought he could play through his shoulder problems but eventually couldn't go on.

"It wasn't that good, but I thought it was going to be fine," he said. "I didn't feel comfortable. I didn't feel comfortable with the stick. My motion is different, and I couldn't do anything with the puck like I wanted."

Several months later, Eddie Johnston, the colourful assistant general manager, and I were having a conversation about building a Stanley Cup–winning team. He casually mentioned "Ziggy quitting" as one of the reasons things hadn't turned out as planned this season. He was the first person in the Penguins organization to say on the record that Palffy hadn't quite "retired."

"I think maybe some people have more of a stomach for getting through the tough times, and other people don't want to go through it," Johnston said. "And Palffy, he didn't really want to keep going like this, so he quit."

After practice, Sidney asked Keith Wehner if he could get a spare copy of a poster-sized photograph that was taken by the *Pittsburgh Post-Gazette* on the night of Crosby's first goal. It showed Crosby celebrating against the boards, and Palffy, who passed him the puck, skating in to embrace him. Sidney wanted to sign it and send it to Palffy as a memento of their time together.

Palffy's retirement was good for Konstantin Koltsov, a second-year winger and first-round pick from Belarus who had twenty-nine points in his rookie season with the Penguins before the lockout. The twenty-four-year-old had spent most of the winter in the minors, but would get a chance on the top line with Crosby and Tomas Surovy in the next night's game against the Rangers. Therrien liked Koltsov's forechecking and play away from the puck. He wanted to see how he handled himself with it, and if the line combination could yield any magic.

At the pre-game skate the following day, as Crosby and Koltsov practised together for the first time and tried to get familiar with each other, the media relations staff alerted everyone that Mario Lemieux would be making an announcement in the lounge outside the players' dressing room.

That morning, January 19, 2006, the *Pittsburgh Post-Gazette* reported that Lemieux had decided once and for all to sell the Penguins. He had always been clear about not wanting to own the team for life, but it was surprising nonetheless, given his earlier commitment to getting a new arena built. The story played at the top of the front page under the headline: Penguins Up for Sale.

In a week in which the Steelers were on their way to the AFC championship game, a front-page hockey story was a rare sight.

It was the latest chapter in the long-running saga that made the Penguins more reminiscent of a nighttime soap opera than a National Hockey League team. Already, the chronic melodrama seemed like far more than Crosby or any of the other Penguins who joined the team expecting great things had bargained for.

The list of seismic events was getting longer by the day. In the past month, Eddie Olczyk had been fired and Michel Therrien hired. Crosby had moved from wing to centre, been made an alternate captain, and weathered heavy criticism. He went from a scoring slump that began after he hurt his foot in Florida to a streak born when Therrien took over and really gathered steam after he was snubbed for the Olympic team.

He had to deal with more and more on-ice bullying, and was left largely to fend for himself until Craig Patrick traded for Eric Cairns, a towering defenceman, to protect his star player and shore up. In another smart personnel move, the young but talented goaltender Marc-Andre Fleury was finally told he would remain with the big league club for the rest of the season and not be sent to Wilkes-Barre, even if it meant the team might end up paying him three million dollars in bonus money.

The team had continued to struggle under Therrien. They were playing better, which pleased the coach, but still weren't winning. On that front, he seemed willing to be more patient. There were three things Therrien looked for, win or lose – commitment, effort, and work ethic. He repeated the words so often over the season they popped into my head as a mantra even when I was away from the rink. "The results, they aren't always there," he said. "But if the other things are, it will come."

In Washington, Alexander Ovechkin had pulled seven points ahead of Sidney in the rookie scoring race and was now the favourite to win the Calder Trophy.

Even the sad-sack Capitals, whom no one had any hopes for, their only star Ovechkin, ranked higher in the standings than the Penguins, who were easily supposed to make the playoffs. And the Penguins' future in Pittsburgh was suddenly more in doubt than ever with Lemieux putting the club up for sale.

"It's been a lot, no doubt," Crosby said. "But I'm here to play. And the team being put up for sale, it's big, but it's not something I think is my concern," Crosby said. "I play. I don't try to interfere with that stuff. That's not what I'm here for. That's the way hockey goes sometimes, and you can't control it. There's things in life you can't always prepare for."

The press conference at the Igloo that morning was a circus. The Rangers were in town for a game later that night, so the New York media combined with the Pittsburgh

crew, which included sports and news crews from newspapers, television, and radio stations across the city, made
for about forty reporters and eight cameramen, a few standing atop chairs to get a better shot. They crowded into the
lounge area, pressing Lemieux and Ken Sawyer, the team's
president and new chief executive officer, against the wall.
John Davidson and Sam Rosen, Rangers analysts for the
Madison Square Garden network, watched from the back
of the scrum as Lemieux confirmed what the paper had
already reported.

"I'm out," he said, nodding slightly. "We are now in a situation where we are going to look at all our options."

The Hockey Hall of Fame legend said he had received
inquiries from "several groups interested in buying the
team" but declined to name them.

It was well-known that groups from Kansas City, Las
Vegas, and Houston were keen to acquire an NHL team and
move it, but Lemieux said he hoped to find a buyer that
would keep the team in Pittsburgh.

But anyone who purchased the club – and Lemieux said
he would let bids set the market value – would be bound to
the Penguins' recent proposal for an arena and casino with
a Biloxi, Mississippi–based gambling operation named Isle
of Capri that had already committed $290 million for an
arena if it won the slots licence to be awarded by the state
early in 2007. Why couldn't Lemieux just hang on a little
longer and see how that played out?

"This is not being done out of frustration," Sawyer said.
"Nobody expected for Mario to own this team forever.
He's done more than he should. He's teed us up perfectly

to move ahead. We have the next generation of Penguins players here, and we want the next generation of owners to run with that ball."

Sawyer, in his sixth year as a Penguins executive, also wanted to keep the team in the city but said, "We're not going to sell the team for a third of the value just to make it a local transaction."

Lemieux had been excited about playing this season with Crosby on what he had hoped would be a serious playoff contender. Instead, he was looking at a team that had the second-worst record in the NHL and he was unable to help, sidelined with heart problems.

Palffy had retired. Defenceman Sergei Gonchar had been a disappointment. Veteran goaltender Jocelyn Thibault was both injured and underachieving. But the youthful talent on the Penguins, led by Crosby, Fleury, Armstrong, and Ryan Whitney, in addition to Russian star Evgeni Malkin, the Penguins' second overall pick from 2004, likely to join the club next season, all promised a brighter future, though perhaps that future wouldn't be in Pittsburgh.

Lemieux strained to be unsentimental about selling the team. "We think the time is right with the way things have unfolded. We've got a new CBA that levels the playing field for all teams. We've got a strong base of young talent, and now we've got a tremendous arena plan on the table that can deliver a new arena at no cost to taxpayers."

The Penguins' lease at Mellon Arena expired in June, 2007, and if plans to build a new rink weren't in place by then, the team would almost certainly relocate.

Sawyer was installed to oversee the operation of the club

and lead the sale process. Lemieux remained chairman of the board until the Penguins could be sold.

They were an interesting contrast – Lemieux in black T-shirt, fleece, grey cotton gym shorts, and sockless in white sneakers; Sawyer in a smart navy sports coat and khaki slacks; both businessmen and both millionaires; both Montrealers who were now Pittsburghers.

"We've done everything we can as an ownership group as far as setting up the franchise for the long-term here in Pittsburgh," Lemieux said. "We have a plan to fully fund construction of an arena without taxpayer money and make sure this franchise stays in Pittsburgh forever. That's always been my goal."

Afterwards, everyone wanted to hear Sidney's thoughts on the team being put up for sale. As usual, he was politically correct and uncontroversial. He and Lemieux never talked business at home. He said he didn't want to think about the team moving. He just wanted to play hockey and win games. He was, after all, just a kid.

"What it means for us, I don't know," he said of the sale. "But I know I'd like to stay here in Pittsburgh."

17

AU REVOIR, LE MAGNIFIQUE

I've done it before, so I know what it feels like.
But not like this. This hurts.

ON JANUARY 23, the Penguins lost 4-2 in Philadelphia, extending their losing streak to ten games. Crosby had managed to score nine points in the stretch, but just two goals. He seemed to be struggling, but it probably had a lot to do with the upheaval on his line.

After Palffy left, Therrien still hadn't found a combination that really clicked.

The following morning, I was at the Philadelphia airport waiting for a flight back to Pittsburgh when I got a message on my cellphone from *Globe and Mail* sports editor Steve Mcallister. The wire had moved a notice that the Penguins had just announced a news conference for two o'clock that afternoon. It could only be about one thing: Mario Lemieux was about to retire from hockey.

It was too difficult to believe that in a single week Ziggy Palffy retired, Lemieux put the franchise up for sale, and he was now ready to call it a career.

228

That Lemieux would retire, even at the end of this season, was not about to shock anyone. He was, even by his own admission, a shadow of his former greatness on the ice and had only played twenty-six out of forty-nine games this year.

He had been battling the condition that made for his irregular heartbeat since before Christmas. He was forty years old. He had beaten cancer. He had rebounded from and played through chronic back and hip injuries. He had already retired and made a comeback. He had 690 goals and 1,033 assists in 915 games and was the number seven scorer in NHL history.

Mario Lemieux had nothing left to prove. And yet the sudden announcement of his retirement seemed jarring, even though it had been on almost everyone's mind at some point during the season. In many ways, it was a no-brainer. Despite working out intensely and skating to get back into game shape, he had still not set a date for his return to the lineup. It made sense this season would be Lemieux's last in the NHL. It was really just a matter of timing; when would it happen?

Standing behind a podium in front of a deep crowd of cameras and reporters, Lemieux's soft voice cracked as he stared down at notes that didn't contain words deep enough for his emotions. His blue eyes filled with tears, but they didn't fall.

With most of his teammates, including Crosby, looking on, the Hall of Fame legend announced to the world that after seventeen seasons, 1,723 points, two Stanley Cups, three MVP awards, and six NHL scoring titles, he was retiring because of his health and diminishing abilities.

"This is always a difficult decision to make for any athlete, but the time has come, and it's in the best interests of myself and my family and the Penguins," Lemieux said. "I can no longer play at the level I was accustomed to in the past, and it's been very, very frustrating to me in this past year.

"It's been a part of my life since I was three years old. To have it taken away some days is difficult to accept, but we all have to go through that. I have some experience at it; I've done it before, so I know what it feels like. But certainly not like this. This is it. It hurts."

He retired in 1997 for three seasons with his back problems and missed another year battling Hodgkin's disease. He came back from that. But he wouldn't come back this time.

He played his last game December 16 against Buffalo, during which he suffered heart palpitations. It was then he began thinking seriously about hanging up his skates for good.

"I don't feel great every day when I get up," he admitted. He said he was considering surgery to correct the problem. He had talked to Toronto Maple Leafs coach Pat Quinn, who had successful surgery for a similar problem.

Lemieux had been working out hard and skating in practice. He said the previous week he wanted to get back into the lineup. But he just couldn't.

"Not feeling 100 per cent was the most frustrating thing," he said. "Trying to play and practise with it and get back to where I need to be, it wasn't going to happen."

A legend in the hockey world and a treasure in Pittsburgh, he rescued them from bankruptcy in 1999. He won two Stanley Cups and led Team Canada to a gold medal at the

Salt Lake City Olympics in 2002 and the World Cup in 2004. His fondest memories were as a twenty-two-year-old playing in the 1987 Canada Cup with Wayne Gretzky, Mark Messier, Paul Coffey, and Ray Bourque.

"They were in their prime, and I was just a young guy learning the game," Lemieux said fondly. "Playing with Gretzky gave me a lot of confidence going back and playing in Pittsburgh. It gave me an opportunity to start my career and really learn what it meant to be a champion and the best in the game.

"It would have been nice to get 700 goals, but more important was winning two championships. That was my goal growing up. Statistics are nice, but they aren't going to change how people view me."

He scored his last goal November 10, in a 3-2 win over Montreal, the game Crosby won in a dramatic overtime shootout and, in hindsight, the moment the torch had passed from one to the other. "I realize the new NHL is really for the young guys," Lemieux said. "It's a young man's game now."

He was talking to the more than two dozen television cameras and still photographers and some forty reporters, but he was really speaking to Crosby and Armstrong, Fleury and Whitney, and the rest of the team he was leaving behind.

"All I can say to the young players is, enjoy every moment of it," he said haltingly, almost in tears. "Your career goes by very quickly. It's a great game, and you guys are all very special to be in the NHL. I'm very privileged."

Although the Penguins' season, at 11-29-9, had been a colossal disappointment, Lemieux said he was "just happy having a chance to play a few more games."

"When you get to the end of your career, every time you're on the ice you try to do the best you can with your abilities, and I'm just sorry I didn't feel any better or play any better, but that's what happens towards the end," he said.

Crosby told reporters that Lemieux's announcement had "come up over the breakfast table that morning." I later learned he had known for a week. He was devastated.

"It's never an easy day to see him walk away from the game," Crosby said. "The most important thing for him is to be happy. To see him walk away on his own terms is good.

"The passion he had for the game, what a down-to-earth person he is, what he's been able to do on the ice and off has been so good for hockey. There aren't many guys who can change the game like he did."

A day later, as Lemieux watched from his owner's box at the Igloo, the National Hockey League's best young hot-shots battled once again for bragging rights, points, and badly needed victories for their teams.

Crosby and Ovechkin reunited in front of 14,415 fans. Many held up signs wishing Lemieux well, and thanking him for the memories and for winning two Stanley Cups. A touching video tribute played on the scoreboard and launched a lengthy ovation.

To tease the crowd for the upcoming young guns' show-down, the scoreboard also showed clips of Ovechkin bullying his way through defenders like a freight train and scoring on his back, and of Crosby jitterbugging and faking to beat goaltenders with his backhand.

For the second time, the game belonged to Sidney. Though Ovechkin was spectacular at moments and scored one terrific goal, Crosby had four points, a goal and three assists, and the Penguins dominated to win the game 8-1 and snap their ten-game losing streak.

It was Crosby's first four-point game. Later, he confessed that Nathalie Lemieux became superstitious about the tomato-based pasta sauce she had made for his pre-game meal that afternoon and tried to repeat the magic with future meals of it.

It didn't show that these two were on teams mired at the bottom of the standings. They came out skating as though they were in game seven of a Stanley Cup final.

Crosby had an excellent scoring chance on the first shot of his first shift and so did Ovechkin, but goaltenders Olaf Kolzig and Marc-Andre Fleury denied both.

Ovechkin hit the stats sheet first, scoring his thirty-fourth goal on the power play early in the second period to tie the game 1-1, and it was a beauty. He missed his first chance and then got his own rebound, scooping up the puck and drifting back towards the top of the red circle. Repositioned, he sent a rocket past Fleury.

A few minutes later, Crosby struck. On a power play and working above the circle, he wonderfully faked a slapshot and slid the puck across to Mark Recchi, who flipped it past Kolzig to regain the lead. Crosby combined with Recchi again later in the period, and set up Tomas Surovy in the third period.

Crosby's goal was pretty too. With the puck on his stick, he skated around the back of the Capitals net and then darted out in front, moving the puck between the skates of Washington's defenceman Bryan Muir before stuffing it past Kolzig.

It wasn't a great night for the Capitals or Ovechkin, who had a frightening moment when he was accidentally speared between the legs by Penguins defender Ryan Whitney near the end of the second period. Ovechkin had to be helped off the ice but returned for the third period, and appeared no worse for wear.

After the rout, the Russian was in a bad mood and refused to speak to reporters. In the Penguins' room, Crosby conceded that playing Ovechkin motivated him. He now had fifty-seven points to the Russian's sixty-three points.

But he thought the biggest reason for the win was that the Penguins finally managed a complete game, one of the first all season. "All our hard work paid off. When everyone chips in, this is what happens."

He did enjoy seeing his rival perform. A week earlier, Ovechkin had scored a goal against the Phoenix Coyotes that was so unbelievable many sportswriters decided then and there that the Russian should win the Calder Trophy. It was a diving, highlight-reel effort, the best, most acrobatic goal scored by anyone all season. Crosby said he enjoyed watching it. It pushed him to be better. "It was an incredible goal," he said. "It's fun to see goals like that. It was so creative. That's what you want to do as a scorer. Players like him inspire you to be better, work harder. It's so good for hockey to have all these young guys playing and scoring like that."

The two had made plans to trade autographed sticks after the game, but the lopsided outcome of the game kept Ovechkin from seeking Crosby out. However, they would get a chance to swap them the next time they played each other. Ovechkin made a point of visiting the Penguins' locker room. He got one for himself and asked Sidney to sign a second stick for a friend back in Russia. Crosby gamely obliged.

By the end of January, the Steelers were headed to the Super Bowl in Detroit and the whole city seemed to be celebrating. The Steelers receiver Hines Ward, an ardent Penguins fan, showed up at a few games wearing a Sidney Crosby jersey, much to the crowd's delight. So did kicker Jeff Reed. Quarterback Ben Roethlisberger, who had godlike status in Pittsburgh, also showed up, waving to the crowd from Lemieux's box. Crosby hopped on the Steelers bandwagon and hockey fans loved him for it. After the Washington game, he was named first star and took his victory skate waving a Terrible Towel, the iconic terrycloth Steelers souvenir.

The irony wasn't lost on anyone. The Penguins were the last team to bring a championship to the city of Pittsburgh when they won the Stanley Cup in the spring in 1992. And they were about to lose that honour. But it was all for one.

"I'm a big Crosby fan," Ward said. "You want to be a part of that excitement. You just hop on. We're all one big family. It's a big little town."

With the Penguins still in a free fall, the team for sale, and Lemieux retiring, they needed all the love they could get.

In the meantime, a couple of things happened that showed Crosby hadn't become overwhelmed by his growing NHL stardom.

In January, his mother mentioned that Halifax regional council had proposed a vague bylaw aimed at curbing behaviour that might impede traffic. It risked being interpreted as banning street hockey. So Crosby e-mailed Halifax Mayor Peter Kelly and members of council urging them to consider rewording the bylaw, which they ultimately did.

"It was just one of those things where I could relate to the topic and I had a strong opinion about it," he said. "Growing up, we played every day. It's a sport we all love, and we don't want to lose that."

A few days later, he received a request from the Cole Harbour Wings, a peewee Triple-A team Crosby had played for as a boy. They were heading to the Quebec International Peewee Hockey Tournament and wondered if Crosby might be able to donate something for the players, a token to send off the team of twelve-year-olds.

When Trina Crosby phoned back Bill Morris at the Cole Harbour Minor Hockey Association, she advised him to bring a truck. Crosby had arranged with Reebok to supply the kids with gloves and helmets, hockey bags and sticks, and even toques.

"Being from a small town, when you go to those international tournaments, it's not the same," Crosby said. "It's kind of looked upon as a small place, and you don't always have the matching equipment teams from bigger cities or bigger teams have. I tried to help out with some things.

"No matter where you are or where you go in life or where it takes you, you always have to remember where you are from," he said. "For me, it's just a way of trying to support a place that I loved growing up and am proud to be from."

LESSONS IN LOSING

A lot of things happen in a season
and you can't always win.

THE PENGUINS LOST their last game of January against the Rangers in New York. It was one of their most embarrassing efforts of the year, a 7-1 defeat in which they mustered only fourteen shots the whole game. Crosby scored the lone goal. Michel Therrien was so disturbed by his team's performance that when he finally strolled into the hallway outside the visitors' dressing room, he could barely bring himself to speak. The look of disgust on his face said everything. "I don't have anything to say. It was an embarrassing performance . . . an embarrassing performance." A scheduling quirk had the Penguins off for three days and then returning to Madison Square Garden for a rematch to start February. There wasn't much to do except return to Pittsburgh and practise. And Crosby caught a cold.

MADISON SQUARE GARDEN, NEW YORK, NEW YORK, FEBRUARY 1, 2006: While his teammates practised the morning of the Rangers game, Sidney sat out with a cold and chatted with Nathan

Welton, a boyhood friend from Cole Harbour who played with the Moncton Wildcats of the Quebec league. The Wildcats were on a team trip to New York. Crosby enjoyed seeing old friends on the road. It gave him a lift.

Sitting in the visitors' dressing room, he looked as though he had lost some weight. He had a throat so sore it hurt to talk. He sat out the morning skate, padding around the bowels of the Garden in his black athletic underwear and bright yellow Crocs. He cupped a spray bottle of Cepacol in his hand to nurse his sore throat. I asked him how he felt. "Not good," he said, barely above a whisper. "Not good." But he still sat and talked, softly, to the New York reporters for more than a half-hour before Keith Wehner came over, as he always did, and urged him into the shower. Crosby was always the last guy on the bus.

Crosby played that night, lining up alongside Jani Rita and Tomas Surovy. Sick and tired and feeling almost entirely depleted, he probably should have sat out. It wouldn't have made any difference. He had four goals and eleven assists in thirteen games, but the Penguins had only won one game in that stretch. He was learning that no matter how hard he played and how much he contributed, he couldn't do it all. The Penguins now had a 12-30-10 record, the fewest wins in the Eastern Conference, and the second-worst record among all thirty teams, just ahead of the dreadful St. Louis Blues.

The evening began badly for Sidney, whose timing was off in his illness. During a Penguins power play early in the game, his pass along the blue line was intercepted by Rangers forward Steve Rucchin. The six foot two, 211-pound winger from Thunder Bay, Ontario, raced up the ice on a short-handed breakaway and scored, giving New York a 1-0 lead just four minutes into the first period. The Penguins would go on to lose 3-1. They had won just once in their last fourteen games.

In particularly trying times, Crosby would look to a handful of motivational sayings and poems he had collected over the years. They helped him focus his goals. Some of them hung on his bedroom wall at the Lemieux house, given to him by family and close friends. He modelled himself after his favourite, from Paul "Bear" Bryant: It's not the will to win that matters, everyone has that. It's the will to prepare to win that matters. "That covers not just hockey, but life. It's a good one for me. The way I look at it, I want to win, but the thing that keeps me sharp and able to rise above is to prepare. No matter what you have accomplished before, you can accomplish more. You're never too good, you can always prepare more."

Another favourite is from the tennis player Arthur Ashe: Success is a journey, not a destination. "This is more of a team one. You can win five games in a row and it doesn't mean anything. You have to look at it over a long period of time."

One from Oliver Wendell Holmes also resonated for him: Greatness is not in where we stand, but in what direction we are moving. We must sail sometimes with the wind and sometimes against it, but sail we must and not drift, nor lie at anchor. He kept it framed in his childhood bedroom.

"That's one I really like," he said. "It tells you there are tough times and good times, but if you just focus on your goal, that's the main thing. To be honest, I don't seek that stuff out too much. Sometimes people in my life give them to me, and those are meaningful. But the ones I've found I like, I just kind of stick to those. I've had the same calendar for three years. I found stuff I like and can relate to, and they're just little reminders when I need them."

This winter, one of the toughest of his life so far, his father gave him one about the importance of not giving up. He took it to heart nearly every day.

"Sometimes things seem so far away and really they're so close," Crosby said. "Sometimes when things seem the toughest, the easy part might be just around the corner. The quote was perfect for this year, because when things seemed so bad, and losing all the time, and never having gone through it before, the easy thing to do would be to give up. Then you feel twice as bad, because you feel bad when you're losing, and you'd feel bad because you gave up. Digging deep and trying to make positives out of it, you have more fun playing, and you can look yourself in the mirror. There's a Lance Armstrong quote I like. He said quitting lasts forever. That's true. When you quit, there's no way after that to make it better. Even if you regroup and make good on it, eventually you still have to live with the time that you quit. Me, I'm so hard on myself I'd never be able to live with that."

SCOTIABANK PLACE, KANATA, ONTARIO, FEBRUARY 6, 2006:
By now, the Penguins were just limping towards the Olympic break that would see the NHL shut down for two weeks.

The week before, Ottawa had scored three short-handed goals against the Penguins in Pittsburgh, but the Penguins struck first in this rematch when Ryan Malone and John LeClair rushed in and lured goaltender Ray Emery out of his crease. Malone put the puck into an open net. It was his thirteenth goal of the season.

Ottawa evened things up a short time later, and on the Penguins' first power play, Crosby rang one off the post. With two minutes left in the second period, Dany Heatley dragged Sidney to the ice with a high stick in the face near the Ottawa blue line. This time referee Eric Furlatt called a penalty and even skated over to check on Crosby. He was still fighting a low-grade cold.

A sign in the crowd announced in big block letters: Nova Scotia misses you. Go Sidney Crosby! And that night, Crosby was the answer to a question on *Jeopardy*.

By a minute into the third period, the Senators had scored five goals and would eventually win 7-2.

There were several bright spots in those long weeks leading up to the Olympics, and they emerged the weekend before the scheduled break began.

The Penguins won big road games against the high-flying Carolina Hurricanes and beat the Capitals again, this time in Washington. And Crosby ranked among the top five Canadian scorers in the NHL with twenty-eight goals and sixty-five points. In goals, he trailed only Philadelphia's Simon Gagné, Carolina's Eric Staal, Ottawa's Dany Heatley, and San José's Jonathan Cheechoo.

Although many Canadians roundly agreed that Crosby might be a bit young when there were so many experienced veterans to choose from before the Olympics opened, that view promptly changed when the chosen players flopped and Team Canada was prematurely bounced from Turin by the Russians. Canada fell in a stunning 2-0 loss in the quarter-final and failed to even make the medal round.

In a cruel irony for the Canadians, Alexander Ovechkin scored the game-winning goal while Todd Bertuzzi, the most controversial selection to the team, was in the penalty box serving time for a needless infraction.

When Russia's Viktor Kozlov pounced on a loose puck and fed it up to Ovechkin to fire, Martin Brodeur, who was playing with a lingering knee injury and was Canada's best player in Turin, didn't have a chance. The game-losing combination of Ovechkin and Bertuzzi was painful but poetic for those who believed in Crosby.

The Penguins defenceman Sergei Gonchar, who drew the Bertuzzi penalty, told reporters in Turin that Crosby would have been a huge asset for the Canadians. "The big ice would be an advantage for a guy like him. He has great speed, great vision. His style fits this game perfectly."

In an interview with NBC's Bob Costas after the loss, Wayne Gretzky defended his decision to leave the teenager off the team. "Sidney Crosby is going to get his chance, and he's a phenomenal young player. I mean this with great respect, you take a player like Ovechkin; he's twenty years old. Sidney is eighteen. Two years is a huge difference. Experience and everything goes with that. We quite honestly thought, why put Sidney in this position? We know in 2010 he's going to be one of the leaders and maybe even the captain of this hockey club."

Crosby didn't watch every game Team Canada played. He spent part of his week off at home in Cole Harbour with his parents and sister, and then flew to Rimouski to visit old friends from the Oceanic. There he skated to keep in shape. He watched three of Canada's five games – the easy win over the Italians, the loss to Switzerland, and the final game against the Russians that sent Team Canada packing. Even as the embarrassment in Turin caused Canadians to cry Where was Sidney?, they also wondered why Staal and Spezza, who were on the taxi squad but didn't play, weren't given a chance.

Crosby didn't waste the break pouting in front of the television. His sense of self was too finely tuned. He had dealt with the feelings over being snubbed by the selection committee long before the Olympic torch had even been lit. He was pretty pragmatic for a teenager. "I got past it," he said. "The first game, I was wishing I was there, but once the first game was over, I realized I wasn't going to be part of it and just became more of a fan, watching it, and just pulling for them. It was so tight toward the end. They were pressing and I was pulling for them. It was tough to see them go out like that."

He would not criticize Gretzky's decision to leave him at home. Did he think he could have made a difference? "I don't think I asked that of myself. I knew I wasn't going to be there. I would have loved to have tried to have helped, to be a part of it, but it is way too hard to tell when the level of play is so high. I don't think it's right to question. I'm not going to put myself in a situation I'm not in. But I would have loved to have been there."

Many Canadians felt the same way. Reader mail started to pour onto the *Globe and Mail*'s Web site minutes after the loss, second-guessing Gretzky's choices and questioning whether he was capable of building a winning team for 2010.

Even though Team Canada boasted $97.9 million worth of NHL talent and thirteen forwards who had scored more than 280 goals so far this season – big-time offensive threats such as Joe Sakic and Jarome Iginla, Dany Heatley and Joe Thornton – they were shut out in three of their last four games. They couldn't score. They managed three goals in the first period of a 3-2 win over the Czech Republic in the preliminary round, but that was it. Even Gretzky was flummoxed. "It's one of those questions we don't have an answer to. When you lose, typically people point fingers at the quality players, superstars. But to go eleven of twelve periods without scoring, it's not one or two or three players, it's collectively the whole team."

The power play was dreadful; Canada was zero-for-eight against Russia, and five-for-thirty-nine in six games. Sidney's creativity and jump would surely have helped. It was the first time Canada failed to reach the semi-finals in the three times since full participation of NHL players began with the 1998 Games in Nagano, Japan, where Canada lost the bronze medal game.

Gretzky had bet on experience to defend the gold medal won in 2002 when Mario Lemieux was captain. Crosby, who watched hockey as a fan – something he didn't get to do too often because he was usually playing – felt as pained as the average Canadian. "It was tough, being Canadian, and just kind of being in that mode of being a fan, you want to see them win. I guess when you're Canadian, your expectations are a gold medal. It's always been like that. I don't think it's going to change. I think that's a great way to be, but it does put a lot of pressure on the guys playing. I think, as a fan, it was tough to see. From a player's point of view and having played for them before, I can feel close to what the players are going through, because it's never easy when you lose, especially when you're Canadian, when the expectations are so high. I guess I felt that a little bit too.

"You have to kind of go through your tough times to make the other ones better. I think we all learn from those. But definitely, there's a lot of pressure to play when you're Canadian."

He was surprised Team Canada failed to score many goals, but also empathized. As he was learning the hard way this year, sometimes in hockey your best intentions, for whatever reason, simply don't work. "The one thing you can't overlook that some people maybe just watching as fans might not realize – maybe from a player's point of view it's easier to see – is it's different ice out there. It's bigger ice. A lot of those guys on a lot of those [European] teams grew up playing on that bigger ice, and that's something that if you really watched the tournament, a lot of teams seem to, right from the start, try to use that to their advantage. That was their thought process, especially playing a North American team, to control that ice. If anything was a weakness of Canada, I think it was that they probably weren't able to adapt to that as fast as maybe other guys. Since they weren't used to playing on that ice, they maybe didn't know how to use it as well."

The Europeans were faster and better skaters. They used the big ice to their advantage, and they used it against the Canadians, who looked flat-footed, and slow, and unresponsive far too often. Crosby may have been watching as a fan, but he had made mental notes as a player.

"In the games they lost, from what I watched, teams were taking away the middle, keeping shots to the outside. If you get a goalie that plays well and you do that, it's anyone's game. It's a tight game when that happens. It can be any-one's game. I think that was where the difference was. In the years before, they seemed to get ahead of teams and it was easier. But when it's close like that, it only takes one mistake, and it's in your net and it's tough to get back into it."

Was Canada too slow?

"From watching it, there were certain times . . . but there were certain times when they were dominating too. I don't think it's fair to say they were a step slow, because there were times when, for half a period, they were in the other team's end, cycling and getting chances. I think the main thing is, it's always easy to criticize after the fact and say 'What if?' But the reality of it is, you can't win every time. You can't win every gold medal in hockey. That's the expec-tations of playing for Canada, to win gold, but sometimes it's not going to happen. Maybe sometimes it takes those mistakes to make you want it more the next time."

Did he expect to see himself playing for Team Canada and leading them in 2010 when the Olympic Games came to Vancouver? He answered cautiously.

"I have no idea. That's up to the guys who are going to make the decisions, to pick the team. But especially with the Olympics being in Canada, I'm sure they're going to want to put on a great performance, really put a good team together. That's a long way away. You have to realize it also has to do with who's having great seasons at that time, who has momentum. A lot of things can happen. We'll have to just wait and see what pans out when the time comes."

Even though Crosby thought of himself as more of "a small ice player," he was looking forward to having a chance to represent Canada at the International Ice Hockey

Federation World Championship tournament being held in Riga, Latvia, in May. Canada finished second to the Czech Republic the previous year in Vienna. Teams at this annual event were made up of the best players not participating in the NHL playoffs; some deeply patriotic players such as Detroit's Brendan Shanahan flew over to join Team Canada as soon as the Red Wings were bounced from the playoffs. Others, such as Calgary's Jarome Iginla and Toronto's Mats Sundin, had played at the Olympics and passed. Crosby hadn't yet received an invitation, but the Penguins weren't going to the playoffs. He almost definitely would be hearing from coach Marc Habscheid.

"I'd love to go if I'm asked," he said. "It's going to be tough not being in the playoffs, but I just want to keep playing hockey as long as I can."

If he had a good tournament, it would show up Gretzky's decision to pass on him for the Olympics and cement him in the minds of Canadians as the future of Team Canada.

The atmosphere in the Penguins' dressing room was much lighter when the NHL got back to business after the Olympics.

They had two days before their next game against the Ottawa Senators, and had been practising for four days in what had felt more like a training camp and less like serious practice with games on the horizon.

Even though the Penguins had finished the pre-Olympic leg of the season strong with road wins at Carolina and Washington, they were still 14-34-11 and all but mathematically eliminated from the playoffs. There was no realistic chance they would recover from the horrible start that doomed their season. It was over weeks ago. But until now, the players had found it impossible to admit. Suddenly, it seemed okay to acknowledge that they weren't making the playoffs and that some guys might be playing for other reasons, like pride, or their jobs next season. Maybe it was the cheering effects of the beach vacations many of the players had been on. As they shucked their sweaty practice sweaters and shin pads aside, you could see Ric Jackman's chest was burned bright red. Ryan Malone's calves were tanned. Even Colby Armstrong, the fairest-skinned of all the Penguins, sported a pink nose. Marc-Andre Fleury's flexible frame was the colour of honey. Most of the guys had gone to Jamaica with their girlfriends; a few others went to Aruba. Mark Recchi was also tanned. He had taken his family to Turks and Caicos. Everyone seemed relaxed and rested. Even I felt refreshed. I sensed the remainder of the season was going to go by quickly.

Crosby sat in his dressing stall and pulled off his jersey, tossing it into the laundry cart. He kidded Armstrong about his pale chest and legs, but Sidney's complexion was also winter white. He split his week off between his parents' home in Cole Harbour and old junior hockey friends in Rimouski, where temperatures fell to minus thirty-four degrees Celsius for a couple of days, and a snowstorm left him stranded in a buddy's house for a day and a half.

"I wasn't really into going south," he said. "I like the beach, but I kind of thought I needed something else. That's the kind of thing I'd do at the end of a season, rather than in the middle of it. It's fun, but for me . . ." His voice trailed off. "It wasn't the right time for that."

His former junior team, the Oceanic, was having a parallel season to the Penguins', that is to say an awful one. While Crosby had led them to the Memorial Cup finals the previous year, where they lost to the Ottawa 67s, this season they had plummeted to last place in the QMJHL standings.

Crosby's former coach and his friend Donald Dufresne asked him to come and talk to his old team about something he was also learning this year: losing and how to live with it.

It was part pep talk, part counselling session, and Crosby found it helpful to talk things over out loud.

"It was like a big self-help group," he said with a knowing smile. "It was funny, because all the things I was trying to tell them are what I've been trying to tell myself all year. It just made me realize a lot of things happen in a season, and you can't always win. To go back there, you realize really how far you've come. Some guys there are wanting so bad to be drafted, and it's even tougher for them to have a season like that. And you realize you could be losing there or losing in the NHL. It puts things in perspective."

Much of the time in Rimouski was spent with his close friend Mark Tobin. Tobin was a twenty-year-old, hulking left-winger on the Oceanic and a Tampa Bay Lightning prospect from St. John's, Newfoundland, who hadn't been able to break into the NHL as easily as Crosby had. "It was good to talk to someone who is going through the same thing, who can relate," he said. "We all feel the same thing when we don't win, when things don't go right."

On what amounted to the closest thing he had had to a mid-winter holiday since he was a toddler, in the frigid Quebec countryside Tobin and Crosby forgot about their problems and reverted to acting out their boyhood dreams.

Donald Dufresne built an outdoor rink at his home each winter, and Crosby and his friends and teammates played shinny for fun and competed for their own, make-believe Stanley Cup. A few years ago, Crosby fashioned a replica Stanley Cup out of a small garbage can and a bowl, using a label-maker to add the winner's names. Who won this time? "I did," he giggled. "I always do." It would have to do for now. Crosby was the brightest of a few bright spots in this awful season, but he had weathered his own problems, and even for someone with his innate optimism and uncanny perspective, these were titanic ups and downs for a teenager.

John Muckler, the Ottawa Senators general manager who won five Stanley Cups as an assistant and head coach with the Edmonton Oilers in the eighties, had watched Gretzky struggle with some of the very same issues – diving and problems with the officials, for two – up close. And he also watched as Gretzky's fame exploded and he became the best player in the game. To Muckler, Crosby's early career was following a similar trajectory and in some ways was even tougher.

"The expectations for him were so high, probably unfairly so," Muckler said one day when I approached him with the question during a Senators morning skate at the Igloo. "He's had an exceptional year for an eighteen-year-old player. He put a lot of pressure on himself. He came in with the expectation he was going to carry this hockey club, and good for him. You've got to respect that. But it's the NHL, and you're going to find out the hard way it's going to be difficult."

Muckler, a white-haired maven who had a reputation as one of the wisest hockey men around, said he thought Crosby was learning very well how to rise above the challenges.

In practice with his teammates, Crosby looked refreshed. And even though they started things off with a loss to the Senators, he had a fresh view. Crosby thought maybe the Penguins were trying too hard. "Sometimes we're looking for a perfect play. It's a pretty simple game. Sometimes we try to be too fancy."

There were twenty-two games left in the season, and he had sixty-five points, six behind Ovechkin. He said he wasn't thinking about the Calder Trophy, because it wasn't something he had any control over.

A few people who were close to him shook their heads when I asked about it. He was too competitive not to want it, but he would chase it in his own quiet way.

Near the end of the awful 2003-2004 season, the Penguins made an improbable stretch run, going 12-5-3 to finish after losing seventeen of eighteen games. It seemed unlikely that history would repeat, and at this point it might have been better for the Penguins to finish dead last and have the best chance of winning the first pick in the draft. That would see their season come unexpectedly full circle, right back where it began last July.

With twenty-two of their twenty-three remaining games against teams still fighting for a spot in the playoffs, it was going to be tough. Still, guys like Colby Armstrong and Michel Ouellet and Ryan Whitney were playing for jobs. Crosby was playing for the rookie scoring title.

19

THE KIDS ARE ALL RIGHT

I can't save the league all by myself.

IT WAS SOMETHING to ponder that after Crosby was left off the Olympic team, it was Alexander Ovechkin who scored the goal that sent Canada home. Evgeni Malkin, the phenomenally gifted nineteen-year-old who was the Penguins' number two draft pick in 2004 and would likely suit up for Pittsburgh in 2006-2007 when he was released from his Russian team, had also been a big asset for the Russians in Turin.

"They're not your typical rookies or younger guys," Crosby said. "They play a lot older. They obviously have the chance to go there, and they're trying to do their best to show that they belong. It's great for hockey in general to have young guys who can bring some excitement, who can contribute at such a young age, because those guys are only going to get better."

Whenever talk surfaced about Crosby saving the NHL, he was quick to point out that he was not the only rookie or young star on the rise deserving of attention. He knew the expectations that were on him, and he was willing to do his part, but as he said one day, "I can't save the league all by myself." As it turned out, he wouldn't have to.

With Ovechkin, Dion Phaneuf, the terrific Calgary Flames defenceman, and Henrik Lundqvist, the New York Rangers goaltender, there were plenty of rookie players this season to entertain and usher in the new league. But most of the focus was on the one-two rookie scoring leaders, the ones with the most highlight reel clips, Ovechkin and Crosby.

The last game before the Penguins broke for the Olympics brought the rookie rivals together again in Washington, D.C.

The Penguins were flying as high as they had been all year. The night before, in Carolina, they had beaten one of the best teams in the NHL, a squad that had managed to find an almost perfect balance of youth and experience and used their speed to simply overwhelm opponents on their way to the Stanley Cup finals. But the Penguins prevailed 4-3 in their last meeting through effort and hard work. They looked like a different team. Crosby had scored and held his own against Rod Brind'Amour, one of the best faceoff men in the business.

The first two times Ovechkin and Crosby had met had been in Pittsburgh at the Igloo. Their first meeting in the U.S. capital was also the first time in three games that Crosby's and Ovechkin's lines played opposite each other for part of the game. Sergei Gonchar, who had previously played for the Capitals, was heckled every time he touched the puck. Gonchar, who was still struggling, was going to the Olympics, where he would play with Ovechkin on the

Russian team. The Penguins were quietly hoping he might rediscover his game and return more like his old self.

In the first period, Marc-Andre Fleury made a spectacular pad save on Ovechkin, who blew through three Penguins on his way down the ice, stickhandling the puck at top speed.

The Penguins won 6-3. Crosby had a goal and an assist, and Ovechkin also scored. They both played well, but it was another former number one pick who really shone. Marc-Andre Fleury had one of his best games of the year, stopping thirteen unanswered Capitals shots and making thirty-six saves in the game. The veterans came up big too. Recchi had a goal and four assists, Gonchar had a goal and three assists, and LeClair had a goal and two assists.

Therrien was happy with the effort. The Penguins killed all five Washington power plays. As badly as everyone wanted the break, they also felt momentum was striking at an inopportune time. Recchi, who was in charge of shadowing Ovechkin during the game and did a fine job, wanted to keep on playing after a win like that.

Sidney was happy in the press scrum. He was looking forward to the break. "I'm just glad to be going home." His dad had a friend with a four-wheeler who could groom the pond, and Crosby was hoping he might get a chance to get out on Bissett Lake in Cole Harbour for some pond hockey.

Tomas Surovy had packed up and was leaving for the airport, where he would fly to Turin to join the Slovakian team. Crosby leaped up and sprinted across the room to shake his hand and wish him luck. Going to the Olympics would have been great, but Crosby was now looking forward even more to relaxing and getting away from hockey for a bit. He needed to recharge. It had already been a long season, and there were still two months left to go. The Penguins' fourth and final meeting with the Capitals in Washington was won by Ovechkin, who led a 6-3 victory. He had a goal and two assists. Crosby was held to just one assist. But the season edge easily went to Sidney.

The rookie seasons of top draft picks in every sport, from hockey to football, baseball, and basketball, have unfolded with both greatness and ignominy, with stops everywhere in between.

A few special players, like Mario Lemieux, are spectacular from their very first seasons or, in his case, his very first shift. In a definite sign that the new era had arrived and Lemieux would never play again, during the Olympic break he underwent successful surgery to restore his natural heart rhythm, a procedure known as ablation. He spent one night in the hospital and returned home to recuperate. It wasn't too long before he was out on the golf course, his other passion, a good sign he was on the mend.

As March got underway, Crosby had twenty-eight goals and thirty-seven assists. He was averaging better than a point a game; it was already a given that he would finish the year with one of the better rookie seasons on record under his belt. It was difficult to ignore what he was accomplishing, especially given his age.

"The age difference is a big, big thing," John Davidson said. "It's impossible to compare."

Teemu Selänne was twenty-two when he scored 132 points for the Winnipeg Jets in 1992-1993. Peter Stastny had 109 points for the Quebec Nordiques in 1980-1981, and he was twenty-four years old. Joe Juneau of the Boston

Bruins was an ancient twenty-five in 1992-1993, his rookie year, and put up 102 points.

Dale Hawerchuk of the Winnipeg Jets had the best rookie season in history for an eighteen-year-old, putting up 103 points in 1981-1982. He turned nineteen on April 4, the last day of the season. Lemieux was also nineteen years old when his rookie season ended.

Mike Bossy put up ninety-one points as a twenty-one-year-old rookie for the New York Islanders in 1977-1978. A decade later, Joe Nieuwendyk of the Calgary Flames, also twenty-one, scored ninety-two.

For every Mario Lemieux, there is an Owen Nolan, a highly touted rookie winger who was drafted by the Nordiques, but had just thirteen points before being demoted to the minor leagues for much of the season.

For every Hawerchuk, who led the Jets to the greatest single-season turnaround in NHL history, there is a Joe Murphy, the Detroit Red Wings centre from Michigan State University who in 1986-1987 had just one assist in five games and spent the rest of the season in the minors, his career never reaching the heights expected of him.

Eric Lindros, whose start in the NHL was delayed for a season when he refused to report to the Nordiques because he didn't want to play in Quebec, had a good freshman year when he finally did play with the Philadelphia Flyers in 1992-1993. He had forty-one goals and thirty-one assists for seventy-two points, even though he only played in sixty-one games. He had size and skill, soft hands and a scoring touch, but his promising career was repeatedly set back by serious concussions and an ongoing feud with Flyers general manager Bobby Clarke. Lindros, for all his talents, seemed star-crossed. Indeed, he missed most of this season with the Maple Leafs because of an injured wrist.

Guy Lafleur had sixty-four points in seventy-three games for Montreal in 1971-1972; Rick Nash had thirty-nine points in 2002-2003 for Columbus.

But highly touted Vincent Lecavalier, who, like Crosby, also came out of Rimouski, struggled to put up just twenty-eight points in eighty-two games on a terrible Tampa Bay Lightning team in 1998-1999. Lecavalier developed into a worthy NHL star, team captain, and won a Stanley Cup with the Lightning in 2003-2004.

Much-hyped Alexander Daigle was considered a colossal failure when he scored fifty-one points with the Ottawa Senators in 1993-1994. His career never really recovered. He was supposed to save the Senators franchise; they were accused of deliberately losing late in the season in order to win the right to draft him. He never lived up to his potential and bounced around to five teams, including the Minnesota Wild for this season.

Some kids are just horribly unlucky. Ilya Kovalchuk was on a steady scoring pace with fifty-one points through sixty-five games when a shoulder injury ended his season.

But no one had it tougher than Joe Thornton, the rangy centre from St. Thomas, Ontario, who was supposed to save the Bruins as an eighteen-year-old in his first season. He broke his forearm in the pre-season and battled several viruses throughout the season. He scored just three goals and had only four assists, and spent much of the fifty-five games he played in on the bench. When he was still in Boston, before he was traded in November to San José, he reflected on his rookie year and the sore luck he weathered.

How did he think Crosby would handle the Penguins' losing ways?

"He's going to be fine," said Thornton, the top pick in the 1997 draft. "He's so good and so explosive. He plays a lot and he's playing well. They'll turn it around for him. It's rough right now for him, I'm sure, but he's got so much going for him, he's already one of the best players on the team. My first season, man, it was terrible. I spent most of it watching from the bench. In hindsight, I probably learned a lot. At the time you don't realize that, but you still would rather have been playing."

Thornton, at twenty-six years old, would get his day, however. In the stunning trade that sent him to the Sharks for three youngsters, the centre would go on to lead all skaters in points with 125 and turn linemate Jonathan Cheechoo into the league's top sniper with fifty-six goals along the way.

Even though Ovechkin had been staying ahead of him in the scoring race, Crosby was having a memorable rookie season. He had only missed one game with the flu; eighty points was well within reach.

Although most number one draft picks come into the league with high expectations, very few come in bearing the pressures that Crosby did. There are few in sports history – LeBron James may be the only parallel – who came in with the attention that Crosby had.

"The world has changed," Ken Sawyer said. "He's had media coverage far greater than Mario or Gretzky ever had."

The lockout created a double cohort of draft classes, the strongest crop of rookies in years, arguably ever.

Ovechkin and Crosby grabbed most of the headlines, but

other kids impressed immediately. Phaneuf, Brad Boyes in Boston, Marek Svatos in Colorado, Lundqvist in New York, Thomas Vanek in Buffalo, and Cam Ward in Carolina, who led his team to the Stanley Cup finals, performed better than expected. How else to explain that Crosby was on pace for 100 points but not actually considered the front-runner for the Calder Trophy?

In the 2003-2004 season, ten first-year players scored more than thirty points, with Newfoundland's Michael Ryder of the Montreal Canadiens on top with sixty-three, including twenty-five goals. He was the Calder runner-up to Boston Bruins goaltender Andrew Raycroft.

In a nod to the double draft class, and also to the increase in scoring, in the 2005-2006 season, thirty players had thirty points or better, and two, Crosby and Alexander Ovechkin, had 100 in their sights.

The best part for NHL general managers was that the new collective bargaining agreement meant that these players came at bargain prices.

Among rookie goaltenders, the Rangers' Swedish wunderkind Henrik Lundqvist posted thirty wins and a remarkable 2.24 goals-against-average and .922 save percentage.

The Sabres' Ryan Miller, the Senators' Ray Emery, the Flyers' Antero Niittymaki, and the Hurricanes' Cam Ward had terrific regular seasons and did well into the playoffs. Miller carried Buffalo to the Eastern Conference finals.

In a season that saw veteran stars such as Jagr and Thornton rediscover their scoring prowess, the rookies left the biggest impression. It signalled a generational shift. "I'm really impressed with the rookie crop, not just the obvious ones, but there have been so many rookies this year who have added depth and played great," John Davidson said. Crosby was already one of the most important players in the NHL, he said. He couldn't wait to see what happened next season.

"I didn't even know how to write out a cheque properly in my first year," Davidson said with a laugh. "Sidney's come such a long way already. In some ways, it's really remarkable. Can you imagine how much he'll understand about the business going into next season? How the league works, how to beat defencemen, how to beat goaltenders, how to prepare, how to practise, how to travel, how to live?

"He's already got it going on. The Calder is a nice reward, but it's not that big of a deal. I think Sidney is probably very happy in his own skin and with what's happened this season."

Hockey was recovering well, and the kids were a big reason why.

Jack Riley, the former general manager of the Penguins in the late sixties and early seventies, believed that Crosby's playing style would eventually define a whole new type of hockey player for generations to come.

At eighty-six, Riley figured to have watched some 5,000 hockey games over the years, and has seen all the greats up close. He said Crosby's speed and strength, timing and vision, coupled with his well-measured mix of grit and finesse, make him unlike anyone who has come before.

"I've never seen a kid like him," he said. "He doesn't play like Mario; he doesn't play like Gretzky. He has a little of Peter Forsberg in him. He passes like Orr. But really, he's one of a kind. He plays like Crosby. And one day in the future, I think we're going to see a whole crop of young players coming up who are compared to him.

"The first time I saw him, I didn't believe he was eighteen years old. And sometimes I still don't. He's got a thirty-five-year-old head on an eighteen-year-old body."

He had already done much more than anyone expected, even if that was true of Ovechkin as well.

"The young players in the league are the best players in the league right now," Eddie Johnston said. "Crosby, Phaneuf, Ovechkin, Staal, Spezza . . . they are the most exciting to watch of everyone out there. They're all great. All of them."

Before the Senators and Penguins met again in March, Senators forward Daniel Alfredsson told the *Ottawa Sun* that Ovechkin wasn't simply the best rookie, but that he was the best player in the whole league and worthy of MVP. He said he admired the Russian's toughness and took a shot at Crosby.

"He doesn't get frustrated if he gets hit, either. He gets up and keeps playing. Not like the other rookie, Crosby, who starts crying. I think there's a big difference in the attitude."

On the day of the game, after making reporters who wanted to talk to him about the matter wait for an hour, Alfredsson snappishly said he hadn't expected "such a big deal" to be made of his words. "It got overblown. I don't know how he's going to think about it. I think he's a great player, and there's no question about it. I wouldn't make a big deal out of it. But that's what I would do."

I asked if he regretted calling Crosby a crybaby. "I didn't call him a crybaby," Alfredsson snapped. "Don't put words in my mouth. But with the media, sometimes you have to really pay attention to what you say. When I said it, I knew right away the way it would be made a bigger deal than I wanted it to be. But that's the way it goes. I should know better, I guess."

Crosby couldn't be drawn into talking about Alfredsson's comments, but they had pissed off Therrien. After the game, which the Senators dominated to win 5-2 – Crosby was held to one assist – the Penguins coach said he'd had enough of comments like Alfredsson's. He was perplexed why anyone felt they had to knock Sidney in order to compliment Alex.

"We hear a lot of comments and look . . . the kid's been terrific. He's doing more than he's been asked of by the NHL. It's sad to hear the comments. He's only eighteen years old. I don't want to take anything away from Ovechkin. He's a great player and has been really good for the league, but you have to understand that two years is such a big difference at that age."

Crosby gamely talked about the Calder race when asked, but after the Olympic break he seemed convinced he wasn't going to win it. Ovechkin was ahead of him by eleven points with ten games left. Crosby seemed more relaxed, as if the pressure was finally off him with everyone expecting him to come in second. He seemed as carefree as he had been all season.

On March 9, Mark Recchi was traded. It wasn't a surprise. He and LeClair had been the Penguins' main trade bait. Recchi, who had signed a three-year contract with a no-trade clause in 2004 to return to the team where he started his career, waived his no-trade clause when the playoff-bound Hurricanes called. In return, the Penguins would get Niklas Nordgren, Krystofer Kolanos, and a second-round pick in 2007. They also picked up Andy Hilbert on waivers from the Blackhawks and sent Ric Jackman to the Panthers, turning the Penguins overnight into one of the youngest teams in the league. In saying goodbye to Recchi, they lost a proven winner and a veteran leader whose vocal personality may have hurt his relationships with some of the Penguins' younger players, including Crosby, who was tactful discussing Recchi's departure. He called him a "great leader."

Later that afternoon, Crosby left the stick he had used to score his first NHL point next to Mark's mailbox with a note attached. Sidney wished him well and asked him to sign the stick for his collection. "Rex, good luck in Carolina, they have a heck of a team. I'll be cheering for you," the note read. If there had been bad feelings between them, they certainly seemed in the past.

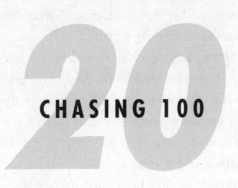

CHASING 100

He may downplay it, but I'm thinking about it for him.

ON MARCH 29, Sidney Crosby was sitting on eighty points, a prodigious production for any hockey player of any age in any era, never mind a teenaged rookie on a bad team.

Before the season began, *The Hockey News* predicted Crosby would lead all rookie scorers with eighty-one points – thirty-three goals and forty-eight assists. He was already almost there with thirty-two goals and the number of assists called for by hockey's bible. He had already done better than even the experts anticipated, and there were still ten games left to play.

By any measure, except maybe Crosby's own, he had already guaranteed himself an outstanding rookie season. Although with so few games left, it seemed unlikely that even if all went reasonably well he would finish with many more than ninety points. But after the Olympic break, Dee Rizzo made a bold prediction to Sidney's father: his son would finish with at least 100 points. Troy thought his buddy was crazy – 100 points?

The last stretch of the season would be hectic. Between March 31 and April 11, the Penguins would play a game on Long Island, return home to face the Devils, and then set out for four games in New Jersey, Florida, Tampa, and Philadelphia. It was the second-longest road trip of the season, but the team was looking forward to it. They played the Panthers at home on Friday night, the Lightning on Saturday. They had been promised a day off on Sunday, and would practise Monday morning in Tampa before flying to Philadelphia. The scheduled break in the sunny south at the end of a long season was a rare treat, and everyone, including the writers and broadcasters making the trip, was dying to get the next few games over with and get down to Florida. Crosby was looking forward to seeing what he could do with the final ten games of his rookie season.

NASSAU VETERANS COLISEUM, UNIONDALE, NEW YORK, MARCH 31, 2006: The Penguins shut out the Islanders 4-0, giving Sebastien Caron his first shutout of the season and moving Crosby ahead. He scored his thirty-third goal of the year and set up two others. The three-point night gave him eighty-three with nine left to play. March was going out like a lion.

Two nights later, at the Igloo, Crosby scored his thirty-fourth goal just 1:55 into a game against the Devils and set up Colby Armstrong for his fifty-first assist just as the first period was winding down. The Penguins would go on to lose 3-2 to the Devils, who were on the playoff bubble in the Eastern Conference and fighting to stay alive, but

Crosby now had eighty-five points and showed no signs of slowing down.

CONTINENTAL AIRLINES ARENA, EAST RUTHERFORD, NEW JERSEY, APRIL 5, 2006:

It was six months to the day since the season had opened, here in the same place Crosby had played his first game as a Pittsburgh Penguin, where he had registered his first NHL point.

It was hard to believe how much had changed since the first game. The Penguins roster barely resembled the one from opening night. Only ten players who were listed on the roster October 5, 2005, were still listed on tonight's roster – Caron, Crosby, Gonchar, Koltsov, LeClair, Malone, Melichar, Orpik, Roy, and Scuderi. By now, even though Crosby was the team's youngest player, he was one of its most veteran members.

Twenty-seven seconds into the game, Crosby pushed past his defender and raced through the slot. He accepted a crisp pass from Armstrong and fired the puck between the pads of Martin Brodeur. The game was barely underway – most of the fans were still making their way to their seats – and Crosby had his thirty-fifth goal of the season.

The Vancouver Canucks scout Lucien DeBlois sat next to me in the press box. He couldn't take his eyes off of Crosby.

"Oh my, he's so strong on his skates," he said, as Crosby fought for the puck near the boards with Devils defenceman Brad Lukowich. His opponent was two inches taller and a dozen pounds heavier but did not look at all stronger.

Crosby plucked the puck from Lukowich's stick and then pulled it through his skates in a figure-eight motion.

He spun 180 degrees away from the Devil, using him as a springboard, and skated away with the puck.

"And to think, he's only eighteen!" DeBlois said. "He's just a phenomenal player. He's everything we expected and heard about, but more. He's got a fifth gear, a quickness that is incredible. It's hard to take him out. Even when he seems off balance, he hardly ever goes down. He's so strong. Young players are often weak on the puck. They haven't grown into their strength potential. Not him. He's so strong."

The Penguins lost again, this time 6-4, but again Crosby kept up the pace with two more points, a goal and an assist. After seventy-five games, number 87 had eighty-seven points.

"It's winding down, and it's going to be a long off-season," he said. "I don't want to have any regrets that I pulled up too early just because we weren't in the playoffs. I want to be able to look at myself in the mirror and know I played the most complete season I was capable of."

In Florida, the Penguins were all over the Panthers, all but eliminated from the post-season. Crosby scored his thirty-sixth goal and added three assists in a 5-1 blowout, giving him ninety-one points on the season with six games left. His efforts in Sunrise, Florida, made him the youngest player in NHL history at eighteen years, 243 days, to reach ninety points, beating Dale Hawerchuk by 100 days. It was an extraordinary mark. Wayne Gretzky managed to score just forty-five points in sixty-nine games before his nineteenth birthday. Hawerchuk scored 103 in seventy-nine games. And now Crosby was second on that list.

He wasn't done yet, but to reach 100 points Sidney would need to average 1.8 points per game before the season ended eleven days from now in Toronto.

He was matter-of-fact. He knew he wasn't going to the playoffs. He knew his rookie season wasn't going to last much longer. He was determined, however, to play as hard as he could. "I'm just going to try and play my best for the rest of the season," he said. "If it happens, it's meant to happen, and if not, that's just the way it goes. I don't want to let up here. The season's not over. This is basically my playoffs, and I want to leave it all out there and finish the best I can."

The Penguins had just twenty wins to their credit, but Crosby was playing the most consistent hockey of the season. He had eleven points in his past five games and had scored at least two points in six of his past eight games.

Meanwhile, in Washington, Ovechkin had stalled. His 100th point was his first goal in seven games, but he was still widely considered the favourite for rookie of the year.

"Regardless of the Calder, we'll have to sit back and marvel at what Sidney has done at eighteen," Tom McMillan marvelled. "Even when you're around hockey for years, it's staggering. Rarely has a teenager played so well. You break into the league when you break in, you can't help when your birthday is, but it's remarkable what Sidney's doing so young with a team in last place. Mario played on a last place team too, but he was old for his draft class. He turned nineteen before the season started."

"One hundred points is huge, huge, especially for an eighteen-year-old," Armstrong said. "It's unbelievable. It's definitely something I want to help him achieve. Maybe he's kind of downplaying it, but it's on my mind for him and it's something I hope he can get to."

Sometimes they would sit around their hotel rooms on the road at night and talk. "We figured out how many games we have left, how many points do we have, how many do we need. It's a big thing for him. It would be a great achievement to get 100 points, and I'm going to try and help get him there."

The desire to help Crosby reach 100 was infectious in the Penguins' dressing room. Everyone wanted to help. It was really fun, those last few weeks, to be around the team. This gave them something to play for, something historic to pursue.

Then, in Tampa, Crosby suffered a mysterious injury that the team would only describe as a lower body injury. Sometime during the first period – no one saw what happened – he left the ice. On television he was shown in his socks, and without his jersey or shoulder pads on, walking slowly.

One of the Lightning equipment managers insisted he use the dressing room telephone to call his parents. He was hungry, and wolfed down an ice cream sandwich. He was still hungry, so the equipment guy brought him a hot dog and a hamburger from the concession stand. He hadn't eaten a hamburger in over a year. When he returned briefly in the third period to see how he would fare on the power play, he felt like throwing up.

After the game, when he came out to talk with a bottle of anti-inflammatory pills tucked into his palm, Crosby kidded good-naturedly about the team's secrecy. "I'm sorry I can't say more," he said. "But I just can't. I'm not trying to be a dickhead."

It was curious. His walk gave nothing away. Whatever his injury was, he kept it well hidden. And it didn't seem to be affecting his play.

He had a goal and an assist against the Flyers in a 4-3 loss, and came out two nights later at home against the Rangers for another goal and three more assists. Everything he touched was perfect that night, and the Penguins beat Jaromir Jagr's Rangers 5-3 to get him to ninety-seven points with three games left. He didn't get any points in the next game against the Islanders, and he wasn't very happy with the way he played. But he only needed three, and there were still two games left.

On April 17, 2006, at the last home game of the year, the Penguins romped over the Islanders, winning 6-1. Crosby wasted no time in taking over the game, assisting on three of the Penguins' first four goals. His first pass set up Andy Hilbert for the game's first goal just sixty-four seconds after the opening faceoff. Nearly five minutes into the second period, he put the puck on Tomas Surovy's stick for a goal. A half-minute later, he touched off the loudest ovation of the season from a standing-room-only sellout crowd.

The point that pushed him to 100 came at 15:44 of the second period. John LeClair knocked the puck over to Crosby, who made a routine, twelve-foot pass to Ryan Malone for the goal on Garth Snow.

With the pass, Crosby joined elite company. Only Dale Hawerchuk, Mario Lemieux, Peter Stastny, Teemu Selänne, Joe Juneau, and Alexander Ovechkin have ever hit triple figures as a rookie.

Crosby shouted and grinned and jumped into Malone's arms. John LeClair rushed to embrace him. Ryan Whitney gave him a bear hug from behind. The crowd went crazy, waving white Penguins T-shirts they had been given at the door and tossing them to the ice. They chanted his name. The game stopped for nearly ten minutes.

"You're only a rookie once," Crosby said afterwards in the dressing room. "You only get one opportunity to do this, and it was nice to be able to, especially here. I scored my first goal here, and it felt very similar. It's nice the way the guys were really pushing for me the last few games, helping me accomplish it. I can't say enough about what they've done to support me."

In the dressing room, his teammates were ebullient. "It's a story I'm going to tell my friends this summer, and one day my kids," Malone said afterwards in the dressing room. "I have no idea what the ceiling is with him. He's already a leader and one of the best I've seen. But he's also a great teammate. He's one of us. He doesn't think he's better than anyone. But he's also unbelievable."

"Imagine how good he is going to be in four or five years," Ryan Whitney enthused. "It's going to be scary."

A few days later, Crosby's memory of the moments after he got his 100th point was the snowstorm of twirling T-shirts as they fell to the ice, the ear-splitting din. "As I was getting closer to 100 and it was building up each time, I can remember with each, ninety-seven, ninety-eight, ninety-nine, I can remember hearing my name and it being very loud. That was awesome."

He had looked up at the scoreboard to watch the replay, and a video of the highlights from his season that Billy Wareham, the team videographer, made the previous day in case Crosby hit 100. It was set to the Rolling Stones song

"Sympathy for the Devil," a fitting, understated choice. Sidney Crosby had definitely introduced himself. And there was no doubt he had been around for a long, long year.

He had some input into the highlight video. His only instruction to Wareham was to make sure it featured plenty of footage of his teammates, especially Colby Armstrong.

Troy Crosby had flown in to see the game, which made Sidney feel proud. He wanted to hit the mark at home, in front of family and friends, and he considered the Igloo crowd a little bit of both. "It was really nice to have my dad there," he said. "It was nice just to do it in front of the home fans. Once I was close, I really wanted to do it. It was a tough year for everyone, not winning games. I don't want to judge myself by points; it doesn't make the season. But it's a pretty nice accomplishment."

The win pulled the Penguins into twenty-ninth place in the NHL, ahead of the St. Louis Blues. No matter what happened now, they would not finish as the worst team in the league. It diminished their chances of winning the first pick in the NHL draft lottery by about 30 per cent.

Sidney won four of a possible seven team awards that night, including best rookie, most valuable player, and the "good guy" award for the patient hours he spent at the disposal of the media through some trying times.

The next morning, shortly before seven o'clock, aboard US Airways flight 4207, I left Pittsburgh for Toronto, the last game of the season. Troy and Dee Rizzo were also on the flight. As we took off, I couldn't believe the journey was almost over and wondered if Troy was feeling the same way. A half-hour into the flight, almost halfway to Toronto, the flight attendant came on the loudspeaker and told us we had to turn around immediately for Pittsburgh because there "was smoke in the cargo hold." On the ground twelve minutes later, a fire truck met us on the runway, and we deplaned and wandered around the airport. It took four hours and many confusing telephone calls to get rebooked on Air Canada, all three of us feeling a little antsy that, after eighty-one games, the idea we might not arrive in time to see the last one simply wasn't acceptable, smoke in the cargo hold or not.

At the Air Canada Centre, a few hours before the final game of his rookie season, Crosby felt wistful. His name was in the NHL record book, and he had little if anything else to prove. It felt as though the season were ending suddenly.

"I tried not to think about it too much because I didn't want to waste my last game," he said. "It's hard for it not to cross your mind. This might be your last time with this group of guys. You don't know what's going to happen next year."

Trina and Taylor also flew in from Halifax to see the conclusion of the trip that began eight months earlier on a crisp autumn night in New Jersey. Crosby scored a goal in the second period and added another assist. His 102 points bettered Mario Lemieux's team rookie record of 100. Lemieux wasn't there; he was on a golfing vacation, but he and Crosby had been text messaging and Lemieux had sent various messages of encouragement, including some good-natured ribbing about his own record perhaps falling. Once again, Crosby felt a little overwhelmed.

"I was trying to be him when I was ten years old," Crosby said with a smile. "So to pass him is pretty special. It's something I'll have for the rest of my life."

He was also in a reflective mood. On the one hand, he couldn't believe it was over. He had only won twenty-two games, but he had 102 points and was his team's best player, pretty much from day one.

"I had no idea what to expect. My goal was just to get comfortable and adjust. I just tried to improve off of that. That was the main thing. In your first year in any league, you want to get your confidence there. I stayed pretty consistent. I think I've gotten better."

Losing so much was easily the worst thing about the season; one of the best was just being here.

"Getting to play against players I've been seeing on TV for so long has been really special," he said. "I finally got a chance to play against them and beat some of them."

Dale Hawerchuk, who holds the record for most points scored by an eighteen-year-old – he scored 103 with the Winnipeg Jets in 1982-1983 and led the club to the biggest single-season turnaround in NHL history – said when I called him up that he had been suitably impressed by Crosby's first season.

"Records are made to be broken," said Hawerchuk, now living on a horse farm in Orangeville, Ontario. "But having said that, it's a lot of points. It was back then and it still is. I think what he's done this season is pretty amazing, considering how much the team struggled. He's definitely worth the price of admission."

The day after the season ended, with players cleaning

out their lockers and taking final meetings with Therrien and getting their summer workout plans from Stephane Dube, Crosby and I sat down to talk one more time before saying goodbye.

On April 8, on a muggy, rain-soaked night in Tampa, with ninety-one points and five games left, Crosby collided with Lightning defenceman Cory Sarich, a six-foot-four, 210-pound brick wall, behind the Tampa net.

The hit did not do damage to his lower body. It separated his shoulder.

"I just hit him and my shoulder popped," Crosby said. "I thought my season was done. When I left the ice that night, I was convinced of it. It's gotten a little bit better, but it's still pretty sore."

With three days between the Tampa game and the Penguins' next game in Philadelphia, Crosby decided to assess the injury day by day and see if the team doctors thought it was okay to continue playing. The team was adamant Crosby's injury be kept a secret. They didn't want opposing players – especially the Flyers – taking a run at their star, aggravating an injury that could affect his career long-term. He also didn't want opposing players at the World Championships, where he was headed after the season, to know.

It was a first-degree separation; his shoulder didn't pop out of the socket, but the joints and tendons spread wide and were badly bruised. He took a non-narcotic to help with the pain but declined a shot to numb it, worried that if he couldn't feel his shoulder he might injure it again. The doctors told him he wasn't likely to separate it again, unless he took the exact same hit. So they called it a lower body injury, and he played with the pain.

"I didn't want to do anything that was going to hurt me for the rest of my hockey career," he said. "But I wanted to get to 100 if I could do it without causing more damage. I was kind of nervous playing in the Philly game."

He scored eleven points in five games with a separated shoulder. He played a slightly gentler game, lurking around the perimeter more, not bullying into the centre of the action. He didn't dish out any big hits for the rest of the season. Crosby chuckled. "I don't know how I did it. I just tried to play and not worry about it. I tried not to be obvious when I hit it. It probably made me skate a lot faster."

Did the kid who grew up on *Rocky* movies feel a little bit the same way this year? Did he think the hard part was finally over? "Yeah, I think so. It's never easy at the end of a season, especially when you're not in the playoffs. It's been a fun year that went by too fast. I don't have any regrets. Next year, my mindset will probably be a lot different. Coming in, I was nervous. I didn't know what to expect. I just wanted to go out there and prove myself, gain confidence and adjust, and I did that.

"Next year I'm not going to be happy just to be playing in the NHL. I'm going to want to win."

21

FOLLOWING SIDNEY CROSBY

Do you think Sidney would go to the prom with me?

THE SEASON I SPENT writing about Sidney Crosby turned out to be a little bit what I imagined following a young Elvis Presley for a year might have been like back in the days when the King was beginning to discover his growing celebrity.

And it also called to mind the book Ed Greenspon had insisted I read when I began the assignment, Gzowski's account of a year spent with a teenaged Gretzky and the Edmonton Oilers. From the first day of Penguins training camp, it was obvious that one of the season's recurring themes would be the crush of attention Crosby weathered and how he would respond with so many eyes on him, especially when all the best-laid plans began to fall apart.

The parallels were frightening at times. Gretzky's and Crosby's stars rose as their respective teams circled the drains. In that year Gzowski chronicled, the Oilers had won just nine games by January. I passed both this tidbit and a copy of the book on to Crosby one day, thinking he might find the resemblances insightful. His eyes bulged. "Nine games? No way. Seriously? I hope we do better than that!" They did, just barely, winning ten by the new year.

Men who had been around hockey a long time, such as Senators general manager John Muckler, and Terry Jones of the *Edmonton Sun*, who reported on Gretzky from his earliest days, saw the parallels too. If Sidney was a whiner, as some said, then he was in awfully elite company.

Crosby, who had given his first newspaper interview to a Halifax daily at seven years old, had gotten used to being the big story as a junior in Rimouski. He was used to mobs of autograph hounds. He was used to planning his outings in the real world. He didn't mind. He loved the NHL life, flying to big cities, staying in hotels. He was playing a game for a living and he didn't take a moment for granted. All of his closest friendships had come from hockey. When pressed, he admitted he might have been a firefighter or a police officer if a job in hockey hadn't been an option, but he didn't want to imagine a life doing anything else.

The thing that stuck with me most from the season was the joy, a simple, pure pleasure that Sidney Crosby took from the game. It was his livelihood, but it was also his love and, in many ways, his life. It is rare to see an athlete in this day and age who takes so much pleasure from playing that he would, in all seriousness, suggest he could help pay part of a teammate's salary if the organization couldn't afford to keep everyone. Crosby wanted the core of young guys – especially Armstrong, Fleury, Hilbert, Murley, Ouellet, Surovy, and Whitney – to stay together and build a Stanley Cup team, just like Gretzky's young Oilers did in the eighties. Over the season, Crosby exhibited untold pragmatism, but he could also be a dreamer. He could afford to be because he understood something about making dreams come true.

When I e-mailed Keith Wehner, the Penguins media relations director, in August 2005 to tell him I hoped to spend the season in Pittsburgh, he and the rest of the organization were intrigued by the idea and were warmly receptive. I fell into step with the regular beat writers, attending home and away games, daily practices, and game-day skates. I had covered sports at the *Globe* for nearly five years before moving to Halifax to work in the Atlantic Canada bureau in 2002. I had covered some big events: Wayne Gretzky's last week in the NHL, Mark McGwire's chase of the home run record held by Roger Maris, several Super Bowls. Covering a team, and in my case focussing almost solely on one person, is admittedly a strange job. You see them almost every day, sometimes several times a day. It makes for an odd and vaguely familial relationship. With most stories, the scene around the centre is often part of the tale. With Sidney, the scene often *was* the story. In those cases, I faded into the background to watch it unfold.

The demands on Crosby's time were a little unreal for a rookie player on a bad team. He had been a big story for years in Canada; he was used to attention and had been through IMG's extensive media training course, learning how to answer questions and deflect controversy. Crosby considered his daily dealings with the press a necessary part of his job as a hockey player. "How are you handling the media attention?" was the naval-gazing query posed to him almost daily for months. "It's like putting on my skates," he would respond.

When he was criticized in the press, as he was in newspapers in Philadelphia and Toronto over perceived whining to officials and diving accusations, he shrugged it off and never fought back with words in the papers. He accepted the attention – good and sometimes bad – with pretty much the same, even demeanour.

"I want to be the best, and whatever comes with that, I have to accept it," he said. "There will never be a time where I step back and say I wish things were different. This comes along with being a hockey player."

At eighteen, he had prepared himself for athletic stardom. The Penguins, however, weren't quite prepared for the level of madness that would surround Crosby and the team the entire season. There was no predicting the drama. With the uncertainty over the team's future, the fight for a new arena, Lemieux's illness and retirement, and the personnel changes, being immersed in the Pittsburgh Penguins' season was not unlike living a sports soap opera.

Sometimes, at the beginning of practice, I would say to Tom McMillan or one of the other writers, well, such-and-such happened yesterday, so nothing else could possibly happen this week, right? But then something would happen, like the week in January when Ziggy Palffy retired, Lemieux put the team up for sale, and then retired himself, all in a span of six days. Things quietened down considerably after that, at least for a while.

I felt lucky to have been a part of Crosby's season from day one. For maybe the first time in my reporting career, instead of being on the outside of something looking in, I felt I was on the inside looking out. At the start of training camp, when I first introduced myself to Sidney and explained that I would be hanging around all season, he was upbeat about it. I told him it was a new kind of assignment for me and that I would be feeling my way along as it went. I told him that if he ever felt claustrophobic about my presence, he should let me know and we could talk about it. He was fine with that. When we were done chatting and he turned to head for the showers, he stopped suddenly and looked back to me. "I just hope I give you something to write about."

That didn't turn out to be a problem.

Covering Crosby's rookie season afforded me almost daily access to the young hockey star. I had not been that intently focussed on an eighteen-year-old boy since I was an eighteen-year-old girl. And at thirty-eight years old, I was suddenly the envy of teenaged girls from Halifax to Harrisburg.

It became a game-night ritual among a few of us in the press box to search for fetching young women in the crowd holding up signs with messages for Sidney. They ranged from sweet to blush-inducing, and some were downright dirty. Among our favourites:

Sidney, score a goal and I'll give you a kiss.

Sidney, will you be my prom date?

Sidney, will you marry me?

Sidney, I love you.

Sidney, put it in my 5 hole.

One young brunette offered up her phone number, written in big black digits so large it could be read and copied down

by the entire crowd. "Sidney, call me at 412-XXX-XXXX."
Crosby didn't call, but someone else might have.

A lot of the e-mails I received from readers at the start
of the season were hockey-themed: how good was he, was
he overrated, was he the best rookie? A few months into
it, my in box got a little more interesting. On the morning
of January 10, an e-mail arrived. It was the first of many
like it.

Hello,
My name is ***** ***** and I'm from Charleroi,
Pennsylvania about 45 minutes away from Pittsburgh.
I am 21 years old and attend ***** University. The
reason I am writing you probably like most other girls
is I L-O-V-E Sidney Crosby. L-O-V-E! I know that you
get your information first hand and was looking for
a few pointers. I know this is a long shot but I am
running out of ideas. I got his address and wrote him
a letter but never got a response. I figured every other
girl around here has done the same thing. I go to
almost every game and once it gets a little warmer
plan to wait in the parking lot for him to come out
after the game. If anything just to meet him and get an
autograph. I know that he drives a Land Rover. What
I was wondering from you is if you know any other
way to get a hold of him or even where he hangs out.
See, the other part about this is I'm probably not what
he looks for in a woman. I am short only about 5'2
and I weigh 150 pounds. So, a short chubby girl! Oh
I forgot to say I have brown hair. I probably don't even

stand a chance and I know I am wasting my time.
Thanks for your time. I don't expect any email back.

Sincerely,
***** *****

Hi Ms. Richer,
Just wanted to let you know how much I enjoyed your
coverage this past season.

I'm a fan of Crosby and the Penguins but really I'm
a diehard Leafs fan. It's a shame neither of them made
the playoffs. Hopefully they'll have better runs next
season. Since you seem to know Crosby well, I was
wondering what you would think about me asking
Crosby to my prom?

Sincerely,
******* ****

Dear Ms. Richer,
My name is ***** *******, and as a seventeen year
old in high school, I am pondering my career. I have
done much research in areas that interest me and I
keep coming back to sports journalism.

Since the beginning of this hockey season, I have
read every one of your articles. As I enter the second
half of my junior year, I am beginning to do research
for my senior project, as a requirement for gradua-
tion. My project will be based on career exploration.
A portion of my project must include job shadowing.

I would very much appreciate it if you could arrange to allow me to observe your work. I live close to Pittsburgh and can be available any time the opportunity arises.

Sincerely,
***** *******

Hello Ms. Richer,
My name is ***** ********* and I am a huge fan of the Penguins and Sidney Crosby. I read all your stories and I know this sounds crazy but my goal is to marry Sidney one day.

The problem is I haven't met him yet. But I know when I get to meet him that I will be the future Mrs. Crosby. This is where I am hoping you can help me. I've tried waiting outside the arena but the crowds are large and I have only gotten an autograph, not a chance to talk to him. Do you have his phone number or an email address that I could use to contact him? I promise if you share it with me I won't give it to anyone else. You can help me meet the man of my dreams! I hope you don't think I am crazy. I'm a freshman at the University of Pittsburgh.

Sincerely,
***** *********

As of the day after his rookie season ended, Sidney Crosby did not have a girlfriend. Although he did see a girl who worked as a lifeguard at a local pool in Rimouski during his first season there for about five months, hockey had occupied most of his time, and this season was no different. "That was the only long-term relationship I've really had," he said with a smile. "It's not something I've really had a lot of time for so far."

Most of his socializing over the season was done with teammates – movies and trips to the mall with his closest friends Armstrong, Whitney, Talbot, Murley, and Christensen, dinners at Ryan Malone's place, sometimes having the guys over to Mario's. He went to see Bon Jovi at the Igloo and met the rock star afterwards, "a very cool moment."

He hadn't met a girlfriend during the season but hadn't really tried either. "It's really tough. It's such a big city, and it depends where you want to meet your girlfriend."

I asked if he spied the signs in the crowd. His eyebrows shot up and he laughed nervously. "Those aren't girlfriend material! I don't think I'm going to meet any of my girlfriends through signs in a hockey arena," he said, turning sombre. "I'm a pretty picky guy. I'm picky about everything. Especially when it comes to something that affects your life. It's like living with a family or choosing your friends. You want someone who complements you well. You want to be around good people and someone who influences you the right way. I don't want to get married at eighteen. If you're a young person at a job, you don't want to be preoccupied with other things. I'm preoccupied with hockey.

"I'm not saying I don't want to meet girls. If the right one came along, I'd do it, but if it's going to get me away from what I'm doing here, it's not the right time."

Sidney Crosby's ideal girl is independent, upbeat, and athletic. "Independent is most important, because I'm so busy and I have a lot going on," he said. "It doesn't mean I don't want to hear from them, but at the same time, they'd have to have some things going on, because if they didn't, they're going to be nuts and I'm going to be nuts. For me, that's the most important."

His view of girls, which wasn't at all typical of a teenaged boy, is a view that's been honed as his fame has grown. "I know probably some things can hurt me a lot more than help me. It's tough sometimes, because even when you meet some girls, it's not a normal situation. A nineteen-year-old girl puts you so far up on a pedestal. It's not like me talking to a girl at school who's a friend. I want to talk to someone who treats me like a normal person who just happens to play hockey. At the same time, it's not their fault they are impressed. I would be in the same situation. If I met Maria Sharapova, even as a hockey player who isn't really star-struck, I could easily look at her and go, 'Whoa.'

"When you're meeting girls, it's nice if they know who you are and what you do, but the less shocking it is the better."

Girls be warned: He doesn't want a girl who wants him because he's a hockey player. "That's the number one turnoff for me."

Crosby wants to get married and have lots of kids; his mother came from a family of eight children. "I envision a big family supper at holidays. That was always a fun time for me. I see [Mario's] four kids buzzing around all the time and it's probably really tiring for Nathalie because he's been on the road so much, but they play together and it's really fun. I'm not looking for four kids of my own now, but down the road, yeah."

Not everyone who wrote was a teenaged girl, though they made up at least half of my e-mail. Canadians living at home and around the world – from Papua New Guinea, Northern Ireland, Australia, and Great Britain, as well as across the United States – wrote to offer opinions. Almost everyone had something to say about the kid, and not all of it was good.

Most of the reader input was kind and positive. But some was over-the-top in its hostility. One person from Philadelphia – yes, them again – who was fixated on Flyers rookie Jeff Carter, called me a one-woman Sidney Crosby publicity department. I had e-mails from people wanting me to settle arguments they were having with their neighbours about whether or not Crosby was a good guy. It was amazing how much emotion an eighteen-year-old hockey player could stir up. There were the hateful e-mails from Philadelphia, and there were many wonderful comments from across the United States, even places where a Canadian might think hockey a little off the radar.

The *Globe*'s project, however, got plenty of attention in the U.S., including in *Sports Illustrated*. Even the Penguins' program featured a four-page spread, written by their beat writer Joe Sager, about my stay in Pittsburgh. The rookie had good buzz in more ways than one.

A few times during the length of the series that ran in the *Globe and Mail*, I received grouchy e-mails from readers accusing me of not being objective about Crosby. I went into the assignment without expectations or preconceived notions. But objectivity, as my wise colleague and friend Christie Blatchford pointed out one day, is not necessarily a worthy goal. To be objective in the literal sense would be to remove all emotion from the coverage, and sportswriting at its best can only be worthwhile by embracing and exposing emotion and all the things that fuel it. Fairness, Blatchford lectured, is the tone you want to strive for.

One of my duties for the *Globe*, in addition to writing the series, was to keep a blog about Crosby on the Web site and update it four or five times a week. One night, after a game in Philadelphia, I wrote a little item about Flyers general manager Bob Clarke not allowing any of the dozens of reporters on deadlines to ride with him in a freight elevator. The blog was kind of a breezy, inside-baseball type of thing, just to give hockey fans a sense of what it was like to follow Crosby around for the year and cover hockey games for a living. I'll never do that again. Comment on the Flyers that is. A touchy bunch, those Philly sports fans are, famous for once booing Santa Claus at a football game.

About a day after the item appeared on the *Globe*'s Web site, the e-mail poured in. Some agreed with me, but soon they were outnumbered ten to one by Flyers fans in the City of Not-So-Much-Brotherly Love. Mentioning Bob Clarke's arrogance was hardly breaking news, but insults arrived by the bushel, filled with obscenities, venom, and most troubling, unabashed misogyny. Some suggested I commit anatomically impossible acts, and some suggested I had learned to whine from Crosby himself. Some encouraged me to get back to the kitchen on the double and stay away from hockey arenas, which are better suited to men. One sorry fellow who ached to be a hockey writer, but worked instead in Manhattan at a crummy job, scolded me and said I was not an inspiration. One suggested I should perhaps consider killing myself. Even some of the Flyers beat writers chimed in. So did one of Clarke's neighbours. Almost everyone assumed I was from Toronto, and taunted me about "the last time I'd won a Stanley Cup."

Being a resident of Halifax, Nova Scotia, and not in a position to compete for the Stanley Cup, what could I say? When poked and prodded, there is no surlier beast than a Philly sports fan. I found this out firsthand. Initially, it was upsetting; who really wanted to be called unprintable things by strangers? Fairly soon, I stopped reading and filed the e-mails unopened into a folder I titled Psycho Flyers Fans. So there it was. With fifty games under our belts, I finally felt as though Sidney Crosby and I had something in common: we were both hated in Philadelphia. A few days later, a reader and native Pittsburgher living in Boston wrote telling me not to worry. "Flyers fans," she stated matter-of-factly, "don't even like themselves."

It was another world in cities such as Montreal, where even as an opposing player, Crosby was widely appreciated. He was such a star in Montreal he couldn't even go out for a meal with his parents. It would have caused a mob scene.

I saw many great moments throughout the year.

There were the little kids who came into the dressing room frozen with excitement about meeting Sidney. He often fetched those kids a stick. He gravitated towards kids in a mob of autograph seekers, signing until they were all happy or he had to get on the bus, whichever came first.

He was always the last guy to leave the dressing room after games but also practices. He would sit in his stall, often in his sweaty equipment, talking to reporters and the team broadcasters and his teammates. He just liked hanging out in the dressing room.

He wore the same hockey pants the whole season, and near the end, when they had ripped and been stitched and trainer Steve Latin was teasing him, he slumped in his locker with an almost drunken smile. "I don't want to take off my equipment," he said with a giggle. "Just take me home like this." Sidney Crosby might have been a hockey star, but at heart he was a rink rat.

"Everything is hockey," the Penguins strength coach Stephane Dube said. "When he's not playing it, he's watching it, and when he's not doing either of those, he's talking about it. I've never known anyone who loved it so much. He gets a light in his eyes."

Colby Armstrong, Sidney's linemate, road roommate, and close friend, said Crosby even talked in his sleep about hockey.

He grew up never letting his mother wash his hockey equipment, preferring instead to air it outdoors, because he loved the smell so much. More than anything, he just loved being at the arena. It was where he was most comfortable. Sometimes, when we were in cities where his media duties were more onerous than others, he stayed on the ice longer than he normally might have, and he was almost always the last one off. The hockey rink was his sanctuary.

Later in the season, Phil Bourque said he was stunned by how "aware" Crosby was for his age. The Penguins' colour commentator on their radio broadcasts was not a stereotypical athlete. He was bright and intuitive about people, and he was most impressed by how Crosby handled himself.

"He's incredibly aware," Bourque said one day as we walked from the dressing room after practice. "He was constantly in tune with everyone who was in the room around him. He let his guard down around certain people; he always knows what's going on. That's incredible for an eighteen-year-old. He's a natural, but he's so tuned in."

Of course I had noticed. For eight months in 2005 and 2006, Sidney Crosby was my raison d'etre.

EPILOGUE

BY THE TIME the regular season came to a close, the NHL landscape had changed considerably from two years earlier. The fans had returned, overwhelmingly in Canada and with some promise in the United States. Things still weren't perfect, but there was no doubt that the game seemed in much better shape than it had been before the lockout.

Now the focus was almost entirely on speed. The game was faster and wide open and more exciting, night in and out. Offence had exploded, and the numbers told the story. Scoring was up by more than 1,000 goals and 1,300 assists from the 2003-2004 season. Forwards had taken 5,200 additional shots. Even-strength scoring was up 17 per cent. On average, 6.1 goals per game were scored, up 18 per cent, the largest boost in seventy-six years. The new rules made for 13,000 fewer stoppages in play. Fighting was down. Tedious ties were a thing of the past.

On the opening night of the season, the Dallas Stars overcame a 4-0 deficit to beat the Los Angeles Kings 5-4 in a thriller. On the final night, the New Jersey Devils, down 3-0 and fighting for a playoff position, rallied heroically to beat the Montreal Canadiens 4-3. Outcomes were often in doubt until the dying seconds of the game. For the most part, fans were delighted. The NHL's prospects looked encouraging.

And if the game was in superior shape, there was no doubt it was also in excellent hands. The most significant sign of its promising future was the rookie class. Sidney Crosby and Alexander Ovechkin combined to have the greatest offensive seasons by a pair of rookies in NHL history. It was the first time in the modern era that two first-year players finished in the top ten in league scoring. Until then, only five rookie players had reached the 100-point milestone and never more than one in a single season.

Ovechkin finished on top with 106 points. Crosby followed with 102 points. Promising Boston Bruins forward Brad Boyes finished a distant third with sixty-nine. And they weren't the only rookies to enjoy terrific outings. Dion Phaneuf in Calgary had forty-nine points and became only the third blueliner in history to score twenty goals. Jussi Jokinen in Dallas and Marek Svatos in Colorado each put up fifty-plus points. Henrik Lundqvist of the Rangers starred on Broadway with thirty wins and a 2.24 goals-against-average to lead all rookie netminders. Ryan Miller backstopped Buffalo to the Eastern Conference finals. Cam Ward, just twenty-two and a sleeper in the regular season, was the playoff star of the Carolina Hurricanes. They made up what was arguably the deepest, most achieving crop of rookies since the league formed in 1917.

Evidence that fans had noticed this fun, entertaining product was reflected at the gate. The NHL claimed the best attendance in its eighty-eight-year history, drawing more than 20.8 million fans to 1,230 games, up 2.4 per cent from the previous season.

Crosby turned out to be the league's biggest draw. The Penguins' attendance increased more than any other team, with an average of 15,804 fans per game, up 33 per cent from 2003-2004. Even though the Penguins won only twenty-two games, they played to twelve standing-room-only sellouts, and twenty-one of forty-one home games drew crowds larger than 16,000. They filled Mellon Arena to more than 93 per cent capacity. It may not have been enough for the Penguins to turn a profit, but it left no doubt that the Steel City was a hockey city and wanted their NHL franchise to stay put.

And Crosby did wonders for other teams' attendance. The Penguins drew on average more than 17,000 fans at road games, and packed arenas where NHL sellouts were as rare as a snowstorm in Florida.

Carolina and Calgary, Buffalo and Boston, Tampa Bay and San José, Nashville and Ottawa also enjoyed large leaps in attendance.

In Montreal, the Canadiens set a single season league record by selling out all forty-one home games and drawing 872,193 fans. The Habs, Flames, Avalanche, Red Wings, Oilers, Kings, Wild, Rangers, Senators, Flyers, Lightning, Maple Leafs, and Canucks all played to 98 per cent capacity or better over the season. Twenty-four of the league's thirty teams finished with attendance ahead of their performance in 2003-2004.

As had been the league's hope when it tinkered with the rules, the most skilled forwards saw mammoth break-throughs in scoring. Carolina's Eric Staal went from thirty-one points to 100 points. San José's Joe Thornton, who won the league scoring title with 125 points, had scored seventy-three the previous season. Thornton, sent to the Sharks from the Bruins in the season's most blockbuster trade, had more assists (ninety-six) than top scorer Martin St. Louis of Tampa Bay had points (ninety-four) in 2003-2004. Five players scored fifty or more goals; seven reached 100 points, the most prodigious scoring totals in a decade. Last season, not a single player hit either mark.

All kinds of players rediscovered their scoring touch – Jaromir Jagr posted 123 points; Dany Heatley had 103.

In many cities, hockey still had a long way to go to capture the fans' imagination. An old joke that there were 18,200 hockey fans in New York – the seating capacity at Madison Square Garden – could still apply to places such as Carolina and Tampa Bay. There was work to be done. The Stanley Cup final featured two small-market teams – Carolina and Edmonton – that indicated, as Bettman said before game one, "that market size had become irrelevant." But a small-market team won the year before, and Carolina was also in the final in 2002. This year's matchup was failing to draw a decent television audience south of the border, evidence that the NHL had plenty of work to do in the U.S. The salary cap would rise to around forty-four million dollars, which Gary Bettman credited to rising profits.

"After the Rangers won the Cup in 1994, we had a lockout, and that was like taking a sledgehammer to the toes," John Davidson said. "Then we had another lockout.

And it could have been really devastating. But we're back a lot quicker than I thought we'd be. I think we're definitely doing really well."

Sidney Crosby did not win the Calder Trophy.

At the NHL Awards on June 22 in Vancouver, he finished the runner-up to his Russian rival, Ovechkin, who was chosen best rookie by the Professional Hockey Writers' Association. Phaneuf finished third in the voting.

Although Crosby wasn't selected the top rookie, he had a season for the ages, the youngest player in NHL history to reach 100 points and was sixth in scoring among all NHL skaters.

After the Penguins finished their season on April 18, he spent two weeks in Pittsburgh nursing his separated shoulder and then travelled to Riga, Latvia, to participate in the World Hockey Championships.

The second-youngest player to represent Canada since the event began in 1920, he was the team's best player from the opening game in which he scored two goals, including the winner. An exhausted Canadian team fell 5-0 to Finland in the bronze medal game, but Crosby led the tournament with eight goals and sixteen points and was named top forward.

He may have failed to win a medal, but his spirited performance guaranteed Sidney Crosby would never again be left off a Team Canada roster.

Crosby took a vacation in Prague after the World Championships, returned briefly to Pittsburgh to pick up some belongings, and then headed home to Cole Harbour to relax and then begin training, every day until his return to

Pittsburgh in mid-August. Not his favourite part of the year, he confessed after the season. "Ugh," he said. "My favourite part of the summer is the weather. It's harder than the hockey season, those two months. I like the day after one o'clock. But from 8 a.m. until then, I don't like it. Training with Andy [O'Brien], I'm a mess. He makes things sound so easy and normal."

Sidney Crosby has a fear about running the mile. A fear so deep it has kept him awake at night and has caused him to vomit in dread and exertion. He doesn't think he's a good runner but is "okay" with that. Something else gets under his skin.

"The mile run is my ultimate nightmare," he said and shrank lower into his chair. "It's something I can't get over. It's a phobia."

He hates that it's just him against the clock. He cannot chase anyone. No one chases him. He doesn't consider competing against himself true competition.

"I'm not a good runner, and I'm okay with that. But I want to win so badly it bothers me that I can never beat the clock. Even if I beat myself, I haven't accomplished anything."

O'Brien has never told him to start running. He starts his stopwatch when Crosby decides to go. Sidney has stood on the start line for fifteen minutes unable to move. "That's how much it scares me."

When Crosby was chasing 100 points, O'Brien left him a message that if he made it, Sidney could pick the date to run his first mile.

The previous year, he ran at a track in the Dartmouth neighbourhood where his grandmother Linda Crosby used to reside, in the same house Sidney and his parents lived in when he was just a baby.

"I liked that. It helped me by reminding me why I was there," he said. "Now I always run there. But I still get freaked out. I'll never be able to change that."

In other developments over the summer that would have serious implications for Crosby and the Penguins, general manager Craig Patrick, after failing miserably to build a competitive team, was let go after seventeen seasons. Ray Shero, the up-and-coming Nashville assistant general manager, was hired in Patrick's place. In June, Russia ratified a transfer agreement with the NHL that was meant to clear the way for the Penguins to bring Evgeni Malkin to Pittsburgh, but ultimately the Russians refused to sign the deal, wanting to keep the twenty-year-old superstar to themselves.

In late July, a group led by Connecticut real estate developer and Toronto native Sam Fingold, which also included concert promoter Michael Cohl, signed a letter of intent to purchase the team from Mario Lemieux and pledged to keep it in Pittsburgh. The Penguins' home in the Steel City still wasn't a lock – the gaming commission that would award the slots licence in the coming months would decide that for certain – but the future looked far rosier than it had just one year earlier.

The Penguins re-signed some of their most talented youngsters – Colby Armstrong, Marc-Andre Fleury, Ryan Malone, and Brooks Orpik. They brought back Mark Recchi, who contributed sixteen playoff points in Carolina's Stanley Cup victory. Recchi said his heart was in Pittsburgh, and on the day his return was announced, the veteran sounded as hopeful about the club's prospects on the ice as he had the previous summer. They also drafted the gifted and towering forward Jordan Staal with their number two pick in the June entry draft. The youth movement in Pittsburgh was well underway.

And in mid-August, perhaps evidence that so much drama might remain forever a part of the Pittsburgh Penguins, reports surfaced that Malkin, who desperately wanted to play in the NHL, had disappeared from his Russian team's training camp in Finland with his belongings and his Russian passport only to surface in Los Angeles.

The Penguins would start training camp in September among friends in Halifax, Nova Scotia, and Moncton, New Brunswick, with two pre-season games virtually in Crosby's backyard. They would open the regular season at the Igloo against their archenemies, the Philadelphia Flyers.

Before the season began, the venerable *Hockey News* projected Sidney Crosby as the favourite to win the Art Ross trophy as the league's top scorer with 116 points.

What was certain at the conclusion of the 2005-2006 National Hockey League season was that even as Crosby's arrival launched a new era and foreshadowed great hockey moments and quite possibly history, it marked the moment he left his boyhood behind for good. The upheavals of his rookie season could finally become part of his past, even as Sidney chose to take the lessons learned with him.

When his second turn at the NHL began, he was all of nineteen years old. He could reasonably remain Sid the Kid for at least a few more years. But he was a boy no more, and a man no less.

WHAT A DIFFERENCE
A YEAR MAKES

ON THE EVENING of June 14, 2007, a warm and nearly perfect summer night in Toronto, the coronation of Sidney Crosby as hockey's newest and greatest superstar was complete.

At the tender age of nineteen, still two months shy of his twentieth birthday, the Pittsburgh Penguins centre – who had already won the Art Ross Trophy as the NHL's leading scorer, the youngest winner in league history – cleaned up at the NHL awards ceremony.

Crosby, handsome and looking like a young Hollywood star in a black Giovanni Valentino tux, was the centre of attention, walking the red carpet and signing autographs outside the Elgin Theatre; his bright, wide smile was befitting a superstar, and his demeanour was anything but. He had brought his parents and his little sister, and even though he was heavily favoured to win everything for which he was nominated, he later appeared surprised when his name was called, and was humble in his thanks and his praise of fellow players.

Crosby started the night at the podium. He won the Lester B. Pearson Award for the most outstanding player, as voted by the seven-hundred-plus members of the National Hockey League Players' Association, and became the youngest player in history to receive the honour (Gretzky was twenty when he captured it in 1982). He also ended the evening at the podium, accepting the Hart Memorial Trophy as the league's most valuable player to his team, as voted by 1,200-plus members of the Professional Hockey Writers' Association, for leading the Penguins into the play-offs for the first time since 2001. He was the youngest player to win all three accolades – the Art Ross, Pearson, and Hart – in the same season.

The proceedings cemented the opinion, had there been any doubt remaining, that Sidney Crosby was no longer The Next One, but The One.

As Sidney accepted the Hart and thanked his family, Sidney's father Troy sat in the audience and fought back tears of pride, eventually giving in to them and letting a few slide down his cheeks.

Sidney Crosby's sophomore season in the NHL unfolded nothing like his first. Sure, there were a few similarities: he was the best player on the Penguins from the beginning, and the season started with the team's future in the Steel City very much in doubt. But little else remained the same.

His phenomenal but occasionally nerve-wracking first year behind him – 102 points in eighty-one games had made him the youngest player in NHL history to record 100 points – Crosby could, for the most part, put the hype and attention of being the No. 1 draft pick behind him, and focus strictly on hockey.

After the World Championships in Latvia, during which Crosby set a record for being the youngest player to win the tournament's scoring title (sixteen points in nine games), he spent much of his summer at home in Nova Scotia, visiting his family and working out. He bought a big house just outside of Halifax, a lakeside spread with plenty of privacy and room for his new yellow Labrador puppy, Sam.

And when he and his teammates regrouped to open training camp in September 2006, everyone was focussed on putting the woes of the previous season, in which they won just twenty-two games, behind them.

It didn't seem like it would be all that difficult. Coach Michel Therrien would be running his structured system and diligent practices from the first day. And the team featured a new distraction for the media – the arrival of towering Russian forward Evgeni Malkin, who had bolted his Magnitogorsk team during training camp and headed for Los Angeles, where, despite a controversy over his eligibility to sign with the Penguins, he would do just that after a judge ruled in the club's favour.

No one was more excited about the prospect of playing with Malkin than Crosby, who had only ever played against the Russian at the World Junior Championship and that summer's World Championship tournaments.

"I can't wait. I played against him and have seen him play a lot. I am looking forward to getting out there and hopefully learning from him, too. He is a great player and you can always learn things. I want to learn from him. Hopefully we can build some chemistry and make some things happen out there."

It didn't even seem to matter that they didn't speak the same language.

Crosby was impressed by his new teammate's determination to get to the NHL, and he admired Malkin for the risks he took in fleeing his Russian team.

"It's a pretty amazing story. What he went through was pretty unbelievable. He showed a lot of guts to go through that and come over here. I think everyone is just looking forward to having him here and making him feel as comfortable as possible.

"For anyone who has a dream to play and the passion to play, this is the league you want to be in. For him, I think when you get that opportunity, you'll do whatever it takes and take those risks to get here. It shows that he wants to be here. He went through a lot of adversity to get here. I think he is going to want it bad and want to play well and expect a lot out of himself. It's only going to make everyone else around him better."

Everyone couldn't wait to see what having that kind of 1-2 punch at centre ice could do for the Penguins, and what the swift-skating Canadian and hard-shooting Russian could do together on the power play.

On September 5, Malkin, the second overall pick in the 2004 NHL entry draft, signed his first NHL contract with the Pittsburgh Penguins. It was a symbol of the team's bright future.

"We have two great players here in Sid and Malkin," said Mario Lemieux. "It's going to be a very exciting time here for the next ten to fifteen years. I think this team is ready to step up and be a force in the NHL. It may take a year or two, but I am looking forward to more championships here in Pittsburgh."

Lemieux didn't really know for sure how long it would take things to turn around in Pittsburgh, but it's safe to assume that even he, once a maker of miracles in the Steel City, couldn't have imagined things happening so quickly.

The Pittsburgh Penguins opened their 2006-2007 training camp at West Point, the United States Military Academy in New York. It was a far cry from Crosby's first NHL training camp experience, as First Sergeant J.B. Spisso, a former army ranger and member of the New York National Guard, put the Penguins through a gruelling, four-day training session that began with hour-long sunrise runs, punishing rifle drills, paintball, pushups, pushups, and more pushups. They participated in buddy drills – pulling a Jeep out of a hole and carrying each other – that were designed to build a team chemistry that had been lacking so often in the previous season. Sessions ended with jumping jack drills, after which the players were so exhausted that they fell out of formation, Crosby laughing hard, as chaos overtook the tired group.

"It was funny because we were all watching each other and were perfect for the first twenty," Sidney said. "Suddenly, everyone's sliding a bit. Then, when we were at a hundred, [Spisso] said a hundred more. You could just see everyone's head drop."

But Crosby took a lot away from the West Point trip, and not just in regard to the team-building. "[Spisso] just put a lot of things in perspective for us. He said when you are playing and you have a bad game or a bad day, you can go to bed that night knowing you will see your family and friends and knowing you can come to the rink tomorrow and do things all over again.

"If you're in a battle in a war, it's not always like that. He just made us realize when things turn tough, it is tough for us, but it's a lot tougher for other people. He just made us realize how lucky we are."

For Therrien, who watched the exercise from the football stands before preparing for the on-ice practices scheduled for later in the day, the trip to West Point accomplished the chemistry-building that he never got a chance to implement when he arrived in the job the previous December.

When the season opened at Mellon Arena against the Philadelphia Flyers on October 4, everyone, especially Crosby, was anxious to get underway. The Penguins lineup looked in promising form. Marc-Andre Fleury was back in goal, and Jordan Staal, the second overall pick in the 2006 draft, was making his NHL debut. It was unfortunate that tough defenceman Brooks Orpik would miss some time with a broken bone in his hand, and Malkin would be out for about a month with a separated shoulder suffered during a training camp game in Moncton.

But some new acquisitions – talented defenceman Mark Eaton, and forwards Jarkko Ruttu, Dominic Moore, and Nils Ekman – had signed as free agents in the off-season, joining Crosby and returning players Recchi, LeClair, Malone, Ouellet, Armstrong, Gonchar, Melichar, Scuderi, and Whitney – and the additions had made the team better and deeper.

The Penguins cruised to a 4-0 win over their hated, cross-state rivals, and Fleury recorded a shutout in his first start of the season. Crosby scored a goal and had an assist in the win, and to the surprise of no one, was off to an auspicious start.

The opening of the season did offer a sizable surprise, however. Hockey obsessed Blackberry guru Jim Balsillie, the chairman and chief executive officer of Research in Motion in Waterloo, Ontario, signed a purchase agreement to buy the Penguins.

Lemieux praised the forty-five-year-old Canadian's commitment to landing a new arena deal and keeping the team in Pittsburgh, and Balsillie charmed everyone with his first trip to Mellon Arena, acting like a giddy kid during the intermission broadcast, even accidentally and good-naturedly dropping a mild curse in his excitement. Even though Balsillie had previously expressed interest in buying an NHL club to move to Hamilton or Kitchener-Waterloo, he seriously downplayed the possibility and said he was committed to keeping the Penguins where they were. And everyone from the current ownership to the media in Pittsburgh seemed convinced that the deep-pocketed Canadian could make the perfect owner.

With the season just one day and one game old, the future of the Pittsburgh Penguins already looked much brighter, on and off the ice.

A week later at Madison Square Garden, Crosby enjoyed his first four-point game of the season, scoring a goal and adding three assists in an emotional 6-5 win. Eighteen-year-old Jordan Staal scored his first NHL goal and nineteen-year-old Kris Letang also had a goal, making it the first time in twenty-four years that three teenagers on one team scored in the same NHL game, and only the ninth time in league history. It hadn't occurred since October 17, 1982, when teens Dave Andreychuk, Paul Cyr, and Phil Housley scored for the Buffalo Sabres in a 6-4 win over the Edmonton Oilers.

The season was only three games old, and the kids, with Crosby as the "seasoned veteran" among them, were making their mark.

A few nights later, in a home game against the New Jersey Devils, Evgeni Malkin, with his shoulder healed, finally made his NHL debut and scored a goal against the best goaltender in the league. With just more than a minute left in the second period, Malkin attacked from the right wing, working a crafty give-and-go play with linemate Mark Recchi.

Recchi took the first shot and Martin Brodeur made the save. But the puck squirted loose and Malkin jumped on it, poking it through Brodeur's pads and into the net.

The rangy Russian leaped into the air, pumping his fist as Crosby charged over to congratulate him. Pittsburgh lost 2-1, but it was clear that the younger generation had arrived. One of Malkin's slapshots that night even shattered the Mellon Arena glass.

He looked comfortable in his first NHL game, and settled in more with each passing shift. And over the next five games, Malkin proceeded to accomplish something no other rookie had achieved in the modern era of the NHL, not even Sidney Crosby.

He scored one or more goals in six straight games – seven goals overall in the span. Before Malkin, only three players in NHL history had done that or better – Montreal's Joe Malone and Newsy Lalonde, and Ottawa's Cy Denneny, all in the 1917-1918 season.

Crosby was having a lot of fun watching the Penguins' newest young star, and wasn't at all bothered to see much of the spotlight focussed on him.

"He's just playing his game," Crosby said of his team-mate. "A lot of times he's able to beat guys with his speed or stepping out of the way. That's just smarts and hockey sense and he has it. It's going to be one of those things he improves on because he's going to get used to the way guys play and the way teams play him. I think he can only get better."

The same could be said of all the Penguins' young players. Eight games into the season, on October 24, Crosby and the rookies Malkin and Staal all scored goals in a dominant 4-2 win over the Devils, giving Pittsburgh a 5-3 record and sole possession of first place in the Atlantic Division with ten points. The buzz was starting in the hockey world – often among the same broadcasters and pundits who had criticized Crosby or withheld praise, or who had called him overrated the previous year – when the Penguins and their young superstar were progressing much faster than anyone had imagined possible.

Therrien, who had inherited a team in spiritual and sta-tistical shambles just ten months earlier, was pleased. He could see his team rounding into shape, and he saw every-one, veterans and youngsters alike, contributing.

"As a coach you have to be proud because [the game] is a real team effort," Therrien explained. "Every line brings something. Crosby's line gave us two goals and Staal's line gave us two goals as well. Guys on the third line like Dominic Moore, John LeClair and Michel Ouellet fore-checked well and they played well. The guys on the fourth line gave us a lot of energy out there. The penalty kill did a great job. Marc-Andre was good. I was really satisfied about our team effort."

Crosby was the unofficial and undisputed leader-in-training, but he didn't feel like everything was resting on his shoulders. He was excited, too, by the obvious chemistry and skill his young teammates were exhibiting. But as always, he was cautiously optimistic.

"We know it's early but we still realize that every game counts. We don't want to follow the standings too much, we have to worry about ourselves. But, first place is nice. We have to continue to take it a game at a time and focus on the next one."

The next one, four nights later, took them to hostile Philadelphia, a place the Penguins were starting to feel they owned. And no wonder, as their dominance over the Flyers continued and Crosby's play against them began to reach mythical proportions.

He scored his first NHL hat trick in the 8-2 blowout. Malkin had a goal and two assists, giving him five goals in as many games. The Penguins were 6-3, and had already beaten the dreaded Flyers twice. They had not won four games in a row since March 2004, and hadn't won three straight on the road since the 1994-1995 season.

By the end of October, in a move that would pay massive dividends, the Penguins had decided to keep Jordan Staal on their roster, rather than return him to his junior team, the Peterborough Petes. The youngest of the Staal brothers (Eric is a star forward with the Carolina Hurricanes and Marc is a promising New York Rangers prospect), Jordan already had four goals and an assist through nine games. As Crosby did in his rookie season, and as Malkin was currently doing, Staal was marking plenty of NHL milestones.

He was already the first player since 1982 to score his first three NHL goals short-handed, and was also the youngest to score two or more goals in one game since Bep Guidolin did it for the Boston Bruins back in 1943. He was also the youngest player to score on a penalty shot. Crosby, himself the holder of so many "youngest ever" honours, was thrilled Staal was staying with the club, seeing him as a crucial building block in the young lineup.

"He has done a great job. He's definitely earned his right to continue proving he can play at this level. He has long strides, but he does have speed. He's a big guy and he's so strong. I think the biggest thing is his work ethic. He's worked really hard to adjust and improve his game as the season has gone on."

November opened with a 4-3 overtime win in Los Angeles, courtesy of a goal 2:45 into the extra frame by Malkin, who had already potted one in regulation. The Penguins now sat at 7-3 and had five consecutive victories under their belt. Malkin had eleven points in only six games. He earned NHL rookie of the month honours for the first month of the season, just as his teammate Crosby had the previous season.

For his part, Crosby already had six goals and a dozen assists – eighteen points in just ten games. At this pace, he would finish the season with 148 points – bettering the

137 points Wayne Gretzky scored as a nineteen-year-old in his 1979-1980 season with the Edmonton Oilers.

By the time he had played his nineteenth game, a 5-3 win at the Flyers on November 20, Crosby, who was tied for fourth in the league in scoring, had amassed ten goals and twenty assists. He was the only player in the top fifteen in scoring not to have played at least twenty-two games. And while he would miss the next three games with a strained groin, it would turn out that he didn't have to worry about losing any ground in the scoring race. Without him in the lineup, though, it also turned out that the Penguins dropped all three games.

On December 14, in a game at home against the Philadelphia Flyers, he turned in a career-best six-point performance as the Penguins romped over their rivals, winning 8-4. He had scored five of those points – a goal and four assists – in the game's first twenty-nine minutes and twenty-nine seconds, and was now leading the league in scoring with forty-seven points, three ahead of Jaromir Jagr.

"It was one of those nights where everything seemed to go in," he said afterwards. "Once I got to five the guys were saying, 'Keep going. It's only halfway through the game.' So I just tried to keep going. It's hard not to want to move the puck a little more when it seems like everyone's burying it. You want to get them the puck and keep it rolling. It was just one of those nights."

The scoring outburst put him atop the NHL scoring leaders with fifteen goals and thirty-two assists in just twenty-seven games. He had scored in five consecutive games and racked up fifteen points in his last six games. Everything was going right.

"It was nice to take over the scoring lead, but it's not something I think about," he said. "There's a lot of the season left. But, it's nice."

The next day, Jim Balsillie pulled the plug on his plans to purchase the Penguins, delivering a notice of termination to Mario Lemieux and announcing that he had stopped negotiating with the NHL. Balsillie wanted to move the team, and the league wasn't going to allow it. Still, this didn't mean the Penguins were sticking around. The uncertainty over a new owner still swirled over the club's head. When the Pennsylvania Gaming Control Board announced a few days later that the Penguins and their partners would not receive a slots license that would allow the funding of the new rink, the future seemed even bleaker, with Gary Bettman saying the Penguins would have to explore all other options, including relocation. Lemieux, furious at Balsillie, took the team off the market and said he would begin looking at moving the team. "After seven years of trying to work out a new arena deal exclusively in Pittsburgh, we need to take into consideration the long-term viability of the team and begin discussions with other cities that may be interested in NHL teams. We will also begin discussions with local leaders about a viable Pittsburgh arena plan."

At least everything on the ice was going reasonably well. The Penguins finished the year by snapping a five-game losing streak – a period that saw Crosby held to just one goal – by crushing the Maple Leafs in a 4-1 victory.

Meanwhile, Sidney Crosby's popularity was growing. His league-leading sixty-five points (twenty-one goals and forty-four assists in thirty-eight games) lifted him above all vote-getters to 825,783 votes in the NHL All-Star Game fan balloting, earning him a starting spot in the game to be held later in January in the non-hockey hotbed of Dallas.

In keeping with the "youngest ever" theme he had gotten used to, Crosby was the youngest player ever voted to start in the All-Star Game. Popular San Jose Sharks centre man Joe Thornton, who had won the scoring title the previous season, trailed Crosby by 161,852 votes to finish second. "To see that much support," Crosby said, "is a great compliment. I really appreciate it, and I'm going to use it as motivation to get better."

The Penguins headed into the All-Star break with an 8-2 romp over the Maple Leafs in Pittsburgh, led by Evgeni Malkin's five points and a hat trick from Mark Recchi. Crosby chipped in a goal and two assists, and the Penguins were lifted to a 21-17-8 record. What was most notable about the game, though, was how the team had finally, really gelled, and how the chemistry was palpable. Their power play was firing on all cylinders as well, with five of the eight goals coming with a man advantage.

They had won three of their past four games and earned seven points in the process. They were in second place in the Atlantic Division, behind the New Jersey Devils, and sat in the eighth and final playoff spot in the Eastern Conference, with fifty points and thirty-six games remaining – one of six teams within four points of each other.

"We're in the hunt," Ryan Malone said. "Last year with the bad start, I don't think the confidence was there. Now the confidence has been there from the beginning. If we even get down a couple of goals we know if we keep playing the right way we have a chance to win a lot of games. Compared to last year, it's definitely a better season."

That was an understatement.

Malkin was leading all rookies with fifty-two points – twenty-four goals and twenty-eight assists through forty-two games – and was four points ahead of Crosby's scoring pace from the previous season. Crosby was top in the league with seventy-two points – twenty-four goals and forty-eight assists through forty-three games – and showed no sign of slowing down.

He was thrilled to be in the All-Star Game, excited about lining up next to great players he had only ever been on the opposing side of – Alexander Ovechkin, Buffalo's Daniel Briere. Twenty-one goals were scored in the game, and though Crosby didn't have one of them, he knew he would have plenty more chances. "There were twenty-one goals, you think I would have had one," he joked later.

As the Penguins headed into the home stretch, everyone appreciated how much things had changed in the space of a year, and they spent a lot of time considering how to keep it going.

"We're in a battle, which is nice," Colby Armstrong said. "Our team has come a long way since last year. If we play well, any night I think we can have a chance to win. It's a different feeling and you can feel it in the locker room. Everyone here wants it and we're right in the thick of things. We're right there. We're on the heels of some teams and we're tied with some teams. We're pretty close and if you win a few or drop a few, you're in or you're out. Hopefully we can keep our streaks rolling and cut our dips to a minimum. The way we started this year, it's kind of cliché, but we wanted to take it a game at a time. If we focus on that, we'll be there by the end of the year battling and that's where we want to be.

"Last year we were out of the playoff race by now. This team has really improved since last year."

Crosby had a goal and three assists against the Phoenix Coyotes, as Wayne Gretzky watched from behind the opposing bench, in a 7-2 win. It was Crosby's third four-point game of the season. A few nights later, in a 3-0 victory against the Florida Panthers, Marc-Andre Fleury was perfect for the third time in the season and the fifth time in his career. The momentum continued to build, and through-out February the Penguins became one of the league's hottest teams. Even with Crosby going eight games without scoring a goal (he had ten assists in that time, however), the Penguins reached a 33-17-9 record after a 3-2 win over the Washington Capitals on the eighteenth, and had earned at least a point in each of their last sixteen games – the second-longest point-earning stretch in franchise history. Jordan Staal was proving to be everything the Penguins thought he would be and more, scoring his first hat trick on *Hockey Night in Canada* in a game at Toronto the previous week, the youngest player in NHL history to do so.

Youth was serving the Penguins incredibly well, but at the February 27 trade deadline, Ray Shero decided that the team needed to add some experience and grit at the forward position if they were going to do anything in the playoffs. To that end, Shero swung a deal to acquire veteran Gary Roberts from the Panthers and tough guy

Georges Laraque, widely considered to be the NHL's best fighter, from the Coyotes.

Roberts, who had been hoping to return to Toronto or join the Ottawa Senators in their serious Stanley Cup hopes, was seen as an enormous coup. Forty years old, with 424 goals, 451 assists, and 2,467 penalty minutes over nineteen NHL seasons, he would bring toughness and a nifty scoring touch around the net, as well as leadership and experience, to the young club.

Laraque, in his ninth NHL season, could also score a little, and he would be charged with defending the team's star, Sidney Crosby. "Look at his fights," Shero said, "I think he's recognized by everybody as the toughest guy in the league." As for Roberts, Shero said, "He plays the game the way it's meant to be played at this time of year. When our players see the preparation that goes into what he's been through for his career with all the games played and playoff series, I think that will only benefit our guys in the future."

Roberts was excited about joining what was unarguably the NHL's most promising club. "You look at the talent here in Pittsburgh. Mark [Recchi] said how much fun he was having playing with this young group of guys. They are basically late for planes and buses because you can't get them off the ice. As an older player that's great to see and fun to be a part of and it actually makes you younger."

Suddenly, the Penguins were young and a little more experienced, what seemed like the perfect combination as they fought to stay in the playoff race in the East.

Mike Emrick, the veteran broadcaster, thought the improvement to the lineup was significant.

"To have somebody like Roberts come in, who won the Stanley Cup in Calgary in 1989 and has been a playoff type player is huge. It's a different game at playoff time. The games are rougher and you're starting to see that now. Georges Laraque is a guy who can play as well as fight. His problem is that he's a heavyweight fighter and he can't get many fights. Guys don't want to mess with him. As a result, if you want a game he's playing, he'd go in the corner and guys would give him at least three feet of room. He could play along the boards and nobody would knock it away from him.

"In the long run, the most important thing is, not only is the team better and potentially great, but the franchise hasn't been on this solid ground with its assets since Jagr and Lemieux, Francis and all those guys fifteen years ago. At a time so critical to the franchise's future, to have assets that anyone can recognize are terrific is outstanding."

Sidney Crosby hit the one-hundred-point mark on March 10 and became only the fifth player in NHL history to reach one hundred points in his first two seasons, joining Peter Stastny, Mario Lemieux, Wayne Gretzky, and Mike Rogers.

"It's something you never think about," he said after tying a game with the Rangers 2-2 that the Penguins went on to win on a goal by Colby Armstrong. "It's nice for sure, but we still have a lot of games left, important ones, so that's where my mind has been."

The Penguins had fourteen games remaining, and Crosby was on pace to finish at the top of the league scoring race with 121 points.

Then, on March 16, something remarkable happened that, like the shoulder he separated during the last season but kept playing with, would not become known until the Penguins' season and playoff run were finished.

Sidney Crosby broke his foot. In a game against the Montreal Canadiens, one that the Penguins won 6-3, Crosby blocked a shot from his teammate, defenceman Brooks Orpik, on the inside of his foot. Then a shot by Mike Komisarek hit him in exactly the same spot later in the game.

He didn't realize it was broken for a week; he did not miss a game. The only people he told were the Penguins' medical staff, his road roommate Colby Armstrong, and his parents.

He managed five goals and nine assists in his last eleven regular season games, and scored three goals and had two assists in five playoff games against the Senators.

"During the playoffs I didn't feel it a lot. I got whacked there once in a while, but it really wasn't anything that changed my game or something. By no means do I want it to be an excuse because it's not. I hope that's not the way people see it."

It would be safe to say no one saw it that way.

As March gave way to April, the final few weeks of the season, it was clear the Penguins had staged a remarkable turnaround from the previous year. They were routinely winning shootouts after winning only one in a total of seven during the previous season – Crosby's famous goal against Montreal being the only winner. Between January 26 and

March 21, the Penguins had won nine of their ten games that had gone to a shootout, including the past seven straight. Crosby and Erik Christensen were winning games on the ice in the shootout, and Marc-Andre Fleury was winning them in net.

It would turn out to have an enormous impact on the Eastern Conference playoff race, with the Penguins picking up ten points in that span to help give them a more comfortable separation from other teams fighting for a spot. "Those ten points? Subtract them and where would we be? Probably not in a playoff spot," Christensen said.

On March 27, the Penguins clinched a spot in the Stanley Cup playoffs for the first time since 2001 with a 4-3 win at Washington. The new era in Pittsburgh had finally, officially arrived.

A few nights later, with a 4-2 victory in Boston, they were sitting on top of the Atlantic Division. And on April 7, what was feeling like a magical regular season finished with a 2-1 win over the New York Rangers, which capped the Penguins' year with a winning 47-24-11 record.

Their 105 points – a forty-seven-point improvement over the previous season – marked the fourth-largest single-season turnaround in NHL history. They had the Eastern Conference's No. 5 playoff seed and would meet Ottawa in the first round.

Crosby earned two assists in the final game to finish the season with 120 points, becoming the youngest Art Ross Trophy–winner as the league's top scorer, as well as the youngest scoring champion in any major professional sport.

But what he really wanted most was a Stanley Cup.

The Penguins were far from favourites to win Lord Stanley's trophy. The Senators were most hockey pundits' pick to go all the way, despite having one of the most chronically disappointing playoff histories in the league. And the Senators were trying to use it to their advantage, especially coach Bryan Murray, who called his team underdogs even though the Penguins boasted sixteen players on the roster who had never been in the NHL playoffs.

Crosby was understandably a bit nervous about making his playoff debut, but planned to keep the same focus he had had all season.

"Whoever I play, whether it's Ottawa or anybody else, I always worry about me. I don't worry about who I'm playing against. It's always a challenge every time you play. You know you're playing against some strong defensive players and you always prepare yourself the same way. I just have to move my feet and skate and I'm confident that when I skate I'm going to create chances or they're going to have to take penalties. It's going to be one of the two. There are probably fewer opportunities to score but you have to make sure that when you get them you put them in. It's just a matter of being focussed and executing."

All the Penguins appeared nervous and a little shell-shocked in the first game, and the Senators did an impressive job of shutting the young centre down and cruising to a 6-3 win in front of a delirious home crowd. Crosby appeared to have scored a goal in the third period that would have cut the score to 3-2 and given the Penguins a huge boost in momentum, but the goal was disallowed. He eventually scored his first playoff goal late in the third with less than a minute left, when the Penguins' hopes for victory were slim.

In Game 2, the Penguins made a furious comeback to win 4-3, and it was Crosby who scored the winner – a tap-in from Mark Recchi and Evgeni Malkin with about eight minutes remaining in the tie game.

It was the best that things would get for the rest of the series. Ottawa won the following game in Pittsburgh 4-2, scoring four straight goals and thoroughly out-playing the Penguins. Crosby blamed the loss on mental mistakes. They responded with a much tighter effort in Game 4, matching the Senators in intensity and goaltending, but a wild bounce that led to a fluky goal by Jason Spezza meant the difference between winning and losing. The Penguins fell 2-1, giving the Senators a 3-1 series lead and a virtual death-grip on the outcome. As the teams headed back to Ottawa, Coach Michel Therrien said it was the first time all series he thought the Penguins looked comfortable.

"It's tough," Crosby said. "We have to be proud of the way we played. We can come into the room and every guy can look in the mirror and say they gave an honest effort and laid it out there. It's playoff hockey. You're not always going to come out with a win. But we laid it out there and I think we showed ourselves and showed them we are a tough team to playoff against when we want to be. Moving forward, we didn't get the win but going into Ottawa, if we bring that game, we have a chance."

Crosby, who already had three goals and two assists, however, seemed realistic about the Penguins' chances of winning the next three games.

"I think we have always felt like we belonged," he said. "It's just a matter of consistency. The consistency was there [in Game 4]. We stuck to the game plan and they got a fluky goal early but we just kept playing the same way. If we keep playing the same way we have a chance."

"You leave it all out there. We have to win the next game. But you can't win three in one. You have to just win the next one. If we do, we're coming back home and then we pour it all out there again. We gave ourselves a real chance and if we do it again there's no reason we can't come home with a win. We just have to focus on that."

It was not to be. The Senators won forcefully, 3-0, to end the Penguins' season.

Inexperience – sixteen players on the roster who had never appeared in a playoff game – doomed the Penguins, but gave this up-and-coming team valuable and necessary post-season knowledge they were sure to use down the road.

Crosby emerged from the playoffs as only the fourth teenager in NHL history to score a goal in each of his first three playoff games – not even Wayne Gretzky accomplished the feat – and he did it on a broken left foot.

"The first two weeks were pretty sore but it didn't have any effect after that," he said.

He played on his broken foot, after receiving assurances from the Penguins' doctors that it wouldn't do further harm, because he couldn't bear not being involved as the team pushed for a playoff spot and then made it.

It meant he wouldn't be able to play for Team Canada at the World Championship in Moscow, but it was a small price to pay for getting through his first post-season appearance.

Meanwhile, the accolades kept rolling in. The sports bible *The Hockey News* named Crosby the NHL's best player and MVP. *The Sporting News* also weighed in with

MVP honours. He was named the most influential sports figure in a Time.com reader poll.

Crosby was nominated for the Hart Trophy as league MVP alongside Martin Brodeur, who won an unprecedented forty-eight games, and Roberto Luongo, who won forty-seven, and also the Lester B. Pearson Award for the most outstanding player, as voted by fellow members of the NHLPA, along with Vincent Lecavalier and Luongo.

Malkin was, of course, nominated for rookie of the year on the strength of his eighty-five points, as was Jordan Staal, and Therrien was a candidate for coach of the year.

By the time Crosby accepted the Art Ross Trophy in early June, he had received clearance from the team's doctors to resume working out, and said he was "looking forward to feeling like an athlete again."

"I really haven't done anything since the season ended. I haven't been able to. It's nice to know I can go work out, without anything holding me back. I'm pretty anxious to do that. I haven't sat around for a month in a long time."

The summer was also expected to bring talks between Crosby and the Penguins about a long-term deal. Crosby is entering the third season of the three-year entry-level contract he signed after being the No. 1 draft pick in 2005, a contract that pays him $850,000 a season plus bonuses in the millions. Ray Shero was likely to open the negotiations when the NHL free agent signing period began on July 1.

"He's our franchise player and a guy we want to be here the rest of his career," Shero said. Crosby said he imagined the negotiations going well; he felt even more connected to Pittsburgh and the franchise after this season.

"It's part of the business side but I'm more than confident everyone's going to be happy," he said.

On May 31, the inevitable happened. Sidney Crosby was officially named the captain of the Pittsburgh Penguins at a press conference at Mellon Arena, becoming the youngest player to be named captain in NHL history.

But it wasn't the first time the topic had been raised during the past year.

In January, the Pittsburgh Penguins' executive vice-president and general manager, Ray Shero, met with Crosby at the NHL All-Star Game in Dallas and offered him the captaincy.

"I met with Sidney . . . and really left it with him to think about and talk to his parents," Shero said later. "Part of what makes Sidney not your average nineteen-year-old kid is that he gave it some thought for two or three weeks and came back to us and said he didn't feel the time was right. He didn't really turn it down, he deferred it. That says a lot about his maturity and where he is at, nineteen years old. It was a team-first mentality.

"When I came here over a year ago, I heard a lot about Sidney Crosby. What I have seen over the past year is a person and a player who is not only the best in the league at what he does, but he is also a player that exhibits the will to win, the passion for the game, the team-first mentality and a player that always strives to be the best.

"At the end of the season when we met, we asked him the same question about the captaincy. Having gone through the second half of the season and having gone through the playoff experience, he feels he's ready for the next step and so do we. It's a perfect fit right now."

Crosby didn't leap at the chance to be captain midway through the season because he said he didn't want to disrupt a dressing room that seemed to have finally found a winning chemistry and been able to keep it going. He didn't think he was quite ready.

"I just thought it wasn't right for me. As a team, we were playing great and you don't want to disrupt things like that. And I felt, individually, I was not ready to accept that responsibility quite yet. Going through the playoffs and having that experience has probably given me more confidence. We have a mix of younger and older guys and I think it's a perfect situation for me to be comfortable and at the same time, learn and grow as a player too."

Shero said: "To me, this is a well-earned honour . . . And when I say 'well-earned,' I mean earned. It's a privilege to announce that Sidney Crosby is the new captain of the Pittsburgh Penguins.

"Sid is a leader by example. As he grows into this, he is going to be a guy who has that communication with the coaching staff and his teammates. He has the respect of the room. Not much will change. As he grows into it, maybe a little bit, but immediately he is going to be the player he is and the person he is and that's what made the choice to do this pretty easy for us."

Before he accepted the C, he talked to Mark Recchi, Sergei Gonchar, and Gary Roberts, the latter two of whom are unrestricted free agents and may or may not return for the 2007-2008 season.

"They had some good feedback and really made me feel comfortable with the whole idea," Crosby said. "I think that's important, when you're a captain, you need to have that respect by your peers."

"I try to lead by example," Crosby said. "I don't think I try to put it solely on my shoulders. As captain, you have to take responsibility, of course, but at the end of the day, it's a team sport. There are a lot of guys I can lean on for advice or help in that area. It takes a team to win. It takes responsibility to be a captain and you're looked upon to lead on and off the ice every day. That is something that I think I am ready to do."

As Ottawa battled in the Stanley Cup finals against the Anaheim Ducks in Canada's capital on June 2, Crosby was at the luxury Brookstreet Hotel a stone's throw from the arena, receiving the Art Ross Trophy at an NHL awards ceremony.

Vincent Lecavalier, who was there to receive the Maurice Richard Trophy for most goals in a season, commented on Crosby's captaincy, announced earlier in the week.

"I don't think I can give him any advice," Lecavalier, who also played his junior hockey in Rimouski, said. "I think he's doing everything right. He's a great leader. He's already shown it. He came into the league at eighteen with a lot of confidence and a lot of leadership. And he's just going to get better and better every year. He's nineteen years old.

"I can't even imagine how good and great he's going to be when he's twenty-six and twenty-seven years old. So just keep doing what you're doing and things will just get better and better."

On that summer night in June, when the awards were handed out and Crosby went home with everything for which he was nominated, he was delighted by, and proud of, all of his accomplishments. Winning the Pearson Award, a nod from his peers, meant so much to him.

"To earn that respect from fellow players, guys you play against every night, it's one of the ultimate compliments you can get. In a way, it's a family, the whole group of guys who battle for their teams. It's a huge honour to get that respect.

"Everybody has to earn respect, no matter the situation, and especially when you're young. I just try to do my best and carry myself in the best way."

As he walked away with the most significant individual awards the NHL has to offer, perhaps Sidney Crosby's most meaningful achievement was taking over the leadership of the Pittsburgh Penguins. They were Sidney's team now, and would be for as long as he wanted them.

APPENDIX I

The Pittsburgh Penguins
2005-2006

THE GOALTENDERS

Number 29 Marc-Andre Fleury, twenty-one: Limber and lanky, the number one pick from the 2003 draft began the season in the minor leagues but was called up for the fourth game of the season to fill in when Jocelyn Thibault was injured. "Flower" was up and down with the club until November 28. Management was concerned about the bonuses his contract would pay if he appeared in too many games. Officially the starter when Thibault needed hip surgery in January. At moments downright dazzling, the soft-spoken francophone occasionally struggled despite his genuine gift for goaltending. But he was growing into his future as the Penguins' franchise goalie.

Number 31 Sebastien Caron, twenty-five: Started the season as Thibault's backup but was sent down in December. "Sea Bass" became number two behind Fleury after Thibault went on injured reserve. A fourth-round pick in his third season, Caron showed plenty of promise and had some terrific starts. Hard-working and earnest, his improvement over the season would go a long way towards earning him a roster spot for the upcoming year.

Number 41 Jocelyn Thibault, thirty-one: "T-Bo" arrived in a summer trade from the Chicago Blackhawks and signed a two-year contract worth three million dollars. The veteran was coming off a hip injury and struggled from the start. Put on waivers in late November. He missed more than half the season after being injured in practice and needed surgery to repair torn cartilage in his left hip. He lost twelve of thirteen starts; his future with the Penguins was uncertain.

THE DEFENCEMEN

Number 2 Josef Melichar, twenty-seven: In his fifth NHL season, the hard-working Czech blueliner posted a career-best season with three goals and twelve assists. Quiet and dependable, "Joe" was one of the Penguins' most solid leaders on the ice and in the dressing room, where his young son Joe was a frequent visitor.

Number 4 Noah Welch, twenty-three: Called up from the minors for three games to fill in for a suspended Eric Cairns, the Harvard graduate was the most promising defenceman in the Penguins system. Big and fearless and a Bruce Springsteen fanatic, Welch had both a best and worst NHL debut when he accidentally scored on his own net, then came out in the third period and scored one for his own side in a victory over Montreal.

Number 5 Robert Scuderi, twenty-seven: In his second NHL season, "Scuds" had three points in the thirteen games he played with the Penguins in 2003-2004. From Syosset, N.Y., the affable blueliner endured a sophomore's struggle to contribute offensively with just four points in fifty-six games, but his reliable, stay-at-home game in his own end showed plenty of promise.

Number 19 Ryan Whitney, twenty-three: Started the season in the minors and called up November 1 to fill in for an injury. An encouraging rookie out of Boston College, the first-rounder was rangy and had good reach. He put up solid numbers, six goals and thirty-one assists, and quickly grew into his role. Bright and funny, "Whit" looked to be a big part of the Penguins' future.

Number 22 Ric Jackman, twenty-seven: In his sixth NHL season, "Jax" put up six goals and twenty-two assists in his second season with the Penguins. His blistering slapshot from the point was a fan favourite, but he was benched repeatedly by both Eddie Olczyk and Michel Therrien before being traded at the deadline to the Florida Panthers.

Number 24 Lyle Odelein, thirty-seven: "Odie" was in his sixteenth NHL season but sat out the last thirty-two games after injuring his knee. The veteran tough guy from Quill Lake, Saskatchewan, had just a single assist in the twenty-seven games he played.

Number 32 Dick Tarnstrom, thirty: In his fourth NHL season and second with the Penguins, "Dickie" requested a trade and was dealt to the Edmonton Oilers on January 26 for Jani Rita and Cory Cross.

Number 33 Eric Cairns, thirty-one: Acquired January 18 from the Panthers to help beef up the defence and protect Crosby. At six foot six and 241 pounds, he was a bear on the ice, but seemed like a gentle giant in the dressing room. He was roommates and buddies with winger Eric Boguniecki. Had 124 penalty minutes and scored his only goal of the season a week after joining the team, against the Islanders. He engaged in the Penguins' best fight of the season when he made short, dramatic work of mouthy Flyers winger Donald Brashear.

Number 44 Brooks Orpik, twenty-five: In his second NHL season, the San Francisco–born blueliner was a first-round draft pick in 2000. "Orp" had two goals, the first a beauty from Crosby in the Penguins' home opener, and seven assists in the season. A nice guy in the room who felt genuinely horrible after a tough but legal hit on Carolina Hurricanes forward Erik Cole that broke his neck and sidelined him through most of the playoffs.

Number 55 Sergei Gonchar, thirty-two: A heralded free-agent signing, "Sarge" struggled much of the season to fulfill his potential as one of the best offensive defencemen in the league. Weathered harsh heckling from fans at home and on the road, but the Russian blueliner began to improve in January under Michel Therrien, tallying ten assists in eleven games. He returned from the Olympics in fine form to finish the season strong with twelve goals and forty-six assists overall. His turnaround was one of the most hopeful signs of a bright future for the Penguins.

THE FORWARDS

Number 7 Michel Ouellet, twenty-four: A rookie from Rimouski, Quebec, who, like Crosby, played with the Oceanic. Started his season in the minors but was called up in November. Displayed a nice scoring touch right away with a close range bullet shot that often found the net, but he struggled to score later in the season. Finished with sixteen goals and sixteen assists; should figure prominently in the Penguins' future.

Number 8 Mark Recchi, thirty-seven: The club's first free-agent signing in June 2004, the seventeen-year veteran winger was Crosby's neighbour in the dressing room and roommate on the road the first month of the season. There was rampant speculation the pair didn't get along, but it was denied by both parties. "Rex" was traded to Carolina at the deadline.

Number 9 Andy Hilbert, twenty-five: Claimed off waivers from the Chicago Blackhawks in March 2006, the young centre immediately showed he could play. Soft-spoken and shy in the room, he scored twelve goals and had fifteen assists in forty-seven games.

Number 10 John LeClair, thirty-six: A former teammate of Recchi's on the Flyers (they were traded for each other at one point in 1995), "Johnny" signed with the Pens in summer 2005. In his fifteenth career season, the left-winger reached an impressive milestone, passing the 400-goal mark. Third on the team in scoring, LeClair reached fifty-plus points for the eighth time. Showed terrific leadership with the rookies.

Number 12 Ryan Malone, twenty-five: A left-winger whose father, Greg, was a Penguins scout and former player, "Bugsy" was a Pittsburgh native coming off a standout rookie season. The second line centre got off to a slow start and was the subject of unfounded trade rumours. Considered valuable because of his size and reach, he was benched by Therrien in January but responded well upon return and finished with twenty-two goals and twenty-two assists. He scored the Penguins' most memorable goal of the season, flat on his back and sliding at the net.

Number 14 Shane Endicott, twenty-three: A rookie centre from Saskatoon, "Endo" was as laidback as they come, kind of the team's Spicoli. He suffered a high-ankle sprain at training camp. Back on the team in early December, he never fully regained his confidence. With just two points in forty-one games, he was put on waivers with six games left in the season.

Number 16 Erik Christensen, twenty-one: A rookie centre, "Crusher" was a third-round draft pick from Edmonton. Smart, sensitive, and sweet-natured, with size and good hands around the net, he was up and down from the minors a handful of times over the season and struggled with his nerve in the NHL. Had six goals and seven assists in thirty-three games.

Number 17 Matt Murley, twenty-five: The rookie left-winger started the season in the NHL and eventually became Crosby's roommate on the road. At six foot two and 205 pounds, "Murls" had the size and fearlessness to be a physical presence, but he was injured in January after suffering a muscle tear in his left shoulder during a fight with the Flyers' Ben Eager and was out the rest of the season.

Number 20 Colby Armstrong, twenty-three: A rookie right-winger from Lloydminster, Saskatchewan, "Army" was called up December 29 and never looked back. A former first-rounder from 2001, he found immediate chemistry on Crosby's line and put up sixteen goals and twenty-four assists in forty-one games. They bonded off the ice as well, becoming road roommates and good friends. His sharp sense of humour and love of dishing out big hits made Armstrong a pest to opponents. He was fun to watch. He was a keeper. By the end of the season, Crosby had affectionately christened him "Armpit."

Number 23 Eric Boguniecki, thirty: A right-winger who came to Pittsburgh in a mid-season trade from St. Louis in early December. At five foot eight, he was the smallest guy on the team but had one of the biggest hearts. Played tough and feisty and finished with six goals and ten assists.

Number 25 Maxime Talbot, twenty-one: "Mad Max" was a physical, promising rookie centre up and down from the minors several times after Therrien took over the club. Frenetic on the penalty kill, he had five goals and three assists in forty-eight games. A jokester with an edge, Talbot's impish charm made him a favourite with female fans and also among the beat writers; he won the media award in Wilkes-Barre. He will play in the NHL.

Number 28 Jani Rita, twenty-four: Finnish right-winger came to the Penguins from Edmonton in a January trade but never quite blossomed in his fourth NHL season, finishing with ten points in fifty-one games. Left the Penguins and signed in the off-season with Jokerit.

Number 33 Zigmund Palffy, thirty-three: A right-winger, "Ziggy" found good chemistry on Crosby's line and had eleven goals and thirty-one assists in forty-one games before suddenly announcing his retirement after twelve NHL seasons. One of the league's most dependable scorers, the pensive Palffy blamed the decision on chronic shoulder pain.

Number 36 Andre Roy, thirty: Big winger won the Stanley Cup with the Tampa Bay Lightning and signed with the Penguins in 2005. A tough guy who liked to break into song in the dressing room, Roy could be a softie, especially when talking about his newborn daughter, Maelie.

Number 37 Ryan VandenBussche, thirty-three: A cheerful, carrot-topped winger from Simcoe, Ontario, "Bushy" spent much of his ninth NHL season on the injured reserve list after straining his neck.

Number 43 Tomas Surovy, twenty-four: The hard-working rookie from Slovakia was a low draft pick in 2001. He showed promise as a sniper after being called up from Wilkes-Barre in December; earned the nickname "Killer" after jumping into a fight in Crosby's defence against the Senators late in the season.

Number 66 Mario Lemieux, forty: "Le Magnifique" suffered an irregular heartbeat and removed himself from the lineup twice before announcing his retirement on January 24. He had seven goals and fifteen assists, and finished his Hall of Fame career with

690 goals and 1,033 assists in 915 games, seventh on the all-time NHL scoring list. He left the game with nothing else to prove.

Number 71 Konstantin Koltsov, twenty-four: A left-winger from Belarus, "Koltsy" moved between Wilkes-Barre and Pittsburgh but came up to the NHL for good in January, where he contributed three goals and six assists.

Number 87 Sidney Crosby, eighteen: Centre had thirty-nine goals and sixty-three assists for 102 points; the youngest player in NHL history to reach 100 and set a Penguins rookie scoring mark. "Sid the Kid" exceeded all expectations.

Although not every player listed spent the entire season with the Pittsburgh Penguins, each played a significant role in the 2005-2006 campaign.

Players' ages listed as of April 18, 2006.

APPENDIX II

Sidney Crosby's Season
Game-by-Game Results and Highlights

October 5, 2005, at New Jersey, 5-1 L
First NHL point in debut; set up Mark Recchi on the power play at 5:36 of the third period and registered three shots on goal, one in each period.

October 7 at Carolina, 3-2 L (SO)
One assist, two blocked shots.

October 8 versus Boston, 7-6 L (OT)
First NHL goal, on the power play at 18:32 of the second period; two assists.

October 10 at Buffalo; 3-2 L (OT)
One assist.

October 14 at Philadelphia, 6-5 L (OT)
One goal, one assist.

October 15 versus Tampa, 3-1 L
One assist.

October 20 versus New Jersey, 6-3 L
Held pointless for the first time.

October 22 at Boston, 6-3 L
Two assists.

October 25 versus Florida 4-3 L (OT)
Registered his tenth assist of the season and six shots on net, a
season high.

October 27 versus Atlanta 7-5 W
Two assists and four shots on goal in the Penguins' first victory
of the season.

October 29 versus Carolina, 5-3 L
Pointless for only the second time in eleven games.

November 1 at New Jersey, 4-3 W (OT)
One assist.

November 3 at New York Islanders, 5-1 W
Two power play goals and an assist; game's first star.

November 5 at Boston, 6-3 L
Held pointless.

November 7 at New York Rangers, 3-2 W
Scored fifth goal of the season; game's first star.

November 9 at Atlanta, 5-0 L
Held pointless.

November 10 versus Montreal, 3-2 W (SO)
Two goals, one on the power play and the game winner in overtime shootout. (Shootout goals do not count towards a player's
scoring statistics.)

November 12 versus New York Rangers, 6-1 L
Held pointless.

November 14 versus New York Islanders, 3-2 L (SO)
Scored seventh goal of the season, five shots on net.

November 16 at Philadelphia, 3-2 W (OT)
Two goals and one assist, including the game winner in overtime,
five shots on goal; game's first star.

November 19 versus Philadelphia, 6-3 L
Scored tenth goal on the power play.

November 22 versus Washington, 5-4 W
One goal, one assist.

November 25 at Florida, 6-3 L
Registered tenth assist; left game in third period after blocking a
shot off his left instep.

November 27 at Tampa Bay, 4-1 L
Held pointless.

November 29 versus Buffalo, 3-2 L
Held pointless.

December 1 at New York Rangers, 2-1 L
Held pointless.

December 3 versus Calgary, 3-2 L
A power play goal, five shots on net.

December 8 versus Minnesota, 5-0 L
Held pointless.

December 10 versus Colorado, 4-3 W
One assist.

December 12 at Detroit, 3-1 L
One assist.

December 13 at St. Louis, 3-0 L
The Penguins' last game under head coach Eddie Olczyk, who was fired the following day.

December 16 versus Buffalo, 4-3 L (OT)
First game under Michel Therrien; one assist, six shots on net.

December 17 at Buffalo, 4-3 L
One goal.

December 23 versus Philadelphia, 5-4 L
Crosby scored two goals in forty-four seconds and registered his twentieth assist.

December 27 versus Toronto, 3-2 L (OT)
One assist.

December 29 versus New Jersey, 6-2 W
Two goals and one assist.

December 31 versus New York Rangers, 4-3 W (OT)
Scored game winner on the power play at 3:31 of overtime, one assist.

January 2, 2006, at Toronto, 3-2 L (OT)
Had an assist in first NHL game on Canadian soil.

January 2 at Montreal, 6-4 W
Crosby scored twice, his twentieth plus the game winner, and was the game's first star.

January 6 at Atlanta, 6-4 L
Notched his twenty-fifth assist and delivered a season-high four hits.

January 7 versus Atlanta, 4-3 L
One assist.

January 10 versus Edmonton, 3-1 L
Held pointless.

January 11 at Columbus, 6-1 L
Held pointless.

January 13 at Chicago, 4-1 L
One assist.

January 15 at Nashville, 5-4 L
One assist, recorded nine shots on goal, most to date.

January 16 versus Vancouver, 4-2 L
A power play goal.

January 19 versus New York Rangers, 4-2 L
Scored a power play goal and registered his thirtieth assist.

January 21 versus Philadelphia, 2-1 L
Held pointless.

January 23 at Philadelphia, 4-2 L
One assist.

January 25 versus Washington, 8-1 W
Win snapped ten-game losing streak; Crosby had one goal and three assists in his second meeting with the Capitals' Alexander Ovechkin; game's first star.

January 26 at New York Islanders, 4-3 L (SO)
One assist.

January 28 at New York Rangers, 7-1 L
Crosby scored his twenty-fifth goal of the season on the power play.

February 1 at New York Rangers, 3-1 L
Held pointless.

February 2 versus Ottawa, 5-2 L
Held pointless.

February 4 versus New York Islanders, 5-4 L (OT)
One power play goal.

February 6 at Ottawa, 5-2 L
Held pointless.

February 8 versus Boston, 3-1 L
Held pointless.

February 10 at Carolina, 4-3 W
His power play goal in the third period was the game winner; one assist.

February 11 at Washington, 6-3 W
Scored on the power play, his twenty-eighth goal, and registered thirty-seventh assist in the last game before the Olympic break.

February 12-28: NHL breaks for Olympic Games.
Held pointless.

March 1 versus Ottawa, 4-3 L
Held pointless.

March 4 versus Carolina, 7-5 L
One assist.

March 7 versus Tampa, 5-4 L (SO)
One power play goal.

March 8 at Washington, 6-3 L
Held pointless.

March 11 versus New Jersey, 6-3 W
Two goals.

March 12 versus Philadelphia, 2-0 W
Two assists.

March 16 at New Jersey, 2-1 L
Held pointless.

March 18 at Montreal, 5-4 W
One assist.

March 19 versus Toronto, 1-0 L
Held pointless.

March 21 at Ottawa, 5-2 L
Had his forty-fifth assist.

March 24 versus New York Islanders, 4-3 W (OT)
One goal, one assist.

March 26 versus Montreal, 6-5 L
Two assists.

March 29 versus Florida, 5-3 L
Held pointless.

March 31 at New York Islanders, 4-0 W
Scored his thirty-third goal and had two assists, including his
fiftieth of the season.

April 2 versus New Jersey, 3-2 L (OT)
One goal, one assist.

April 5 at New Jersey, 6-4 L
Scored his thirty-fifth goal and had his fifty-second assist.

April 7 at Florida, 5-1 W
One goal and three assists; second four-point night of the season.

April 8 at Tampa, 1-0 L
Held pointless after suffering a separated shoulder in the first
period.

April 11 at Philadelphia, 4-3 L
Scored his thirty-seventh goal and added one assist.

April 13 versus New York Rangers, 5-3 W
One goal and three assists for his third four-point game of the
season.

April 15 at New York Islanders, 5-4 L (SO)
Held pointless; still suffering with a shoulder injury.

April 17 versus New York Islanders, 6-1 W
Three assists to reach 100 points.

April 18 at Toronto, 5-3 L
In the last game of the season, Crosby scored one goal and had
one assist to finish with 102 points.

The Pittsburgh Penguins finished their season with a record of 22-46-14, second-to-last overall in the NHL. They never won more than two consecutive games all season and accomplished that on only four occasions.

Sidney Crosby had thirty-nine goals and sixty-three assists and became the youngest player in NHL history to reach 100 points. He also reached the following marks:

- Second in NHL history in points scored before his nineteenth birthday (behind Dale Hawerchuk, 103 points for Winnipeg in 1981-1982).
- Second in NHL history in points scored by players who broke into the league in the year they were drafted (second to Hawerchuk).
- Set a Pittsburgh Penguins rookie scoring record with 102 points, breaking Mario Lemieux's mark of 100 set in 1984-1985.
- Set a Pittsburgh Penguins rookie record for assists with sixty-three, breaking Lemieux's mark of fifty-seven.
- Became the seventh rookie in NHL history to score 100 points.
- Became the first rookie in NHL history to compile 100 points and 100 penalty minutes.
- Finished sixth in the NHL scoring race.
- Finished seventh in the NHL in assists.
- Ranked third among Canadian-born NHL players in scoring (behind Joe Thornton and Dany Heatley).

W = Win, L = Loss, OT = Overtime, SO = Shootout
Source: National Hockey League/Elias Sports Bureau